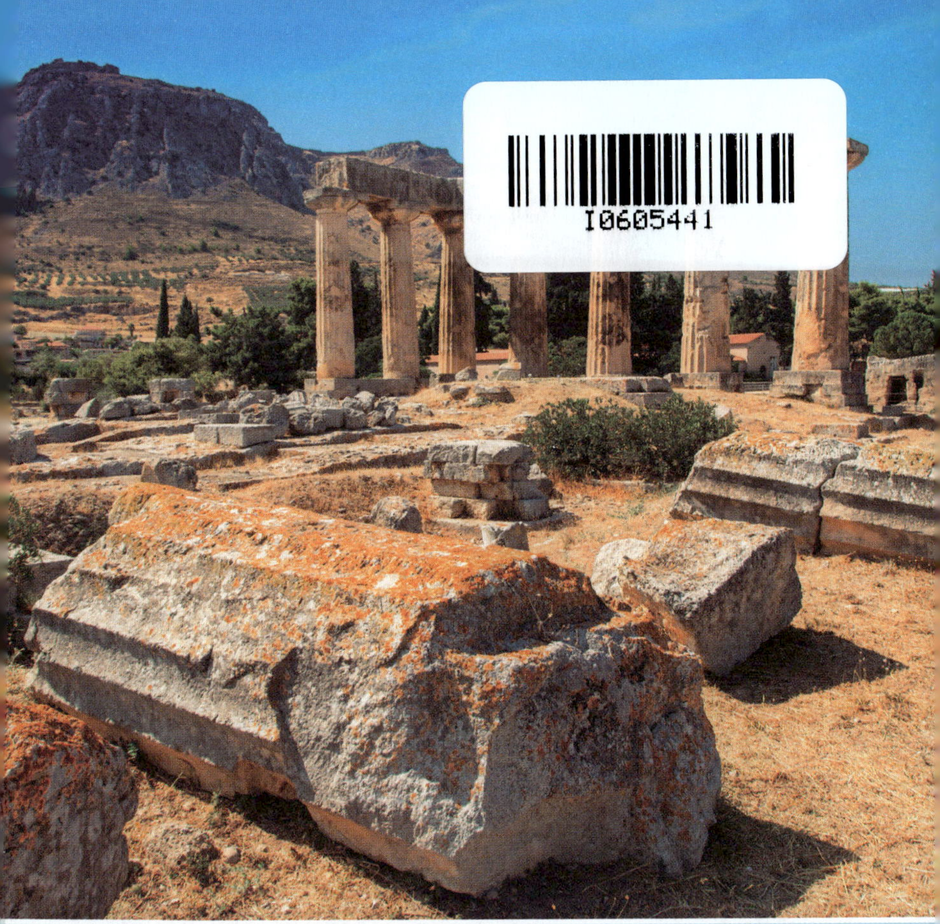

THE ROUGH GUIDE TO THE

# PELOPONNESE

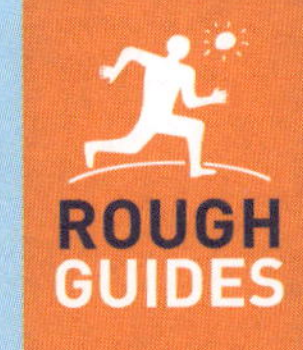


This first edition written and researched by
**Rebecca Hall**

# Contents



AERIAL VIEW OF ANCIENT CORINTH

# Introduction to
# The Peloponnese

The Peloponnese, a sun-drenched peninsula – technically an island since the cutting of the Corinth Canal – is a tapestry of ancient history, dramatic landscapes, and vibrant culture in southern Greece. Shaped like a mulberry leaf (*mouriá*) the region is linked to the mainland by the slender Isthmus of Corinth. Its storied past is woven into the very fabric of Western civilization, from the rise of Mycenaean culture to the epic battles of the Trojan War and the philosophical advancements of the Classical period.

The Peloponnese peninsular, surrounded by coastline on all sides and its mountainous inland, is packed with historical treasures and charming villages waiting to be unveiled. Despite its vastness, many key sites are just a short drive apart, making the region easy to explore.

The cultural riches and natural beauty of the Peloponnese can hardly be overstated. This southern peninsula seems to have the best of almost everything Greek. Ancient sites include the Homeric **palaces of Agamemnon at Mycenae** and of **Nestor at Pýlos**, the best preserved of all Greek theatres at **Epidaurus**, and the lush sanctuary of **Olympia**, **host to the Olympic Games** for a millennium. The medieval remains are scarcely less rich, with the fabulous Venetian, Frankish and Turkish castles of **Náfplio**, **Methóni** and **ancient Corinth**; the strange battle towers and frescoed churches of the **Máni**; and the extraordinarily well-preserved Byzantine enclaves of **Mystra** and **Monemvasiá**.

Beyond the incredible profusion and density of cultural monuments, the Peloponnese is a superb place to relax and wander. Its **beaches**, especially along the west and southwest coast, are among the finest in the country, and the **landscape** inland is superb – dominated by forested mountains cut by some of the most captivating valleys and **gorges** imaginable. Not for nothing did its heartland province of **Arcadia** become synonymous with the very concept of a Classical rural idyll.

PRODHRÓMOU MONASTERY, ARCADIA

# Where to go

There are many sights in the region's secluded hill towns, ancient tower villages, and serene beaches. Exploring the Peloponnese rewards visitors with stunning landscapes, from dramatic **gorges** navigated by **vintage railways** to **ancient caves** steeped in history. Whether you're fascinated by nature or history, there're a wealth of attractions that can be explored at your own pace. If time is limited, focus on the **ancient treasures**, where a short drive from Athens allows you to delve into its rich heritage. With more time, extend your journey to include significant **historical sites** and tranquil **coastal retreats.** Embrace the slower pace, and you'll find this region full of enduring charm and cultural depth.

However, the Peloponnese reveals its true character most clearly when you venture off the beaten track: to the likes of old Arcadian **hill towns** Karítena, Stemnítsa and Dhimitsána; to the **Máni tower villages** such as Váthia; at Voïdhokiliá and Elafónissos **beaches** in the south; or through the **Vouraïkós Gorge** on the old **rack-and-pinion railway.** Nature lovers will love the **ancient caves** such as **Kapsia** – a 55-minute drive inland from **Náfplio** or the lesser-known **Kastania cave**, 1.5 hours from **Monemvasiá.**

No matter how much time you have, the region will amply repay any amount of time you spend here. The **Argolid**, the area richest in ancient history, is just a couple of hours

PELOPONNESE
Mesolóngi
Evinohóri
Kryonéri
Andírrio
Návpaktos
Psathópyrgos
Río
Pátra
Ágios Nikólaos
Erátini
Pendeória
Galaxídi
Desfína
Andikýra
Livadiá
Palovouna
1748m
ÓROS ELIKÓN
Petra
Vágia
Thebes
Athens
Elopía
Paralía
Thísvi
Melissohóri
Erythres
Pórto Germenó
Mándra
Athens
Mégara
Salamína
Perahóra
Loutráki
Kórinthos
Léheo
Isthmía
Saronic
Gulf
Égina
Égina
Angístri
Agnoúndos
Néa Epídauros
Paleá Epídauros
Epídauros
Méthana
Póros
Kórfos
Bari, Ancona & Venezia
Kefaloniá & Zákynthos
Gulf of Patras
Ionian
Beach
Áraxos
Lakópetra
Metóhi
Lápa
Káto Ahaïa
Vasilikó
Várda
Hióna
Gulf of Kórinthos
Égio
Diakoftó
Akráta
Lykoporiá
Xylókastro
Kiáto
ÓROS PANAHAÏKÓ
Petrotó
Ahea
Katarráktis
Flámboura
Káto Vlasía
Vouraïkos
Moní
Méga Spíleo
Agía
Lávra
Kalávryta
Agíou
Georgíou
Feneoú
Helmós
2355m
Spílio Límnón
(Cave of the Lakes)
Stenó
Zíria
2375m
Tríkala
Soúli
Sikyon
Ancient Corinth
Kastaniá
Stymfalía
Neméa
Dervenákia
Mycenae
Mykínes
Fíhti
Ireon
Árgos
Tiryns
Lygourió
Náfplio
Toló
Mýli
Lerna
Kyllíni
Hlemoutsi
Lehená
Andravída
Gastoúni
Loutrá
Kyllínis
Stavrodrómi
Piniós
Amaliáda
Kouroúta
Ládon
Skafidiá
Pýrgos
Katákolo
Levkohóri
Orchomenos
Magoúliana
Langádia
Vytína
Levídi
Kapsia
Cave
Olympia
Olympia
Dimitsána
Karkaloú
MÉNALO
Kréstena
Alfiós
Loúsios
Gorge
Stemnítsa
Trípoli
Ahladókambos
Loutra Kaïafa
Zaháro
Andrítsena
Bassae
Karýtena
Tegea
Káto Figália
Megalópoli
Eléa
Néda Gorge
PÁRNON
Ástros
Agía
Loukoú
Parálio Ástros
Argolic Gulf
Kranídi
Ermióni
Paradhísia
Ág. Andréas
Kryonéri
Kaló Nerό
IONIAN SEA
Kyparissía
Meligalás
Spétses
Ýdra
Ýdra

AEGEAN SEA
MEDITERRANEAN SEA
Gulf of Messíniá
Filiatrá
Messene
Mavromátio
Marathópolis
Gargaliáni
Nestor's Palace
Hóra
Messíniá
Kalamáta
Romanós
Voïdokiliá Bay
Giálova
Boúka
Petalídi
Sfaktiría
Pýlos
Methóni
Finikoúnda
Koróni
Sapiéndza
Shíza
Ákra Akrítas
YGETOS
Trýpi
Mystra
Spárti
Amýkles
Avía
Kámbos
Tsérnia
Kardamýli
Stoúpa
Selenítsa
Plátsa
Nomitsís
Langáda
Ítylo
Kastaniá
Evrótas
Kosmás
Elonis
Pláka
Poúlithra
Geráki
Kyparíssi
Skála
Élos
Rihéa
Mólai
Yíthio
Mavrovoúni
Yéfira
Monemvasiá
Areópoli
Flomohóri
Dhiroú
Máni
Lágia
Geroliménas
Váthia
Pórto Kágio
Ákra Ténaro
(Matapas)
Poúnda
Elafónissos
Neápoli
Ákra Maléas
Ág. Pelagía
Kýthira
Diakófti
Kapsáli
Andikýthira, Kastéli-Kíssamou & Crete
N
Metres
1400
1200
1500
1000
500
200
100
0
0
20
kilometres

from Athens, and if pushed you could complete a circuit of the main sights here – **Corinth**, **Mycenae** and **Epidaurus** – in a couple of days, making your base by the sea in **Náfplio**. Given an extra week, you could add in the two large sites of **Mystra** and **Olympia** at a more leisurely pace. To get to grips with all this, however, plus the southern peninsulas of the Máni and Messinía, and the hill towns of Arcadia, you'll need at least three weeks as the province is approximately the size of Belgium.

## When to go

If anything is God-given to the Greeks, it is their **climate**. With summers increasing in temperatures over the years, most places in the Peloponnese are far more agreeable outside the mid-July to end of August peak season, when soaring temperatures can be overpowering. You won't miss out on **warm weather** if you come in **June or September** – in fact, even earlier can be preferable such as at the end of **April** up until **October**. Greece as a whole is trying to encourage tourism outside of high season when temperatures are more bearable, so places are increasingly staying open beyond the usual peak season.

### FACT FILE

- The **southernmost peninsula in mainland Greece**, the Peloponnese – with a land area of 21,550 sq km – is surrounded by the Aegean, Mediterranean and Ionian seas, plus the Corinth Gulf.
- It's referred to as an **'island within the mainland'** as it's linked by two points: the Corinth Canal to the east and the Rion-Antirion Bridge to the north.
- The **Byzantines**, **Franks** and **Ottomans** have all ruled the region at some point or another, shaping its architecture, culture and gastronomy.
- **Pátra is the biggest city** in the Peloponnese and considered the gateway to the west. Its large port is more of a transport hub, connecting with many Italian destinations, as well as domestic Greek islands. You'll also find a large student population here.
- The famous **Kalamáta black olive** originates from the Peloponnese, said to have been cultivated over five thousand years ago.
- The Peloponnese was a key battleground during the **Greek War of Independence (1821-1829)** against Ottoman rule. **Kalamáta** is said to be the place where, on 23 March 1821, it was the first major Greek town to be liberated.

### AVERAGE MONTHLY TEMPERATURES AND RAINFALL

| | Jan | Feb | Mar | April | May | June | July | Aug | Sept | Oct | Nov | Dec |
|---|---|---|---|---|---|---|---|---|---|---|---|---|
| **NÁFPLIO (COASTAL)** | | | | | | | | | | | | |
| Max (°C/°F) | 13/55 | 14/57 | 18/64 | 22/72 | 27/81 | 32/90 | 35/95 | 34/93 | 30/86 | 25/77 | 19/66 | 14/57 |
| Min (°C/°F) | 4/39 | 5/41 | 6/43 | 9/48 | 12/54 | 16/61 | 19/66 | 18/64 | 15/59 | 12/54 | 8/46 | 6/43 |
| Rainfall (mm) | 64 | 64 | 61 | 33 | 29 | 17 | 8 | 11 | 31 | 40 | 61 | 69 |
| **DHIMITSANA (MOUNTAIN)** | | | | | | | | | | | | |
| Max (°C/°F) | 7/45 | 8/46 | 11/52 | 16/61 | 21/70 | 26/79 | 29/84 | 28/82 | 24/75 | 18/64 | 13/55 | 8/46 |
| Min (°C/°F) | -2/28 | -1/30 | 0/32 | 3/37 | 6/43 | 10/50 | 12/54 | 12/54 | 9/48 | 6/43 | 2/36 | -1/30 |
| Rainfall (mm) | 112 | 89 | 82 | 48 | 53 | 54 | 21 | 16 | 62 | 65 | 81 | 91 |

# Author picks

Our intrepid author has visited every corner of the Peloponnese to bring you some unique travelling experiences. These are some of her personal favourites.

**Fabulous regional food** Sample unique local delicacies such as *lalagia* (fried dough strips) and *syglino* (smoked pork). Kalamáta olives (see page 134), feta cheese, and local seafood are staples, while oranges and honey round off the region's distinct Mediterranean flavours.

**Ancient caves** Jurassic era caves with their unique stalactite and stalagmite formations entice you to explore beyond the beach. Kapsia (see page 122) and Kastania (see page 82) are two such natural wonders.

**Castle heaven** The Peloponnese doesn't disappoint with its countless fortresses, many of them dating back to Venetian times. Koróni (see page 138) in the Messinia region is one such gem, with many houses still intact.

**A sunken city** There's more to Epidaurus than its famed theatre. Take a canoeing trip out to the sunken city, just offshore at Kalyminos Bay (see page 72). It's actually a Roman villa that sunk in CE500, with ancient pots still below the surface.

**World Heritage Byzantine Town** Not only a visually stunning medieval city, this UNESCO World Heritage site of Mystra (see page 96), springing up out of the Taÿgetos Mountains, preserves a superb assemblage of Byzantine frescoed churches and is also a perfect base for hikers as the E4 Trans-European Hiking route meanders through here.

**Wine Route** Lovers of wine must pay a visit to Nemea – a 40-minute drive from Náfplio (see page 70). Enjoy sampling the excellent reds and rosés that come from the *agiorgitiko* grape.

**Deer Island** The coastline offers a profusion of beaches and coves, but a visit to Elafonissos island (see page 83) is a must. It's reached in 15 mins by ferry from Pounta, (see page 76). With undulating sand dunes on beaches such as Simos, you'll find nudism-friendly spots, plus camping is allowed.

> Our author recommendations don't end here. We've flagged up our favourite places – a perfectly sited hotel, an atmospheric café, a special restaurant – throughout the Guide, highlighted with the ★ symbol.

PORK AND FETA SKEWERS

KASTANIA'S BEAUTIFUL ROCK FORMATIONS

# 15

## things not to miss

It may not be possible to see everything that the Peloponnese has to offer in one trip – and we certainly don't suggest you try. What follows is a selective and subjective taste of the island's highlights: superb ancient and religious sites, unforgettable scenery and a variety of activities. All highlights are colour-coded by chapter and have a page reference to take you straight into the Guide, where you can find out more.

1

**1 ANCIENT CORINTH AND CANAL**

See page 46

Visit Ancient Corinth and the fortifications of Acrocorinth, a huge, barren rock crowned by a great fortress. Marvel at the engineering wonder that is the Corinth Canal–with walls of 79 metres, it's the world's deepest.

**2 MYCENAE KINGDOM**

See page 58

Mycenae is the ancient city that gave its name to a civilization whose Homeric heroes have become household names. The palace of legend and alleged tomb of Agamemnon who was murdered upon his return from the Trojan War.

**3 BIRTHPLACE OF THE OLYMPICS**

See page 153

Sports ground of the ancients whose competitive motto "Faster, Higher, Stronger" is as relevant today as it was then, some 1400 years of the Olympic Games are laid bare along the verdant valley of the Alfiós, at Olympia, and the site's museum houses some of Greece's greatest sculptures.

**4 THE ORIGINAL GREEK CAPITAL**

See page 65

Náfplio, with its gently fading nineteenth-century elegance, is a port town and makes a picturesque base for exploring the Argolid region.

**5 A BYZANTINE ROCK**

See page 76

Monemvasiá, the Byzantines' impregnable stronghold – the "Gibraltar of the East"– a castle town still lived in set into rock accessed by walk able causeway out at sea, is now a unique time bubble; stylish and traffic-free.

6

7

## 6 FEUDAL LAW

See page 104

The Máni is a rugged southern peninsula in the Peloponnese that has inspired many visitors with its quirky tower houses and isolated churches. Lord Byron made his home here.

## 7 CLASSY BEACH HOLIDAYS

See page 135

You don't need to head to a built up Greek island for a beach holiday. The Messenian Coast is mainland Greece's answer to any island beach holiday.

## 8 ANCIENT CLASSICS PERFORMED AMONG THE ANCIENTS

See page 70

Epidaurus is one of the most beautifully preserved of all ancient theatres, epitomizing the inspiring views and perfect acoustics for which the Greeks were renowned.

## 9 QUIRKY RAILWAY

See page 167

Cut through dramatic countryside as you chug through the Vouraïkós Gorge on the old rack-and-pinion railway from the coastal town of Diakofto up to the mountain town of Kalavryta with its ski centre in the area.

## 10 MUSEUM OF THE OLIVE AND GREEK OLIVE OIL

See page 95

In the town of Spárti, this unique museum is worth a visit for its insight into the love affair of the Greeks with the olive tree that has provided them with food, heat, soap and medicines for thousands of years.

### 11 MODERN DAY MARATHON

See page 92

The annual September Spartathlon, a 246km run from Athens to Spárti, commemorates the messenger Pheidippides who ran the same route in 490 BC: the current course record is 20hr 25min.

### 12 TEMPLE OF APOLLO EPIKOURIOUS

See page 127

This remarkable little known site occupies one of the remotest and highest (1131m) elevations in Greece. It's one of the best-preserved Classical monuments in the country, thought to have been designed by Iktinos, architect of the Parthenon and the Hephaisteion (Thisseion) in Athens.

### 13 LOCAL DELICACIES OF KALAMÁTA

See page 134

Famous for the black olives that have been produced for thousands of years, giving the region its name, come and sample the local delicacies in this second most populous region of the Peloponnese.

### 14 VISIT PATRICK LEIGH FERMOR HOUSE

See page 115

English writer, scholar, soldier and polyglot, not to mention philhellene, made his home in Kardhamýli, the Mani with his wife in 1964. Since 1996 it was bequeathed to the Benaki Museum and open to visitors.

### 15 MÉGA SPILÉOU MONASTERY

See page 167

The oldest monastery in Greece, Méga Spiléou, is built into the cliff face 120m-high, en route to Kalavryta on the rack-and-pinion railway from Dhiakoftó to Kalávryta. It resembles a 70s hotel, but the views of the Vouraïkós Gorge are a sight to behold.

13

14

15

# Itineraries

The following itineraries will allow you to see highlights of the Peloponnese peninsula, and also allows for deeper exploration of some of the lesser-known areas.

## THE GRAND TOUR

10–14 days in the Peloponnese and not sure where to start? Our Grand Tour puts you on the right track.

❶ **Corinth (Korinthos)** This is a good starting point as you take in Ancient Corinth and the Corinth Canal, its towering sides making it the deepest in the world. See page 46

❷ **Náfplio** Greece's original capital city, Náfplio is a charming seaside town. Take at least a day and a half to explore the towering Palamidi Fortress, wander through cobbled streets and view the Neoclassical houses and Venetian architecture in the Old Town. See page 65

❸ **Epidaurus** This theatre is a masterpiece of ancient Greek architecture. Nearby, the Sunken City of Epidaurus invites visitors to snorkel over submerged ruins. See page 70

❹ **Archaeological site of Mycenae** This site is pivotal in Greek history. Enter it through the imposing Lion Gate and visit the awe-inspiring Tomb of Agamemnon. See page 58

❺ **Monemvasiá** This medieval fortress town is carved into a sea rock. Its cobbled streets, lined with Byzantine churches and stone-built houses, evoke a timeless atmosphere. See page 76

❻ **Neápoli** This small port town is a good base to explore Kastania Cave and the sunken Bronze Age city of Pavlopétri. At Poúnda you can take the ferry across to Elafónissos. See page 82

❼ **Máni** Máni's rugged landscapes, epitomises Greek culture. Base yourself in picturesque Stoupa or Kardhamýli. Explore Cape Ténaro where ancient myths and stunning views combine. See page 104

❽ **Sparti and Mystra** Heading slightly inland, Sparti offers visitors ancient ruins including the Acropolis of Sparta and the popular Museum of the Olive and Greek Olive Oil. Nearby Mystra showcases Byzantine splendour. See page 92

❾ **Olympia** Moving northwest, the birthplace of the Olympic Games is a must-see destination. Explore the impressive Temple of Zeus, the ancient stadium where the Games were held and its insightful museum. A few kilometres away is Brintziki Winery. See page 148

❿ **Kalamáta & Ancient Messene** Spend a few days in Kalamáta, known for its beach, market, museums and the famed olive. Then head north to Ancient Messene. See pages 134 & 137

⓫ **Koróni** Explore its castle and beaches. Then it's south to Methoni. See page 138

**Create your own itinerary with Rough Guides**. Whether you're after adventure or a family-friendly holiday, we have a trip for you, with all the activities you enjoy doing and the sights you want to see. All our trips are devised by local experts who get the most out of the destination. Visit **www.roughguides.com/trips** to chat with one of our travel agents.

## NORTH AND NORTH WEST PELOPONNESE

The north and northwest of the region offers a mix of beach, culture and nature.

❶ **Pátra** Stop for a few days in the capital. Kalogriá beach with its stunning dunes and Strofyliá Forest-Kotýkhi Wetland National Park are also nearby. See page 160

❷ **Kalávryta Express** Base yourself at Dhiakoftó to kick back and enjoy local life before taking the unique Kalávryta Express train through the stunning Vouraïkós gorge. See page 167

❸ **Kalávryta** Spend a couple of days in this historic mountain village before heading back on the Kalávryta Express. The Kalávryta Ski Centre is here, too. See page 168

❹ **Nemea** Visit the Temple of Nemea, Temple of Zeus and the Nemean Stadium. The region is also renowned for its vineyards. See page 55

❺ **Arkoúdhi** Heading back northwest, spend a few days in this coastal village. See page 157

❻ **Khlemoútsi Castle** This Frankish stronghold is one of the best preserved in Greece and has views across to Zákynthos. See page 157

## MOUNTAIN VILLAGES

Uncover this little discovered region.

❶ **Trípoli** A gateway to the mountains. Just north of the city lies Kapsia Cave. See page 120

❷ **Karítena** A traditional town with Frankish, Byzantine and Ottoman roots. See page 124

❸ **Stemnítsa** Three dramatic ravines divide this scenic winter resort. See page 124

❹ **Dhimitsána** Houses here cling precariously to the cliffs. Its Open-Air Water-Power Museum is a popular attraction. See page 126

❺ **Loúsios Gorge** Base yourself at any of the aforementioned villages for this hiking route to Prodhrómou Monastery. See page 126

❻ **Andhrítsena** More of a roadside settlement with a café lifestyle; the Temple of Apollo Epikourios is 14km south. See page 127

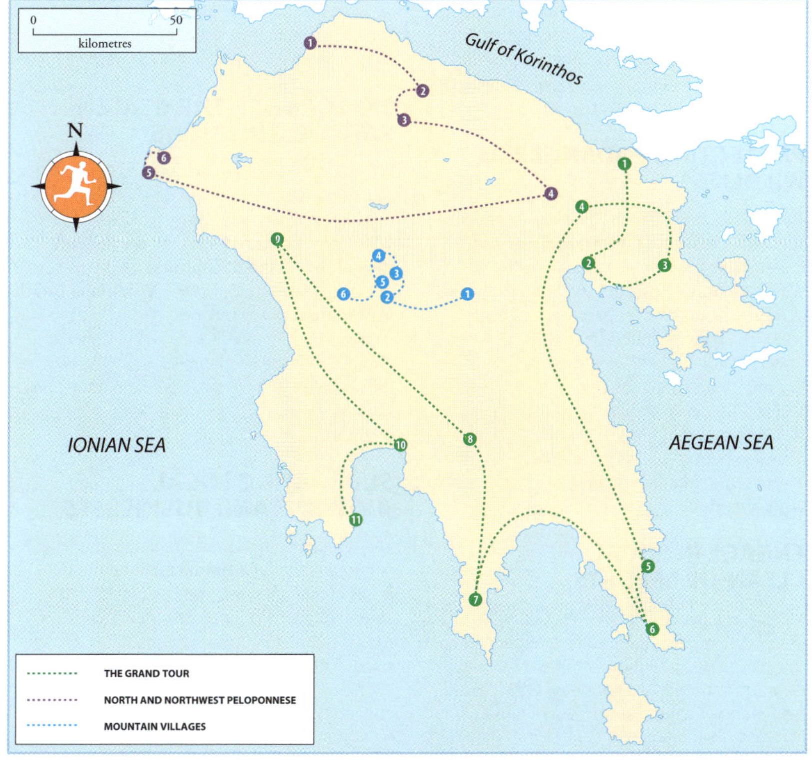

# Sustainable travel

Travellers are ever more aware of the necessity of low impact travel. There are various ways when visiting the Peloponnese – Greece's Green Peninsula – that you can explore its stunning landscapes and rich heritage through eco-friendly practices.

This captivating region in southern mainland Greece boasts diverse ecosystems, ancient ruins, and vibrant communities. Yet environmental challenges – from endangered wildlife to plastic pollution – is ever present. Embracing sustainable travel practices here will not only enrich your experience, but also contribute to preserving this beautiful destination for future generations.

## PROTECTING ENDANGERED WILDLIFE

The Peloponnese is home to some endangered species such as the **loggerhead sea turtle** (Caretta caretta) in the Kyparissia Gulf in the Western Peloponnese. Organizations such as Archelon work tirelessly to protect these creatures. Their Research Field Station, based at Apollo Village – a well-organized campground located right next to the beach in Gianitsochori village – allows visitors to support these efforts by participating in conservation activities such as beach patrols and nest monitoring. In this way, visitors help ensure these species thrive for years to come.

## ENGAGE IN LOCAL CLEAN-UP EFFORTS

The pristine beaches of the Peloponnese are, as in many places, increasingly encroached upon by plastic pollution. Joining local beach clean-up initiatives is a hands-on way to make a difference. Groups like "Let's do it Greece" (http://letsdoitgreece.org/) organise regular clean-up events. Travellers can also minimize their impact by avoiding single-use plastics and carrying reusable water bottles and bags. Every small action contributes to keeping the Peloponnese's coastlines clean and beautiful.

## EXPLORE OFF-THE-BEATEN-PATH DESTINATIONS

While ancient sites like Olympia and Mycenae are must-sees, the Peloponnese is full of lesser-known destinations that offer equally rich experiences without the crowds. Visiting the **traditional mountain village of Dhimitsana** on the slopes of Mount Mainalo, or stunning **Voidokilia Beach** in **Messinia** with its biodiversity not only provides a unique insight into local life and wildlife, but also supports their economies. Engaging with these quieter spots reduces pressure on popular sites and distributes tourism benefits more evenly across the region.

## SUPPORTING LOCAL ARTISANS AND BUSINESSES

The Peloponnese is known for its artisanal crafts – from the famous **Kalamáta olives** and its lesser-known silk woven products sold in this coastal town to honey production in the Mani region. Supporting local businesses helps sustain traditional crafts and contributes to the local economy. Look for community-run markets, craft cooperatives, and women-led initiatives. Buying

BEEHIVES WITH A SEA VIEW

PRETTY DHIMITSANA

locally made products reduces your carbon footprint and fosters a deeper connection with the region's culture and heritage.

## ECO-FRIENDLY ACCOMMODATION OPTIONS

Choosing sustainable lodging options is another way to reduce your travel impact. The Peloponnese offers numerous eco-friendly accommodations, from the Green Key-certified **Kinsterna Mansion in Monemvasiá** that's eliminated the use of oil and natural gas for heating and kitchen operations, installed electric car chargers, and donates a share of the electricity they naturally produce to local institutions such as the church and vulnerable households; to the **Manna Hotel in Arcadia** – in the mountainous central-eastern Peloponnese – which generates both heat and cool air via a geothermal heat pump. Staying in such places not only minimizes your carbon footprint, it also offers a more authentic and immersive experience.

## PARTICIPATE IN NATURE PRESERVATION EFFORTS

The Peloponnese's natural beauty is safeguarded by numerous preservation initiatives. Visitors can join tree-planting projects or assist in reforestation efforts organized by groups like the Peloponnese Parks Network. Hiking in protected areas such as the **Menalon Trail**, a certified Leading Quality Trail, allows you to enjoy nature responsibly. By following marked trails and respecting local guidelines, you help preserve these landscapes for all to enjoy.

## SUSTAINABLE TRAVEL AND TRANSPORT

Opting for eco-friendly transportation can significantly reduce your carbon footprint while exploring the Peloponnese. The region's **scenic train routes** such as the rack rail train journey from the coastal town of Diakopto cutting through gorges to the mountainous village of Kalávryta, and expanding **cycle networks** such as in the coastal town of Náfplio offer green alternatives to car travel. Additionally, many towns are enhancing their infrastructure for electric vehicles. Renting an e-bike or using public transportation not only lowers emissions but also provides a slower, more intimate way to experience the region's charm.

THE BAY OF VOÏDHOKILIÁ, MESSINÍA

# Basics

# Getting there

**By far the easiest way to get to Greece initially is to fly and then onward travel to the Peloponnese (see page 22). There are direct flights to a variety of Greek destinations from all major UK airports. Even if your starting point is North America, Australia, New Zealand or South Africa, the most cost-effective route to Greece may well be to get to London, Amsterdam, Frankfurt or another Northern European hub, and pick up an onward flight from there.**

Airfares are highest in July, August and during Easter week. But May, June and September are also popular, and since far fewer flights operate in winter, bargains are rare at any time. Note that the tourist season is extending though, due to extreme heat in the summer months, so airfares could very well increase earlier/later because of this.

**Overland** alternatives from the UK or Northern Europe involve at least three days of nonstop travel. If you want to take your time over the journey, **driving** or travelling **by train** can be enjoyable, although invariably more expensive than flying. We've included only brief details of these routes here.

When booking flights, it always pays to shop around and bear in mind that many websites don't include charter or budget airlines in their results. Be aware, too, that a **package deal**, with accommodation included, can sometimes be as cheap as, or even cheaper than, a flight alone: there's no rule that says you have to use your accommodation every night, or even at all.

## Flights from the UK and Ireland

Unless you book far in advance, there are **few bargain fares** to Greece. If you can book early, it's a good tactic to check the budget airlines' flight release dates, otherwise their prices are little different from those of the traditional operators and can be higher if you leave it late. If you're heading for **Athens**, easyJet (http://easyjet.com) can fly you direct from Gatwick, Manchester, Bristol or Edinburgh, Ryanair (http://ryanair.com) from Stansted, and Norwegian (http://norwegian.com) from Gatwick. British Airways (http://britishairways.com) have frequent flights to Athens from Heathrow, Aegean (http://aegeanair.com) from Heathrow, Birmingham, Manchester and Edinburgh. From Dublin, Aer Lingus (http://aerlingus.com).

## Flights from the US and Canada

Only Emirates offers daily year-round **non-stop to Athens** from Newark. Seasonal direct flights to the Greek capital are operated by Delta (http://delta.com) New York JFK; American (http://aa.com) from Chicago, New York and Philadelphia; and United (http://united.com) from Newark and Washington, DC. Code-sharing airlines can quote through fares with one of the above, or a European partner, from virtually **every major US city**, connecting either in New York or a European hub such as London, Amsterdam or Frankfurt.

**Fares** vary greatly, so it's worth doing some research online, or using a good travel agent; book as far ahead as possible to get the best price. Expect to pay ten to twenty percent more from the West Coast. Remember, too, that you may be better off getting a domestic flight to New York or Philadelphia and heading directly to Athens from there, or flying to London (beware of changing airports as they are far apart) or another European city and travelling on from there.

As with the US, airfares from **Canada** vary depending on where you start your journey and whether you take a direct service. Air Canada Rouge (http://aircanada.com) flies daily to Athens out of Toronto and Montreal between May and October, while Air Transat (http://airtransat.com) also has summer-only flights two or three times a week from Toronto and Montreal to Athens. Otherwise, you'll have to choose among one- or two-stop itineraries on a variety of European carriers, or perhaps Delta via New York; costs from Vancouver can be double that of Toronto in high season.

### A BETTER KIND OF TRAVEL

At Rough Guides we are passionately committed to travel. We believe it helps us understand the world we live in and the people we share it with – and of course tourism is vital to many developing economies. But the scale of modern tourism has also damaged some places irreparably, and climate change is accelerated by most forms of transport, especially flying. We encourage all our authors to consider the carbon footprint of the journeys they make in the course of researching our guides.

## Flights from Australia and New Zealand

There are **no direct flights** from Australia or New Zealand to Greece; you'll have to change in Southeast Asia, the Gulf or Europe. Tickets purchased direct from the airlines tend to be expensive; travel agents or Australia-based websites generally offer much better deals on fares and have the latest information on limited specials and stopovers.

The shortest flights and best fares are generally with airlines like Emirates (http://emirates.com), in partnership with Qantas (http://qantas.com), and Etihad (http://etihadairways.com) who fly you directly to Athens from their Gulf hubs, though you'll also find offers on Swiss (http://swiss.com), KLM (http://klm.com) and other European carriers. From New Zealand, prices are noticeably higher.

## Flights from South Africa

There are currently **no direct flights** from South Africa to Athens. Alternative routes include Emirates (http://emirates.com) or Etihad (http://etihadairways.com) via the Gulf, EgyptAir (http://egyptair.com) via Cairo, or just about any of the major European airlines via their respective domestic hubs.

## Regional flights

**Kalamáta** is the regional airport of the **Peloponnese** with direct flights from Heathrow, Gatwick and Stansted on British Airways (http://britishairways.com), Ryanair (http://ryanair.com), easyjet (http://easyjet.com) or Jet2 (http://jet2.com), but seasonally only i.e. from the beginning of April through to October. Outside of these months, fly to Athens or Thessaloniki, then take a **domestic connecting flight** with Aegean (https://aegeanair.com), Sky Express (https://skyexpress.gr) or Olympic (https://olympicair.com).

### FLIGHT AGENTS

**Charter Flight Centre** UK 020 8232 9779, http://charterflights.co.uk. Booking for a huge range of charter flights from the UK and Ireland.

**Flight Centre** UK 0870 499 0040, Ireland 01 695 0365, US 1866 977 9341, Canada 1877 967 5302, Australia 133 133, New Zealand 0800 243 544, South Africa 0877 405 000; http://flightcentre.com. Low-cost airfares worldwide from local agencies, plus rail passes and more.

**North South Travel** UK 01245 608 291, http://northsouthtravel.co.uk. Friendly, competitive flight agency, offering discounted fares worldwide. Profits are used to support projects in the developing world, especially the promotion of sustainable tourism.

**Skyscanner** http://skyscanner.net. Comprehensive flight search site that includes charter and budget airlines.

**Trailfinders** UK 020 7084 6500, Ireland 01 677 7888; http://trailfinders.com. One of the best-informed and most efficient agents for independent travellers.

**Travel CUTS** Canada 1800 667 2887, http://travelcuts.com. Popular, long-established student-travel organization, with good worldwide offers; not only for students.

## Trains

As a result of the economic crisis, **Greek rail routes** have been greatly reduced, and for a while all international services were suspended. Travelling to Greece by train is possible, however, and the most practical route **from Britain** doesn't actually involve any Greek trains; you cross France and Italy by rail before embarking on the **ferry from Bari**, Brindisi, Ancona or Venice to Pátra (Patras) (see box, page 22). The quickest route (though still slower and more expensive than using the ferry from Italy) is via Paris, Munich and Zagreb to Belgrade.

Either way, the journey to Athens from the UK takes **two days** at least and will almost always work out more expensive than flying. It also takes a fair bit of planning, since there's no through train and **tickets** have to be bought from several separate operators. However, you do have the chance to stop over on the way, while

### ITALY–PELOPONNESE FERRIES

Sailing from **Italy to Greece**, you will arrive in Pátra at the northwest tip of the Peloponnese. Ferries also sail from Venice and Ancona to Pátra via Igoumenítsa/Corfu. These longer routes are more expensive, but the extra cost closely matches what you'll pay in Italian motorway tolls and fuel to get further south. On most ferries, you can stop over in Corfu for no extra charge.

The following companies operate ferries: schedule and booking details for all of them are also available at http://openseas.gr.

**Grimaldi Lines** http://directferries.co.uk. Ancona, Brindisi and Venice to Igoumenítsa and Pátra.

**Minoan Lines** http://minoan.gr. Ancona and Venice to Igoumenítsa and Pátra.

**Superfast** http://superfast.com. Ancona, Bari and Venice to Corfu, Igoumenítsa and Pátra.

**Ventouris Ferries** http://ventourisferries.it. Bari to Corfu, Igoumenítsa, Kefaloniá and Zákynthos.

with an **InterRail** (for European residents only; http://interrail.eu) or **Eurail** (for all others; http://eurail.com) pass, you can take in Greece as part of a wider rail trip around Europe. Booking well in advance (essential in summer) and going for the cheapest seats on each leg can help reduce costs. Using rail passes will cost you more, but give far more flexibility. For full details, check out the Man in Seat 61 website (http://seat61.com).

## Car and ferry

**Driving to Greece** can be a pleasant proposition if you have plenty of time to dawdle along the way, though fuel, toll and ferry costs ensure it's not a cheap option. It's only worth considering if you want to explore en route, or are going to stay for an extended period. The **most popular route** from the UK to the Peloponnese is down through France and Italy to catch the **ferry** from Bari, Brindisi, Ancona or Venice to Pátra (Patras); this is much the best way to get to western and southern Greece, the Ionian islands, and to Athens and most of the islands except those in the northeast Aegean. The far longer alternative through Germany, Austria, Slovenia, Croatia, Serbia and North Macedonia only makes sense if you're heading to the north, or want to explore northern Greece on the way.

## Tour operators

Every mainstream **tour operator** includes Greece in its portfolio. You'll find far more interesting alternatives, however, through the small **specialist agencies**.

### PACKAGE OPERATORS

**Hidden Greece** UK 020 8004 9095, http://hidden-greece.co.uk Specialist agent putting together tailor-made packages to smaller destinations at reasonable prices.

**Homeric Tours** US 1800 223 5570, http://homerictours.com. Hotel packages, individual tours, escorted group tours and fly-drive deals. Good source of inexpensive flights.

**Olympic Holidays** UK 020 8492 6868, http://olympicholidays.com. Huge package-holiday company specializing in Greece; all standards from cheap and cheerful to five-star, and often a good source of last-minute bargains and cheap flights.

**Sun Island Tours** Australia 1300 665 673, New Zealand 64 9889 6567; http://sunislandtours.com.au. Greece specialist offering an assortment of island-hopping, fly-drives, cruises and guided land-tour options, as well as tailor-made.

**Sunvil Holidays** UK 020 8568 4499, http://sunvil.co.uk. High-quality outfit with a wide range of holidays to all parts of the mainland and islands.

**True Greece** US 1800 817 7098, http://truegreece.com. Luxury hotels and villas, plus cruises, customized trips, weddings and more.

### WILDLIFE HOLIDAYS

**Natural Greece** Greece 0030 21303 46261, http://natural-greece.gr. Birdwatching, bear-spotting, botanical and marine-eco (some including scuba) trips across the country.

**Naturetrek** UK 01962 733051, http://naturetrek.co.uk. Fairly pricey but expertly led one- or two-week birdwatching and botanical tours in the Peloponnese

# Getting around

## By bus

Buses from Athens (daily, hourly; 1hr) to the Peloponnese run along the highway past Elefsína and over the Corinth Canal to the Isthmós KTEL station, 6km east of the modern town of Kórinthos. Most stop there (except for services to Kórinthos town) and then go on to Náfplio, Trípoli, Spárti, Kalamáta, Pýrgos and Pátra. If you don't have a direct service to the Peloponnesian towns, you'll have to change here.

From major departure points, **ticketing** is computerized, with assigned seating, and on inter-city lines such as Athens–Pátra buses often get fully booked at the *ekdhotíria* (ticket-issuing office); some regional KTEL companies have online booking, though it's no cheaper than buying from the ticket office on the day. On secondary rural/island routes, it's first-come, first-served, with some standing allowed, and tickets dispensed on the spot by a conductor (*ispráktoras*). Prices are fixed according to distance: note that return tickets are not always cheaper than two one-way fares.

## By train

Athens' commuter train network, the Proestiakós, runs hourly to Kiáto via Kórinthos (daily 6am–11pm; 1hr 30min), and makes a worthwhile alternative to the bus. There are works underway to extend the line to Pátra, but currently you have to change at Kiáto onto an OSE shuttle bus for Pátra. No other trains operate except the rack-and-pinion railway train to Kalávryta (http://odontotos.com).

## By car

The region is blessed with dramatic mountain and coastal scenery, which is undoubtedly a joy to drive through. You should, however, bear in mind that the country as a whole has one of the highest fatal **accident rates** in Europe. Local driving habits can be atrocious; overtaking on bends, barging out from side roads and failing to signal manoeuvres are common practices. **Drunk driving** is also a major issue, especially on Sunday afternoons, public holidays or late at night.

Drivers heading from Athens to the Peloponnese should take the express tollway to Elefsína/Kórinthos. Once on the peninsula, there are **three highways**: the Kórinthos–Kalamáta highway, which allows you to cross the Peloponnese diagonally in less than 2hr, albeit with several road tolls; the Kórinthos–Pátra highway; and the Olympic Highway from Pátra to Pýrgos.

**Parking** in almost every mainland town, plus the biggest island centres, is uniformly a nightmare. **Pay-and-display** systems, plus residents-only schemes, are common, and it's often unclear where to obtain tickets. **Fuel**, whether regular unleaded (*amólyvdhi*), super or diesel, is more expensive in remoter areas. Be aware that many petrol stations close after 8pm and on Sundays.

### By boat

Arrival for many on the Peloponnese is by hydrofoil from the Argo-Saronic islands linked with the ports of Ermióni and Pórto Héli (see page 72). For details and frequencies of services, which are drastically seasonal, check the Greek Travel Pages website, http://gtp.gr. Pátra (see page 164) is the Peloponnese port of call for arrivals by ferry from Italy, as well as from Igoumenítsa on the mainland (see box, page 22) and from the Ionian islands (see box, page 22). There are also ferries from the island of Kýthira (see page 84) to and from Neápoli.

## Accommodation

**There are vast numbers of beds available for tourists throughout the Peloponnese, yet don't rely on simply turning up and finding something. At Easter and in July and August you'll especially run into problems unless you've booked in advance.**

In cities and the region's towns you'll probably stay in **hotels**, but along the coast, the hotels and self-catering complexes are mostly pre-booked by package-holiday companies for the whole season. Non-package visitors are more likely to find themselves staying in smaller, simpler places which usually describe themselves simply as "**rooms**", or as apartments or studios. Standards here can vary from spartan (though invariably clean) to luxurious, but the vast majority are purpose-built blocks where every room is air-conditioned, and where the minimal furnishings are well adapted to the local climate – at least in summer. As is becoming increasingly popular now, the Peloponnese also has several **boutique establishments** to stay in; many converted historical buildings such as **luxury mansion houses**. Some have been listed here as an option, despite their obvious expense.

### Seasons

There are typically three **seasons** which affect prices: October to April (low), May, June and September (mid) and July and August (high), while **Easter** and the first two weeks of August may be in a higher category still. Urban hotels with a predominantly business clientele tend to charge the same rates all year. Elsewhere, places that have significant domestic tourism such as Náfplio frequently charge significantly more at weekends.

Many of the smaller places offering rooms **close from October to April**, so in winter you may have to stay in hotels in the main towns or ports. In smaller inland villages, there may be just one hotel and a single taverna open year-round.

### Hotels

The tourist police set official **star categories** for hotels, from five-star down; all except the top category have to keep within set price limits. You may still see the old letter system (L, luxury, is five-star, then A to E). Ratings correspond to the facilities available (lifts, dining room, pool etc), a box-ticking exercise which doesn't always reflect the actual quality of the hotel; there are plenty of 2-star hotels which are in practice smarter and more comfortable than 3-star outfits. A "boutique" category allows some hotels to escape the straitjacket on the grounds of location or historical significance.

Hotels with 2-star and below have only to provide the most rudimentary of continental **breakfasts** – sometimes optional for an extra charge – while 3-star and above will usually offer buffets with cheese, cold meats, eggs and cereals.

**Single rooms** are rare, and generally not great value – you'll often have to pay the full double-room price or haggle for a small discount; on the other hand, larger groups and families can almost always find triple and quadruple rooms, and more upmarket hotels may have **family suites** (two rooms sharing one bathroom), all of which can be very good value.

In the cheaper hotels, the price of a basic double room starts at around €35 a night out of season, though the same room may be €60 or more in August. For a bit more luxury and in more touristy areas, you'll probably be paying €50–70 in mid-season, €80–100 if you add a pool and other facilities. Flashier hotels and the growing breed of boutique establishments can cost well over €100, while 5-star hotels charge at least €200 and some exclusive resorts €500 or more.

By law, **prices must be displayed** on the back of the door of your room, or over the reception desk. You should never pay more than this, and in practice it is rare to pay as much as the sign says. If you feel you're being overcharged, say you'll make a report to the tourist office or police, who will generally take your side in such cases. The price is for room only, except where otherwise indicated; fancier places often include breakfast in the price – we indicate this in the listing, but check when booking.

All the usual **online booking engines** include properties in the Peloponnese, including Airbnb, and the majority of places have their own online booking. Even on Airbnb most of the properties in tourist areas are regular commercial rooms or apartments: in theory, any accommodation offered has to be registered and pay tax. The vast majority of hoteliers prefer you to book direct, however, rather than pay commission to a third party and will often offer a better deal for direct bookings.

## ACCOMMODATION PRICE CODES

Throughout the guide the following **price codes** are given for accommodation, based on the cheapest double room during high season but not including the peak times such as August or Easter, when prices can almost double. Conversely, prices can fall dramatically during the off-season if the establishment is still open and it is always worth bargaining at any time of year if you show up on spec.

**€** = under €80
**€€** = €80–150
**€€€** = €151–300
**€€€€** = over €300

## Private rooms

Many places categorized as apartments or rooms are every bit as comfortable as hotels, and in the lower price ranges are usually more congenial and better value. Traditionally, **rooms** (*dhomátia* – but usually marked by a "Rooms for Rent" or "Zimmer Frei" sign) were literally a room in someone's house, a bare space with a bed and a hook on the back of the door, where the sparse facilities were offset by the disarming hospitality you'd be offered as part of the family. Such places are now rare, however, and these days almost all are purpose-built (though many still family-run), with comfortable en-suites, air-conditioning and balconies – at the fancier end of the scale you'll find studio and apartment complexes with marble floors, pools, bars and children's playgrounds. Many have a variety of rooms at different prices, so ask to see the room first. Places described as **studios** usually have a small kitchenette, while **apartments** generally have at least one bedroom and separate kitchen/living room.

If you haven't already booked a room, you may find owners descending on ferry or bus arrivals to fill any space they have, sometimes with photos of their premises. This can be great, though you may find the rooms are much further than you had been led to believe, or bear no relation to the pictures. In some

## AIR CONDITIONING AND HOT WATER

When checking out a room, always ask about the status of **air conditioning** and **hot water**. Almost all modern rooms and apartments have air conditioning (indicated by a/c in our listings), but it's sometimes an optional extra, in which case you'll be charged a small additional amount per night to use it. Hot water is always theoretically available, though there may not always be enough: rooftop solar heaters are popular and effective, but shared solar-powered tanks tend to run out in the post-beach shower crunch around 6–7pm, with no more available until the next day. A water heater, either as a backup or primary source, is more reliable. **Wi-fi** is ubiquitous and invariably free – even the most basic places tend to have it, though the signal may not extend to every room, and it's often pretty slow, especially in mountainous regions of the Peloponnese where mobile phone signal can be somewhat sketchy too.

places, the practice has been outlawed. In the more developed island resorts, room owners may insist on a **minimum stay** of a few days, or even a week, especially in high season.

Rooms proprietors sometimes ask to keep your **passport**: ostensibly "for the tourist police", but in reality to prevent you leaving with an unpaid bill. They'll almost always return the documents should you ask for them.

## Villas and longer-term rentals

Although one of the great dreams of Greek travel is finding an idyllic coastal villa and renting it for virtually nothing for a whole month, there's no chance at all of your dream coming true in modern Greece. All the best **villas** are contracted out to **agents** and let through **foreign operators**. They represent some superb places – from simple to luxurious, and costs can be very reasonable, especially if shared between a few people.

However, if you do arrive and decide you want to drop roots for a while, you can still strike lucky if you don't mind avoiding the obvious coastal tourist spots, and are happy with relatively modest accommodation. Choose an untouristed village, get yourself known and ask about; you might still pick up a wonderful deal. **Out of season**, your chances are much better – even in touristy areas, between October and March (sometimes as late as April and May) you can bargain a very good rate, especially for stays of a month or more. **Travel agents** are a good source of information on what's available locally, and many places have an apartment on the side or know someone with one to rent.

Another good source is local **social media groups** – usually best researched before leaving for the Peloponnese. **The Peloponnese Experience** group on Facebook is a good start where you can post questions and interact with others living in and visiting the region.

### VILLA AND APARTMENT AGENTS

**CV Villas** UK 020 3993 4088, http://cvvillas.com. High-quality villas across the Peloponnese.

**Greek Islands Club** UK 020 8232 9780, www.gicthevillacollection.com. Specialist in upmarket villas with private pools, especially in the Ionian islands and Sporades.

**Oliver's Travels** UK 0333 888 0205, http://oliverstravels.com. Stunning upmarket villas of various sizes scattered across the peninsular.

**Simpson Travel** UK 020 3797 1762, http://simpsontravel.com. Classy villas, upmarket hotels and village hideaways in selected areas.

**Vintage Travel** UK 01954 261 431, https://vintagetravel.co.uk. Classy, cute, villas, most with pools, in the Peloponnese, mostly in the Messinia region.

## Hostels and backpackers

Over the years, most traditional youth **hostels** in Greece have closed down; competition from inexpensive rooms meant that they were simply not as cost-effective as elsewhere in Europe, the **Peloponnese** being no exception. The region has limited hostel or camping grounds, some even listing

### 5 SPECIAL PLACES TO STAY

**Euphoria Hotel & Spa, Mystra** Unique spa retreat fusing eastern and western treatments set right into the foot of Taïyetos Mountain. Relax in their facilities with pool and massage treatments, or take up one of their specially planned packages to help you de-stress. Worth the expense. See page 100

**Kinsterna, Áyios Stéfanos, Monemvasiá** An Ottoman judge's farmhouse around an old cistern, converted into a spa eco-retreat with several seasonal activities such as grape stomping and honey gathering. See page 81

**Ariá Estate Suites & Spa** Just 4km from Areópoli, on the way to the Dhiroú caves lies this gorgeous traditional Maniot manor house turned hotel and spa with sixteen suites, cleverly built amphitheatrically overlooking the Bay with outdoor infinity pool and indoor pool in the spa. See page 110

**Manna Arcadia, Korfoxylia Magoulianon, Arcadia** Unique spa mountain retreat, once the largest TB Sanatorium in the Balkans in the 1920s, retaining much of its original infrastructure and architectural character. See page 128

**Opora Country Living, Pyrgiotika, Nafplio** Rustic luxury 30-acre farmhouse with a small smattering of cottages, large outdoor pool and the chance to become involved in their activities such as olive harvesting. See page 69

### CAMPGROUNDS

#### ORGANIZED CAMPGROUNDS

**Gythion Bay Camping** Near Gythio, Laconia (see page 109); https://gythiocamping.gr/. This campground offers a range of amenities, including a pool, restaurant, and access to a sandy beach.

**Ionion Beach Camping** Near Glyfa, Elis (see page 157); https://www.ionion-camping.gr/. Known for its beautiful beachfront location, it provides modern facilities and various activities.

**Simos Camping** On Elafonisos Island, accessible from Neápolis port (see page 83); https://simoscamping.gr/. Famous for its crystal-clear waters and pristine beaches

#### POPULAR AREAS FOR WILD CAMPING

**Taïyetos Mountains**: Offers stunning landscapes, hiking trails, and remote spots for camping. See page 113

**Máni Peninsula**: Known for its rugged beauty and secluded beaches, it's a great area for wild camping. See page 104

**Kyllíni Beach**: The area around Kyllíni offers some good spots for wild camping near the beach. See page 157

small Pension style hotels on Hostel websites. Check https://hostelz.com/hostels-in/Greece/Peloponnese for specific listings.

## Camping

Partly thanks to the economic crisis, Greek **camping** has undergone something of a revival in recent years. **Officially recognized campsites** range from ramshackle compounds on the islands to highly organized and rather soulless complexes, often dominated by camper vans. The Peloponnese offers a variety of options for camping, including organized campgrounds and opportunities for wild camping. Here are some details and recommendations:

### Wild Camping

Wild camping is generally tolerated in Greece, especially in less populated areas like the Peloponnese. However, it's important to follow some guidelines to ensure a respectful and environmentally friendly experience:

**Legal Considerations:** Wild camping is technically not legal, but it's often tolerated if you are discreet and respectful. Avoid camping in protected areas, private property, or near archaeological sites.

**Leave No Trace:** Practice Leave No Trace principles. Pack out all your trash, avoid making fires, and leave the area as you found it.

**Safety:** Choose a safe and secure location. Avoid camping near cliffs, unstable terrain, or areas prone to flooding.

**Water and Supplies:** Ensure you have enough water and supplies, as wild camping locations may be far from amenities.

# Food and drink

**Although many visitors get by on moussaka or kalamári almost every night, there is a huge range to Greek cuisine, not least its wonderful mezédhes, seafood and juicy, fat olives where the famed Kalamata black olive is from. The Peloponnese, in particular, has its own regional dishes.**

Despite depressed wages, most Greeks still eat out with friends or family at least once a week. The atmosphere is always relaxed and informal, with pretensions rare. Drinking is traditionally meant to accompany food, though a range of bars and clubs exists.

## Breakfast

Greeks don't generally eat **breakfast**, more often opting for a mid-morning snack (see below). This is reflected in the abysmal quality of most hotel "continental" offerings, where waxy orange squash, stewed coffee, processed cheese and meats, plus pre-packaged butter, honey and jam (confusingly called *marmeládha*), are the rule at all but the top establishments. There might be some fresh fruit, decent yoghurt and pure honey, if you are lucky. The

## EATING PRICE CODES

In reality, the vast majority of restaurants have a range of dips and salads for around €8–10 and at least some main courses under €10, meaning the expenditure for one person need not exceed €20 by much. *Psarotavérnas* (fish tavernas) tend to be a bit more expensive and sometimes overcharge (see page 28). Other pricier establishments, including gourmet restaurants and the relatively few places serving foreign cuisine, are mostly confined to the larger cities or ultra touristy spots. Generally speaking, eating out is good value and sharing a number of dishes with other people in true Greek fashion will be even kinder on your pocket, as well as giving you the chance to try more things.

Throughout the guide the following **price codes** are given for restaurants and other eating establishments, based on an average two-course meal with wine for one person, not including any particularly expensive items that might be on the menu.

€ = under €20
€€ = €20–30
€€€ = €31–45
€€€€ = over €45

only egg-and-bacon kinds of places are in resorts where foreigners congregate, or where there are returned North American- or Australian-Greeks. Such outlets can often be good value, especially if there's competition.

## Picnics and snacks

**Picnic** ingredients are easily available at supermarkets, bakeries and greengrocers; sampling produce like cheese or olives is acceptable. Standard white **bread** is often of minimal nutritional value and inedible within a day of purchase, although rarer brown varieties such as *olikís* (wholemeal), *sikalísio* (rye bread) or *oktásporo* (multi-grain) fare better. Olives are ubiquitous; the Kalamáta and Ámfissa varieties usually surpass most local picks in quality.

**Honey** is the ideal topping for the famous local **yoghurt**, which is widely available in bulk, the most famous area for **thyme honey** in the Peloponnese being the regions of the Messinian Mani and the Taïyetos mountains.

Sheep-milk yoghurt (*próvio*) is richer and sweeter than the more common cow's-milk. **Feta cheese** is found everywhere, often with a dozen varieties to choose from, made from goat's, sheep's or cow's milk in varying proportions. Harder *graviéra* is the second most popular cheese.

Greece imports very little produce from abroad, aside from bananas, the odd pineapple and a few mangoes. **Fruit** can be expensive and mainly available seasonally. Reliable picnic fruits include cherries (June–July); *krystália*, small, heavenly green pears (Sept–Nov); *vaniliés*, orange- or red-fleshed plums (July–Oct); and kiwi (Oct–May). Less portable, but succulent, are figs (mainly Aug–Sept). Salad **vegetables** are more reasonably priced; besides the famous, enormous tomatoes (June–Sept), there's a bewildering variety of cool-season greens, including rocket, dill, enormous spring onions and lettuces.

On the fertile lands of the Peloponnese, expect to find lemon, orange, mandarin and apricot orchards as well as fig, cherry, apple, walnut, almond trees, plus vineyards such as Brintziki Organic Winery in Olympia and Illía (see page 156), that grows their own distinctive vintage called the Diapyros, and the Wine Route of Nemea near Corinth (see page 54) where the unique *agiorgitiko* grape is grown. Grapefruits can be found around the Valley of Sparta.

## Restaurants

Greek cuisine and **restaurants** are usually straightforward and still largely affordable. Even when preparation is basic, raw materials are usually wholesome and fresh. The best strategy is to **go where Greeks go**, often less obvious backstreet places that might not look much from outside but deliver the real deal. The two most common types of restaurant are the **estiatório** and the **taverna**. The main distinction is that the former is more commonly found in large towns and emphasizes the more complicated, oven-baked casserole dishes termed **mayireftá** (literally, "cooked").

As one might expect, the identikit tavernas at places dominated by foreigners tend to make less effort, bashing out speedily grilled meat with pre-cut chips and rice containing the odd pea. You should beware of **overcharging** and bill-padding at such establishments too. In towns, growing numbers of pretentious restaurants boast fancy decor and Greek nouvelle (or fusion) cuisine with specialty wine lists, while producing little substance.

Greeks generally eat very late in the evening, rarely venturing out until after 9pm and often arriving at 11pm or later. Consequently, most restaurants operate flexible hours, varying according to the level of custom, and thus the **opening times** given throughout the listings should be viewed as approximate at best.

### Tavernas and psistariés

**Tavernas** range from the glitzy and fashionable to rough-and-ready beachside ones with seating under a reed canopy. Really primitive ones have a very limited (often unwritten) menu, but the more elaborate will offer some of the main *mayireftá* dishes mentioned above, as well as standard taverna fare: **mezédhes** (hors d'oeuvres) or **orektiká** (appetizers) and **tis óras** (meat and fish, fried or grilled to order). **Psistariés** (grill-houses) serve spit-roasted lamb, pork, goat, chicken or *kokorétsi* (grilled offal roulade), and often *yíros* by the portion. They will usually have a limited selection of mezédhes and salads (*salátes*), but no *mayireftá*. In rural areas, roadside *psistariés* are often called *exohiká kéndra*.

The most common **mezédhes** found throughout Greece and the Peloponnese are tzatzíki (yoghurt, garlic and cucumber dip), *melitzanosaláta* (aubergine/eggplant dip), *tyrokafterí/khtypití/kopanistí* (spicy cheese dips), fried courgette/zucchini or aubergine/eggplant slices, *yígandes* (white haricot beans in hot tomato sauce), *tyropitákia* or *spanakopitákia* (small cheese or spinach pies), *revythokeftédhes* (chickpea patties similar to falafel), octopus salad and *mavromátika* (black-eyed peas).

Among **meats**, *souvláki* and chops are reliable choices; pork is usually better and cheaper than veal, especially as *pantséta* (pork belly). The best *souvláki*, not always available, is lamb; more commonly encountered are rib chops (*païdhákia*); lamb roasted in tin foil (*exohikó*) is another favourite. *Keftédhes* (breadcrumbed meatballs), *biftékia* (pure-meat patties) and the spicy, coarse-grain sausages called *loukánika* are cheap and good. Chicken is widely available but typically battery-farmed. Other dishes worth trying are stewed goat (*yídha vrastí*) or baked goat (*katsíki stó foúrno*) – goat in general is typically free-range and organic.

## Fish and seafood

Seafood can be one of the highlights of a trip to Greece, especially the Peloponnese given the peninsular is completely surrounded by water, though there are some tips to bear in mind. When ordering, the standard procedure is to go to the glass counter and pick your specimen, then have it weighed (uncleaned) in your presence. Overcharging, especially where a printed menu is absent, is not uncommon; have weight and price confirmed clearly. Taverna owners often comply only minimally with the requirement to indicate when seafood is **frozen** – look for the abbreviation "kat", "k" or just an

### REGIONAL DISHES IN THE PELOPONNESE

**Arcadia** – PDO (Protected Designation of Origin) *feta* and pasta from Vytina and *graviera* cheese from Tripoli. Baked aubergines (*tsakonikes melitzanes*) with *feta*, slow-cooked cockerel with thick pasta (*hylopites*). Also popular here is the Corinthian raisin, used in dishes such as wild boar with quince and cod *plaki*, a dish with salted cod, potatoes, courgettes and tomatoes.

**Argolid & South West Argolid, inc. Corinth & Náfplio** – Fruits such as PDO pomegranates, melons, apricots and wild cherries made into jams. Lamb *bogana* cooked in an earthen pot with potatoes, tomatoes and herbs, *giosa*, mature goat, gently cooked until it falls off the bone and served in baking parchment and *gourounopoula* (roast pork).

**Máni** – Cured pork with celery (*Syglino*), chicken with red sauce and traditional pasta (*hilopites*), small fried pies with herbs and local cheese (*Tsaitia*)

**Messinia inc. Kalamata** – lamb with oregano (*riganato*), and cockerel with small, square-cut pasta (*hylopites*). Classic vegetable-based dishes include courgette flowers fried with fresh tomatoes, black-eyed beans with spinach and greens and a boiled wheat dish with tomato (*trahanas*).

**Olympia and Ilía** – vermicelli-style noodles with oil, sautéed onion and grated tomato, slow-cooked and served with freshly ground pepper and *feta* (*hondromenoudelo*), beans cooked with courgettes (*tabakali*).

### FAST FOOD GREEK STYLE

Traditional hot **snacks** are still easy to come by, although they are being elbowed aside by Western fast food at both international and nationwide Greek chains such as *Goody's* (burgers, pasta and salad bar), *Everest*, *Grigoris* and *Theios Vanias* (baked pastries and baguette sandwiches), and various pizzerias. Still, thousands of kebab shops (*souvladzídhika*) churn out *souvlákia*, either as small shish on wooden sticks or as *yíros* – doner kebab with garnish in pítta bread. Other snacks include cheese pies (*tyrópites*), spinach pies (*spanokópites*) and, less commonly, minced-meat pies (*kreatópites*); these are found either at the baker's or some of the aforementioned chains.

asterisk on the Greek-language side of the menu. If the price, almost invariably quoted by the kilo, seems too good to be true, it's almost certainly farmed. The choicest varieties, such as red mullet, *tsipoúra* (gilthead bream), sea bass or *fangrí* (common bream), will be expensive if wild. Less esteemed species tend to cost much less per kilo but are usually quoted by the portion.

Fish caught in the summer months tend to be smaller and drier, and so are served with *ladholémono* (oil and lemon) sauce. An inexpensive May–June treat is fresh, grilled or fried *bakaliáros* (hake). *Gávros* (anchovy), *atherína* (sand smelts) and *sardhélles* (sardines) are late-summer fixtures, at their best in the northeast Aegean. *Koliós* (mackerel) is excellent either grilled or baked in sauce. Especially in autumn you may find *psarósoupa* (fish soup) or *kakaviá* (bouillabaisse).

Cheaper **seafood** (*thalassiná*) such as fried baby squid (usually frozen); *thrápsalo* (large, grillable deep-water squid) and octopus are summer staples; often mussels, cockles and small prawns will also be offered at reasonable sums.

In the **Argolid** region and near **Epidaurus** there are several floating marina fish farming units where mostly sea bream and sea bass is farmed.

## Wine

The Peloponnese is renowned for its diverse and exceptional wines with the wine routes of Nemea (see page 54) and Olympia (see page 156) of specific interest to viticulturists'. Blessed with a Mediterranean climate and varied soil, it produces some of Greece's finest wines. Key varieties include the Agiorgitiko grape, known for its deep red colour and rich flavours from Nemea with the Olympia region producing, from its white grapes: Chardonnay, Assyrtiko and Malagousia and from red grapes: Merlot, Syrah, Agiorgitiko and Avgoustiatis.

The region also boasts the sweet dessert wines of Patras, made from Mavrodaphne and Muscat grapes. Peloponnesian vineyards combine ancient traditions with modern techniques, resulting in wines that are celebrated for their complexity, balance, and reflection of the region's rich winemaking heritage.

All tavernas will offer you a choice of bottled **wines**, and most have their own house variety, kept in barrels, sold in bulk (*varelísio* or *hýma*) by the quarter-, half- or full litre, and served in glass flagons or brightly coloured tin "monkey-cups". Per-litre prices depend on locale and quality but are generally cheap by European standards.

## Cafés and bars

A venerable institution, under attack from the onslaught of mass global culture, is the **kafenío**, still found in every Greek town but dying out or extinct in most resorts. In greater abundance, you'll encounter **patisseries** (*zaharoplastía*), swish modern **cafeterias** and **trendy bars**.

### Kafenía, cafeterias and coffee

The **kafenío** (plural *kafenía*) is the traditional Greek coffee house. Although its main business is "Greek" (Middle Eastern) **coffee** – prepared unsweetened (*skétos* or *pikrós*), medium (*métrios*) or sweet (*glykós*) – it also serves instant coffee, ouzo, brandy, beer, sage-based tea known as *tsáï vounoú*, soft drinks and juices. Some *kafenía* close at siesta time, but

### VEGETARIANS

Vegetarians will find scarcely any dedicated **meat-free restaurants** in the Peloponnese. That is not to say that they cannot enjoy excellent food. The best solution in tavernas or *ouzerís* is to assemble a meal from vegetarian mezédhes and salads and, in *estiatória* especially, keep an eye open for the delicious *ladherá*, vegetables baked in various sauces. See box on page 29 for regional dishes.

many remain open from early in the morning until late at night. The chief summer socializing time for a pre-prandial ouzo is 6–8pm, immediately after the afternoon nap.

Cafeterias are the province of fancier varieties of coffee and **kafés frappé**, iced instant coffee with sugar and (optionally) condensed milk – uniquely Greek despite its French name. Like Greek coffee, it is always accompanied by a glass of water. *Freddoccino* is a cappuccino-based alternative to the traditional cold frappé. "Nes"(café) is the generic term for all instant **coffee**, regardless of brand. Thankfully, almost all cafeterias now offer a range of foreign-style coffees – filter, dubbed *fíltros* or *gallikós* (French); cappuccino; and espresso – at overseas prices. Alcohol is also served and many establishments morph into lively bars late at night.

### Sweets and desserts

The **zaharoplastío**, a cross between café and patisserie, serves coffee, a limited range of alcohol, yoghurt with honey and sticky cakes. The better establishments offer an amazing variety of pastries, cream-and-chocolate confections, honey-soaked Greco–Turkish sweets like *baklavás*, *kataïfi* (honey-drenched "shredded wheat"), *loukoumádhes* (deep-fried batter puffs dusted with cinnamon and dipped in syrup), *galaktoboúreko* (custard pie) and so on. For more dairy-based products, seek out a **galaktopolío**, where you'll often find *rizógalo* (rice pudding), *kréma* (custard) and locally made *yiaoúrti* (yoghurt). Both *zaharoplastía* and *galaktopolía* are more family-oriented places than a *kafenío*. **Traditional specialities** include "spoon sweets" or *glyká koutalioú* (syrupy preserves of quince, grape, fig, citrus fruit or cherry).

**Ice cream**, sold principally at the parlours which have swept across Greece (Dhodhoni is the posh home-grown competition to Haägen-Dazs), can be very good and almost indistinguishable from Italian prototypes.

## TAVERNA TIPS

Since the idea of **courses** is foreign to Greek cuisine, starters, main dishes and salads often arrive together unless you request otherwise. The best strategy is to order a selection of *mezédhes* and salads to share, in local fashion. Waiters encourage you to take *horiátiki saláta* – the so-called Greek **salad**, including feta cheese – because it is the most expensive. If you only want tomato and cucumber, ask for *angourodomáta*. Cabbage-carrot (*láhano-karóto*) and lettuce (*maroúli*) are the typical cool-season salads.

**Bread** is generally counted as part of the "cover" charge (€0.50–1 per person), so you have to pay for it even if you don't eat any. Though menu prices are supposedly inclusive of all taxes and service, an extra **tip** of around five percent or simple rounding up of the bill is a decent gesture if you've had good service.

## THE STRONG STUFF

**Ouzo,** *tsípouro* (north mainland and increasingly nationwide) and **rakí** or *tsikoudhiá* (Crete) are simple spirits of up to 48 percent alcohol, distilled from the grape-mash residue of winemaking. The former is always flavoured with anise, the latter two are mostly unadulterated but may have a touch of anise, cinnamon, pear essence or fennel. There are nearly thirty brands of ouzo or *tsípouro*; the best are reckoned to be from Lésvos and Sámos islands, or Zítsa and Týrnavos on the mainland. Note that ouzo has the peculiar ability to bring back its effect when you drink water the morning after, so make sure you don't plan to do anything important (like driving) the next day.

### Bars, beer and mineral water

**Bars** (*barákia*) are ubiquitous across Greece, ranging from clones of Spanish bodegas and British pubs to musical beachside bars more active by day than at night. At their most sophisticated, however, they are well-executed theme venues in ex-industrial premises or Neoclassical houses, with both Greek and international soundtracks. Many Greek bars have a half-life of about a year; the best way to find current hot spots, especially if they're more club than bar, is to look out for posters advertising bar-hosted events in the neighbourhood.

**Shots** and **cocktails** are invariably quite expensive, except during well-advertised happy hours. **Beers**, which can vary wildly in price according to how trendy the bar is, are mostly foreign lagers made locally under licence at a handful of breweries on the mainland. **Local brands** include Zeos Gold Pilsner, Zeos Black Weiss and Zeos Blue Lager from the Argos region with its unique flavour of malt that makes it sweet to hops for the bitterness. Eza Fine Larger and Premier Pilsner are brewed in Kyparissi in the southern Peloponnese, popular due to its aroma of citrus fruits and delicate bitterness.

The town of Loutraki, 5 miles northeast of Corinth, produces its own **mineral water** yet is not esteemed by the Greeks themselves, who prefer various brands from other regions of Greece such as Crete and Epirus. In many tavernas there's a backlash against plastic bottles, and you can now get mineral water in glass bottles. Souroti, Epsa and Sariza are the principal labels of naturally **sparkling** (*aerioúho*) water, in small bottles. Note that despite variable quality in taste, **tap water** is essentially safe all over the Peloponnese. Water comes as standard, even if ordering a soft drink, so if you prefer tap water, be sure to advise the waiter in advance.

# Festivals

**Most of the big Greek popular festivals have a religious basis, so they're observed in accordance with the Orthodox calendar: this means that Easter, for example, is only rarely celebrated on the same weekend and can fall as much as five weeks after the Western festival.**

On top of the main religious festivals, there are scores of local festivities, or **paniyíria**, celebrating the patron saint of the village church. Some of the more important are listed below; the *paramoní*, or **eve of the festival**, is often as significant as the day itself, and many of the events are actually celebrated on the night before. If you show up on the morning of the date given, you may find that you have missed most of the music, dancing and drinking. With some 330-odd possible saints' days, though, you're unlikely to travel round for long without stumbling on something. Local tourist offices should be able to fill you in on events in their area.

## Easter

**Easter** is by far the most important festival of the Greek year. It is an excellent time to be in Greece and the Peloponnese, both for the beautiful and moving religious ceremonies and for the days of feasting and celebration which follow. If you make for a smallish village, you may well find yourself an honorary member for the period of the festival. This is a busy time for Greek tourists as well as international ones, however, so book ahead: for Easter dates, see below.

The first great ceremony takes place on **Good Friday** evening, as the Descent from the Cross is lamented in church. At dusk, the *Epitáfios*, Christ's funeral bier, lavishly decorated by the women of the parish, leaves the sanctuary and is paraded solemnly through the streets. Late **Saturday** evening sees the climax in a majestic Mass to celebrate Christ's triumphant return. At the stroke of midnight, all the lights in each crowded church are extinguished and the congregation plunged into darkness until the priest lights the candles of the worshippers, intoning *"Dévte, lévete Fós"* ("Come, take the Light"). The burning candles are carried home through the streets; they are said to bring good fortune to the house if they arrive still burning.

The lighting of the flames is the signal for celebrations to start and the Lent fast to be broken. The traditional greeting, as fireworks and dynamite explode all around you in the street, is *"Khristós Anésti"* ("Christ is risen"), to which the response is *"Alithós Anésti"* ("Truly He is risen"). On **Easter Sunday** there's feasting on roast lamb.

The Greek equivalent of **Easter eggs** is hard-boiled eggs (painted red on Holy Thursday), which are baked into twisted, sweet, bread loaves (*tsourékia*) or distributed on Easter Sunday. People rap their eggs against their friends' eggs, and the owner of the last uncracked egg is considered lucky.

## Name days

In Greece, everyone gets to celebrate their birthday twice. More important, in fact, than your actual birthday, is the "**Name Day**" of the saint who bears the same name. If your name isn't covered, no problem – your party is on All Saints' Day, eight weeks after Easter. If you learn that it's an acquaintance's name day, you wish them *Khrónia Pollá* (literally, "many years").

The big name day **celebrations** (Iannis/Ianna on Jan 7 or Yioryios on April 23, for example) can involve thousands of people. Any church or chapel bearing the saint's name will mark the event – some smaller chapels will open just for this one day of the year – while if an entire village is named after the saint, you can almost guarantee a festival. To check out when your name day falls, see http://namedays.gr.

## Festival calendar

### JANUARY

**January 1: New Year's Day** (Protokhroniá) In Greece this is the feast day of Áyios Vassílios (St Basil). The traditional New Year greeting is "Kalí Khroniá".

**January 6: Epiphany** (Theofánia/Tón Fóton) Marks the baptism of Jesus as well as the end of the twelve days of Christmas. Baptismal fonts, lakes, rivers and seas are blessed, especially harbours (such as Pireás), where the priest traditionally casts a crucifix into the water and local youths compete for the privilege of recovering it.

## FEBRUARY/MARCH

**Carnival** (Apokriátika) Festivities span three weeks, climaxing during the seventh weekend before Easter. Pátra Carnival, with a chariot parade and costume parties, is one of the largest and most outrageous in the Mediterranean.

**Clean Monday** (Katharí Dheftéra) The day after Carnival ends and the first day of Lent, 48 days before Easter, marks the start of fasting and is traditionally spent picnicking and flying kites.

**March 25: Independence Day and the feast of the Annunciation** (Evangelismós) Both a religious and a national holiday, with military parades and dancing to celebrate the beginning of the revolt against Ottoman rule in 1821, plus church services to honour the news given to Mary that she was to become the Mother of Christ. There are major festivities on Tínos, Ýdhra and any locality with a monastery or church named Evangelístria or Evangelismós.

## APRIL/MAY

**Easter** (Páskha: April 20 2025; April 12 2026; May 2 2027; April 16 2028) The most important festival of the Greek year (see above). Good Friday and Easter Monday are also public holidays.

On Easter Sunday in Kalamata, the custom of the "Saitopolemos" or "paper plane war" takes place where participants are divided into groups of 10-15 people with a banner, a trumpet, and a leader. Many of them wear traditional or military uniforms. The paper planes light up and the deafening noise excites the spectators. According to local tradition, the custom holds from the struggles of the inhabitants of Kalamata against the Turks, who used the planes to drive out the Turkish cavalry.

**Easter Monday** (April 21 2025; April 12 2026; May 3 2027; April 17 2028); The dance of Yem. In the small town of Sofiko in Corinth, every Easter Monday the inhabitants will gather in the square of the church of Evangelistria to sing and dance, the lyrics referring to foreignness, love, and freedom

**April 23: The feast of St George** (Áyios Yeóryios) St George, the patron of shepherds, is honoured with a big rural celebration, with much feasting and dancing at associated shrines and towns. If it falls during Lent, festivities are postponed until the Monday after Easter.

## MAY/JUNE

**May 1: May Day** (Protomayiá) The great urban holiday when townspeople traditionally make for the countryside to picnic and fly kites, returning with bunches of wildflowers. Wreaths are hung on their doorways or balconies until they are burnt in bonfires on St John's Eve (June 23). There are also large demonstrations by the Left for Labour Day.

**May 21: Feast of St Constantine and St Helen** (Áyios Konstandínos & Ayía Eléni) Constantine, as emperor, championed Christianity in the Byzantine Empire; St Helen was his mother. There are firewalking ceremonies in certain Macedonian villages; elsewhere celebrated rather more conventionally as the name day for two of the more popular Christian names in Greece.

**Whit Monday** (Áyio Pnévma) Fifty days after Easter, sees services to commemorate the descent of the Holy Spirit to the assembled disciples.

**June 29 & 30: SS Peter and Paul** (Áyios Pétros & Áyios Pávlos) The joint feast of two of the more widely celebrated name days is on June 29. Celebrations often run together with those for the Holy Apostles (Áyii Apóstoli), the following day.

## JULY

**July 17: Feast of St Margaret** (Ayía Marína) A big event in rural areas, as she's an important protector of crops.

**July 20: Feast of the Prophet Elijah** (Profítis Ilías) Widely celebrated at the countless hilltop shrines of Profítis Ilías. The most famous is on Mount Taïyetos, near Spárti, with an overnight vigil.

**July 26: St Paraskevi** (Ayía Paraskeví) Celebrated in parishes or villages bearing that name, especially in Epirus.

## AUGUST

**August 15: Assumption of the Blessed Virgin Mary** (Apokímisis tís Panayías) This is the day when people traditionally return to their home village, and the heart of the holiday season, so in many places there will be no accommodation available.

## SEPTEMBER

**September 8: Birth of the Virgin Mary** (Yénnisis tís Panayías) Special services in churches are dedicated to the event.

## OCTOBER

**October 26: Feast of St Demetrios** (Áyios Dhimítrios) Another popular name day. In rural areas the new wine is traditionally broached on this day, a good excuse for general inebriation.

**October 28: Óhi Day** A national holiday with parades, folk dancing and speeches to commemorate prime minister Metaxas' one-word reply to Mussolini's 1940 ultimatum: ***"Ohi!"*** ("No!").

## NOVEMBER

**November 8: Feast of the Archangels Michael and Gabriel** (Mihaïl & Gavriïl, or tón Taxiárhon) Marked by rites at the numerous churches named after them.

## DECEMBER

**December 6: Feast of St Nicholas** (Áyios Nikólaos) The patron saint of seafarers, who has many chapels dedicated to him.

**December 25 & 26: Christmas** (Khristoúyenna) If less all-encompassing than Greek Easter, Christmas is still an important religious feast, one that increasingly comes with the usual commercial trappings: decorations, gifts and alarming outbreaks of plastic Santas on rooftops.

**December 31: New Year's Eve** (Paramoní Protohroniá) As on the other twelve days of Christmas, a few children still go door-to-door singing traditional carols for money. Adults tend to sit around playing cards, often for money. A special baked loaf, the *vassilópitta*, in which a coin is concealed to bring its finder good luck throughout the year, is cut at midnight.

### Cultural festivals of the Peloponnese

Throughout the summer you'll find **festivals** of music, dance, theatre, literature and history at venues across Greece, with many of the events taking place at atmospheric outdoor venues. The granddad of them all is the **Athens and Epidaurus Festival** (http://greekfestival.gr; see page 70), which has been running every summer for over sixty years, incorporating numerous events from open-air performances of Classical drama in ancient theatres such as the Theatre of Epidaurus to jazz and contemporary art. Others in the Peloponnese include:

**Kalamáta Dance Festival** July http://kalamatadancefestival.gr
**Kardamyli Festival** Oct https://kardamylifestival.com/
**Paleologia Festival in Mystra** May https://www.greeka.com/peloponnese/mystras/festivals/
**Pátra International Festival** May–July
**Pátra Film Festival** Oct

## Culture and etiquette

**In many ways, Greece is a thoroughly integrated European country, and behaviour and social mores differ little from what you may be used to at home. The same goes for the Peloponnese region. Dig a little deeper, however, or travel to more remote, less touristed areas within the peninsular and you'll find that traditional Greek ways survive to a gratifying degree. It's easy to accidentally give offence – but equally easy to avoid doing so by following a few simple tips, and to upgrade your status from that of tourist to *xénos*, a word that means both stranger and guest.**

In general, Greeks are exceptionally friendly and curious, to an extent that can seem intrusive, certainly to a reserved Brit. Don't be surprised at being asked personal questions, even on short acquaintance, or having your personal space invaded.

### SHHHH! SIESTA TIME

The hours **between 3 and 5pm**, the midday **siesta** (*mikró ýpno*), are sacrosanct – it's not acceptable to visit people, make phone calls to strangers or cause any sort of loud noise (especially with motorcycles) at this time. Quiet is also legally mandated **between midnight and 8am** in residential areas.

### Dress codes and cultural hints

Though **dress codes** on the beaches are entirely informal, they're much less so away from the sea; most Greeks will dress up to go out, and not doing so is considered slovenly at the least. There are some **nudist** beaches in remote places but on family beaches, or those close to town or near a church (of which there are many along the Peloponnese coast), even toplessness is often frowned on. Most monasteries, and to a lesser extent churches, impose a fairly strict **dress code** for visitors: no shorts, with women expected to cover their arms and wear skirts (though most Greek women visitors will be in trousers); the necessary wraps are often provided on the spot if you have none to hand.

Two pieces of **body language** that can cause **unintentional offence** are hand gestures; don't hold your hand up, palm out, to anybody, and don't make an OK sign by forming a circle with your thumb and forefinger – both are extremely rude. Nodding and shaking your head for yes and no are also unlikely to be understood; Greeks use a slight forward inclination of the head for yes, a more vigorous backward nod for no.

Although **no-smoking zones** in restaurants, bars or public offices are beginning to be respected, Greeks are still among the heaviest smokers in Europe, and in outdoor spaces at least you'll very likely be surrounded by people puffing away.

### Bargaining and tipping

Most shops have fixed prices, so **bargaining** isn't a regular feature of tourist life. It is worth negotiating over rooms off-season, or for vehicle rental, especially for longer periods, but don't be aggressive about it; ask if they have a cheaper room, for example, rather than demanding a lower price. **Tipping** is not essential anywhere, though taxi drivers generally expect it from tourists and most service staff are very poorly paid. Restaurant bills incorporate a service charge; if you want to tip, rounding up the bill is usually sufficient.

### Women and lone travellers

Thousands of **women** travel independently through the Peloponnese without harassment or intimidation.

With the westernization of relationships between unmarried Greek men and women, almost all the traditional Mediterranean macho impetus for trying one's luck with foreign girls has faded. It is sensible not to bar-crawl alone or to accept late-night rides from strangers (**hitching** at any time is not advisable for lone female travellers) and in fact, with its lack of high-rise resorts, the Peloponnese doesn't lend itself to this type of tourism. In more remote areas, intensely traditional villagers may wonder why women travelling alone are unaccompanied, and may not welcome their presence in exclusively male *kafenía*. Travelling with a man, you're more likely to be treated as a *xéni*.

# Health

**There are no required inoculations for Greece, though it's wise to ensure you are up to date on tetanus and polio. The main health risks faced by visitors involve overexposure to the sun, overindulgence in food and drink, or bites and stings from insects and sea creatures.**

EU nationals (including British citizens at the time of writing) are entitled to free medical care in Greece upon presentation of a European Health Insurance Card (see box, page 36). The US, Canada, Australia and New Zealand have no formal healthcare agreements with Greece (other than allowing for free emergency trauma treatment), so insurance is highly recommended.

## Doctors and hospitals

For serious medical attention, you'll find English-speaking **doctors** (mainly private) in all the bigger towns: if your hotel can't help, the tourist police or your consulate should be able to come up with some names. There are also **hospitals** in all the big cities; medical standards are high but, in state hospitals at least, you'll only get the most basic level of nursing care – locals depend on family for support. For an ambulance, phone 166.

## Pharmacies, drugs and contraception

For minor complaints it's enough to go to the local **pharmacy** (*farmakío*). Greek pharmacists are highly trained and dispense a number of medicines which elsewhere could only be prescribed by a doctor. In the larger towns and resorts there'll usually be one who speaks good English. Pharmacies are usually closed evenings and Saturday mornings, but all should have a schedule on their door showing the night and weekend duty pharmacists in town.

If you regularly use any form of **prescription drug**, you should bring along a copy of the prescription, together with the generic name of the drug; this will help you replace it, and avoids problems with customs officials. Also, be aware that **codeine** is banned in Greece – if you import any you might find yourself in serious trouble, so check labels carefully; it's a major ingredient of Panadeine, Veganin, Solpadeine, Codis and Nurofen Plus, to name just a few.

**Contraceptive pills** are sold over the counter at larger pharmacies, though not necessarily the brands you may be used to; a good pharmacist should come up with a close match. **Condoms** are inexpensive and ubiquitous – just ask for *profylaktiká* (less formally, *plastiká* or *kapótes*) at any pharmacy, sundries store or corner *períptero* (kiosk). Sanitary towels and **tampons** are widely sold in supermarkets.

## Common health problems

The main health problems experienced by visitors – including many blamed on the food – have to do with **overexposure to the sun**. To avoid these, cover up, wear a hat, and drink plenty of fluids to avoid any danger of **sunstroke**; remember that even hazy sun can burn. **Tap water** meets strict EU standards for safety, but high mineral content and less than perfect desalination on many islands can leave a brackish taste not suited to everyone. For that reason many people prefer to stick to bottled water (see page 32). **Hayfever** sufferers should be prepared for a pollen season earlier than in northern Europe, peaking in April and May.

## Hazards of the sea

To avoid hazards in or by the sea, goggles or a dive mask for swimming and footwear for walking over wet or rough rocks are useful. You may have the bad luck to meet an armada of **jellyfish** (*tsoúkhtres*), especially in late summer; they come in various colours and sizes ranging from purple "pizzas" to invisible, minute creatures. Various over-the-counter remedies are sold in resort pharmacies to combat the sting, and baking soda or diluted ammonia also help to lessen the effects. Less vicious but far more common are spiny **sea urchins**, which infest rocky shorelines year-round. If you step on or graze against one, an effective way to remove the spines is with a needle (you can crudely sterilize it with heat from a cigarette lighter) and olive oil. If you don't remove the spines, they'll fester.

### THE EUROPEAN HEALTH INSURANCE CARD

Despite Brexit having come into effect, British citizens are still covered by the **EHIC** scheme (http://ehic.org.uk, http://ehic.ie) for as long as their card is valid; when it expires, they will be able to apply for a UK GHIC (Global Health Insurance Card) to replace it. Holders of a valid EHIC or GHIC are entitled to free consultation and treatment from doctors and dentists. At hospitals you should simply show your EHIC or GHIC; for free treatment from a regular doctor or dentist, call the IKA (the Social Insurance Institute, who administer the scheme) on their national appointments hotline, 184. For prescriptions from pharmacies you pay a small fixed charge plus 25 percent of the cost of the medicine; if you are charged in full, get a receipt and keep the original prescription to claim it back. You can also claim back for private treatment; take the original receipts and your EHIC to the IKA within one month, and they will reimburse you up to the limit allowed for similar treatment by the IKA.

## Bites and stings

Most of Greece's insects and reptiles are pretty benign, but there are a few that can give a painful bite. Much the most common are **mosquitoes**: you can buy repellent devices and sprays at any minimarket. On beaches, **sandflies** can also give a nasty (and potentially infection-carrying) sting. **Adders** (*ohiés*) and **scorpions** (*scorpií*) are found throughout Greece. Both are shy, but take care when climbing over drystone walls where snakes like to sun themselves, and – particularly when camping – don't put hands or feet in places, like shoes, where you haven't looked first.

Finally, in addition to munching its way through a fair amount of Greece's surviving pine forests, the pine processionary **caterpillar** – which takes its name from the long, nose-to-tail convoys – sports highly irritating hairs, with venom worse than a scorpion's. If you touch one, or even a tree trunk they've been on recently, you'll know all about it for a week, and the welts may require antihistamine to heal.

If you snap a **wild-fig shoot** while walking, avoid contact with the highly irritant **sap**. The immediate antidote to the active alkaloid is a mild acid – lemon juice or vinegar; left unneutralized, fig "milk" raises welts which take a month to heal.

# The media

**Greeks are great devourers of newsprint – although few would propose the Greek mass media as a paradigm of objective journalism. Papers are almost uniformly sensational, while state-run TV and radio are often biased in favour of whichever party happens to be in government. Foreign news is widely available, though, in the form of locally printed newspaper editions and TV news channels.**

## Newspapers and magazines

**British newspapers** are widely available in resorts and the larger towns. Many, including the *Times*, *Mail* and *Mirror*, have slimmed-down editions printed in Greece which are available the same day; others are likely to be a day old. In bigger newsagents you'll also be able to find *USA Today* and *Time* as well as the *International New York Times*, which has the bonus of including an abridged English edition of the same day's *Kathimerini*, a respected Greek daily, thus allowing you to keep up with Greek news too. From time to time, you'll also find various English-language magazines aimed at visitors to Greece, though none seems to survive for long.

## Radio

Greece's airwaves are cluttered with **local and regional stations**, many of which have plenty of music, often traditional. In popular areas, many of them have regular news bulletins and tourist information in English. The mountainous nature of much of the country, though, means that any sort of **radio reception** is tricky: if you're driving around, you'll find that you constantly have to retune. The two state-run networks are ER1 (a mix of news, talk and pop music) and ER2 (pop music).

The BBC World Service no longer broadcasts to Europe on short wave, though Voice of America can be picked up in places. Both of these and dozens of others are of course available as internet broadcasts, although frustratingly for sports fans live events cannot be broadcast digitally by the BBC outside the UK.

## Television

Greece's state-funded **TV stations**, ET1, NET and ET3, lag behind the private channels – notably Mega, Star, Alpha, Alter and Skai – in the ratings, though not necessarily in the quality of offerings. Most foreign films and serials are broadcast in their original language with Greek subtitles; there's almost always a choice of English-language movies and series from about 9pm onwards, although the closer you get to the end of the movie, the more adverts you'll encounter. Hotels and rooms places usually have TVs in the room, but reception can be poor: even where they advertise satellite, the only English-language channels this usually includes are CNN and BBC World.

### Films

Greek **cinemas** show all the regular major release movies, which in the case of English-language titles will almost always be in English with Greek subtitles. In summer, wonderful **open-air screens** operate in all the big towns. You may not hear much, thanks to crackly speakers and locals chatting throughout, but watching a movie under the stars on a warm night is simply a great experience.

# Travel essentials

## Accessible travel

In general, **travellers with disabilities** are not especially well catered for in the Peloponnese, though, as EU-wide legislation is implemented, things are gradually improving. For example, across the country as a whole, over two hundred Greek beaches are implementing the SEATRAC system, a fully remote, controlled system whereby a wheelchair user shifts from their wheelchair to the seat, then presses a button to enable it to move along the track and into the sea. In the Peloponnese beaches in the Corinth area, Nafplio, Kalamata and Kyllini on the west coast, to name but a few, all operate such a system.

The National Tourist Organization of Greece (see page 42) can help; they also publish a useful questionnaire that you can send to hotels or self-catering accommodation. Before purchasing **travel insurance**, ensure that pre-existing medical conditions are not excluded. A **medical certificate** of your fitness to travel is also useful; some airlines or insurance companies may insist on it.

## ATMs and debit/credit cards

**Debit cards** are the most common means of accessing funds while travelling, by withdrawing money from the vast network of **ATMs** in the Peloponnese. Airports in Athens and Kalamata have at least one ATM in the arrivals hall, plus any town with a population larger than a few thousand (or substantial tourist traffic) also has them. Visa, MasterCard, Visa Electron, Plus and Cirrus cards are widely accepted; note that American Express holders are restricted to the ATMs of Alpha and National Bank. There is usually a charge of 2.25 percent on the sterling/dollar transaction value, plus a commission fee of a similar amount. Using **credit cards** at an ATM costs roughly the same; however, inflated interest accrues from the moment of use. When using a card, if you are given the option for the transaction to be calculated in euros or your home currency, always choose euros to avoid disadvantageous rates.

Major credit cards are essential for renting cars plus travel agents may also accept them, though a **three-percent surcharge** is often levied on the purchase of ferry tickets.

## Crime and personal safety

Greece is one of Europe's safest countries, with a **low crime rate** and a deserved reputation for honesty. The Peloponnese is tantamount to this. It's quite possible that if you leave a bag or wallet at a café, you'll probably find it scrupulously looked after, pending your return. Nonetheless, theft and muggings are becoming increasingly common, especially in some of the bigger port cities such as Pátra, a trend that has been increased by the economic crisis. With this in mind, it's best to lock rooms and cars securely, and to keep your valuables hidden. Civil unrest, in the form of strikes and demonstrations, is also on the increase, but while this might inconvenience you, you'd be very unlucky to get caught up in any trouble as a visitor.

Though the chances are you'll never meet a member of the national **police force**, the Elliniki Astynomia, Greek cops expect respect, and many have little regard for foreigners. If you do need to go to the police, always try to do so through the **Tourist Police** (171), who should speak English and are used to dealing with visitors. You are required to carry suitable ID on you at all times – either a passport or a driving licence – though it's understood you probably won't have it at the beach, for example.

The most common causes of a brush with the law are beach nudity, camping outside authorized sites, **public inebriation** or lewd behaviour. Also avoid taking **photos in forbidden areas** such as airports and military zones (see page 41).

**Drug offences** are treated as major crimes, particularly since there's a mushrooming local addiction problem. The maximum penalty for "causing the use of drugs by someone under 18", for example, is life imprisonment and an astronomical fine. Foreigners caught in possession of even small amounts of marijuana get long jail sentences if there's evidence that they've been supplying others.

## Electricity

Voltage is 220 volts AC. Standard European two-pin plugs are used; **adaptors** should be bought beforehand in the UK, as they can be difficult to find locally; standard 5-, 6- or 7.5-amp models permit operation of a hairdryer or travel iron. Unless they're dual voltage, North American appliances will require both a step-down transformer and a plug adaptor (the latter easy to find in Greece).

## Entrance fees

All the major **ancient sites**, like most **museums**, charge **entrance fees** ranging from €2–20, with an average fee of €4–8. From November to March, entrance to all state-run sites and museums is half price and **free** on Sundays and public holidays. In the guide we simply denote whether there is a charge or entry is free.

## Entry requirements

EU citizens (and those from some European countries not in the EU) need only a valid **passport** or identity card to enter Greece and can stay indefinitely (see page 39). UK, US, Australian, New Zealand, Canadian and most non-EU Europeans can stay, as tourists, for ninety days (cumulative) in any six-month period. Such nationals arriving by flight or boat from another EU state party to the Schengen Agreement may not be stamped in routinely at minor Greek ports, so make sure this is done in order to avoid unpleasantness on exit. Your passport must be valid for three months after your arrival date but should ideally have six months left on it.

Visitors from **non-EU** countries are currently not, in practice, being given extensions to tourist visas. You must leave not just Greece but the entire Schengen Zone and stay out until the maximum 90-days-in-180 rule, as set forth above, is satisfied. If you **overstay** your time and then leave under your own power – i.e. are not deported – you'll be hit with a huge fine upon departure, and possibly be banned from re-entering for a lengthy period of time; no excuses will be entertained except (just maybe) a doctor's certificate stating you were immobilized in hospital. It cannot be overemphasized just how exigent Greek immigration officials are on this issue.

### GREEK EMBASSIES ABROAD

**Australia & New Zealand** 9 Turrana St, Yarralumla, Canberra, ACT 2600; 02 6271 0100, http://mfa.gr/canberra.
**Canada** 80 Maclaren St, Ottawa, ON K2P 0K6; 613 238 6271, http://mfa.gr/canada/en/the-embassy.
**Ireland** 1 Upper Pembroke St, Dublin 2; 01 676 7254, http://mfa.gr/dublin.
**South Africa** 323 Alpine Way, Hilside Lynwood 0081; 012 348 2352, http://mfa.gr/pretoria.
**UK** 1A Holland Park, London W11 3TP; 020 7229 3850, http://mfa.gr/london.
**USA** 2217 Massachusetts Ave NW, Washington, DC 20008; 202 939 1300, http://mfa.gr/washington.

## Insurance

Despite the EU healthcare privileges that currently apply in Greece (see page 36), you should consider taking out an **insurance policy** before travelling, to cover against theft, loss, illness or injury. Before paying for a whole new policy, however, it's worth checking whether you are already covered: some home insurance policies may cover your possessions when overseas, and many private medical schemes (such as BUPA or WPA in the UK) offer coverage extensions for abroad. **Students** will often find that their student health coverage extends during the vacations.

Make any claim as soon as possible. If you have medical treatment, keep all receipts for medicines and treatment. If you have anything stolen or lost, you must obtain an **official statement** from the police or the airline which lost your bags – with numerous claims being fraudulent, most insurers won't even consider one unless you have a police report.

## Internet

Other than in major cities and some towns, **internet cafés** have all but disappeared, due to the proliferation of **wi-fi.** Nearly all accommodation, most cafés (but not old-style *kafenía*) and an increasing number of tavernas offer free wi-fi to patrons, and an increasing number of municipalities are introducing free wi-fi hotspots such as at ports.

## Laundry

**Laundries**, or *plindíria*, in Greek, are available in some major towns; sometimes an attended service wash is available for little or no extra charge over the basic cost of €8–10 per wash and dry. Self-catering villas will usually be furnished with a drying line and a selection of plastic washbasins or a bucket. Most larger hotels have laundry services, but charges are high.

## LGBTQ+ travellers

Greece in general is deeply ambivalent about **homosexuality**: ghettoized as "to be expected" in the arts, theatre and music scenes but apt to be closeted elsewhere. "Out" gay Greeks are rare, and "out" local lesbians rarer still, although this is changing. Foreign same-sex couples will be regarded with some bemusement but accorded the same standard courtesy as straight foreigners – as long as they refrain from public displays of affection, taboo in rural areas. There is a sizeable **gay community** in Pátra, plus some gay bars in the student town of **Kalamata**.

## Living in Greece

EU (and EEA) nationals are allowed to stay indefinitely in any EU state, but to avoid any problems – eg, in setting up a bank account – you should, after the third month of stay, get a **certificate of registration** (*vevéosi engrafís*). Residence/work permits for **non-EU/non-EEA nationals** can only be obtained on application to a Greek embassy or consulate outside Greece in your home country; you have a much better chance of securing one if you are married to a Greek, are of Greek background by birth or have permanent-resident status in another EU state. Since 2021, UK nationals can no longer officially work in Greece without negotiating this procedure.

As for **work**, non-EU nationals of Greek descent and EU/EEA native speakers of English have a much better chance than anyone else. **Teaching English** at a private language school (*frontistírio*) is not as well paid as it used to be and is almost impossible to get into these days without a bona fide TEFL certificate. Again, Brexit has made the situation more complicated for UK citizens.

Many people find **tourism-related work**, especially in hotels around the coastline most dominated by foreign visitors; April and May are the best time to look around. Opportunities include being a rep for a package company, although they recruit the majority of staff from the home country; all you need is EU nationality and the appropriate language, though knowledge of Greek is a big plus. Jobs in bars or restaurants are a lot easier for women to come by than men. Another option if you have the requisite skills is to work for a **windsurfing** school or **scuba diving** operation.

## Mail

**Post offices** are open Monday to Friday from 7.30am to 2pm, though certain main branches also open evenings and Saturday mornings. **Airmail letters** take 3–7 days to reach the rest of Europe, 5–12 days to North America, a little longer for Australia and New Zealand. For a modest fee you can shave a day or two off delivery time to any destination by using the **express service** (*katepígonda*). **Registered delivery** (*systiméno*) is also available for a similar amount but is slow unless coupled with express service. Stamps (*grammatósima*) are widely available at newsagents and other tourist shops, often for a small surcharge.

**Parcels** should (and often can) only be handled in the main provincial or county capitals. For non-EU/EEA destinations, always present your box open for inspection, and come prepared with tape and scissors.

Ordinary **post boxes** are bright yellow, express boxes dark red, but it's best to use those adjacent to an actual post office, since days may pass between collections at boxes elsewhere.

## Maps

The most reliable **general touring maps** of Greece are those published by Athens-based Anavasi (http://anavasi.gr) who also produce good hiking and topographical maps of the Peloponnese, Road Editions (http://travelbookstore.gr) and Orama (http://oramaeditions.gr). Anavasi and Road Editions products are widely available in Greece at selected bookshops, as well as at petrol stations and general tourist shops countrywide. In Britain they are found at Stanfords (http://stanfords.co.uk) and the Hellenic Book Service (http://hellenicbookservice.com); in the US, they're sold through Omni Resources (http://omnimap.com).

## Money

Greece's currency is the **euro** (€). Up-to-date **exchange rates** can be found on http://xe.com. Euro notes come in denominations of 5, 10, 20, 50, 100, 200 and 500 euros, and coins in denominations of 1, 2, 5, 10, 20 and 50 cents and 1 and 2 euros. Avoid getting stuck with **counterfeit euro notes** (€100 and €200 ones abound). The best tests are done by the naked eye: genuine notes all have a hologram strip or (if over €50) patch at one end, there's a watermark at the other, plus a security thread embedded in the middle. Note that shopkeepers do not bother much with shortfalls of 10 cents or less, whether in their favour (especially) or yours.

### Banks and exchange

**Banks** normally open Monday to Thursday 8.30am–2.30pm and Friday 8.30am–2pm. Always take your passport with you as proof of identity and expect long queues. Large hotels and some travel agencies also provide a **foreign cash exchange service**, though with hefty commissions, as do a number of authorized brokers in Athens and other major tourist centres. When changing small amounts, choose bureaux that charge a flat percentage commission (usually 1 percent) rather than a high minimum. There are a small number of 24-hour automatic **foreign-note-changing machines**, but a high minimum commission tends to be deducted. There is no need to **purchase euros** beforehand unless you're arriving at some ungodly hour to one of the remoter frontier posts.

### Costs

The **cost of living** in Greece in general has increased astronomically since it joined the EU, particularly after the adoption of the euro and further increases in the VAT rate. Prices in shops and cafés across the Peloponnese now match or exceed those of many other EU member countries (including the UK). However, outside the chintzier resorts of the region, travel remains affordable with the aggregate cost of restaurant meals, short-term accommodation and public transport falling somewhere in between that of cheaper Spain or France and pricier Italy.

**Prices** depend on where and when you go. Larger cities that attract a university crowd such as Pátra tend to be more expensive, as are the trendy tourism spots of Náfplio and Costa Navarino, plus costs everywhere increase sharply during July and August, Christmas, New Year and Easter.

A daily per-person **budget** of €120/£101/$130 will get you basic accommodation and meals, plus a short ferry or bus ride, as one of a couple. Camping would cut costs marginally. On €135/£113/$147 a day you could be living quite well, plus sharing the cost of renting a large motorbike or small car. Note that **accommodation** costs (see page 25) vary greatly over the seasons.

A basic taverna **meal** with bulk wine or a beer costs around €20–€25 per person. Add a better bottle of wine, pricier fish or fancier decor and it could be up to €30 a head. Even in the most developed resorts, with inflated "international" menus, there is often a basic but decent taverna where the locals eat.

## Opening hours

It's difficult to generalize about **opening hours in the Peloponnese**, they're notoriously erratic. Most shops open 8.30/9am and close for a long break at 2/2.30pm. Most places, except banks, reopen around 5.30/6pm for three hours or so, at least on Tuesday, Thursday and Friday but increasingly from Monday–Friday. Tourist areas tend to adopt a more northern European timetable, with supermarkets and travel agencies, as well as the most important archeological sites and museums, more likely to stay open through-out the day. If you need to tackle **Greek bureaucracy**, don't

### PUBLIC HOLIDAYS

**January 1** New Year's Day.
**January 6** Epiphany.
**February/March** Clean Monday (*katharí dheftéra*), 7 weeks before Easter.
**March 25** Independence Day.
**April/May** Good Friday and Easter Monday (see page 32 for dates).
**May 1** May Day.
**May/June** Whit Monday, 7 weeks after Easter.
**August 15** Assumption of the Virgin Mary.
**October 28** Óhi Day (see page 33).
**December 25/26** Christmas Day/ Boxing Day.

## PHONE CODES AND NUMBERS

All Greek phone numbers require you to dial all ten digits, including the area code. Landlines begin with 2; mobiles begin with 6. All landline exchanges are digital, and you should have few problems reaching any number from either overseas or within Greece. Mobile phone users are well looked after – there's even signal in the Athens metro.

### PHONING GREECE FROM ABROAD

Dial 0030 + the full number

### PHONING ABROAD FROM GREECE

Dial the country code (below) + area code (minus any initial 0) + number

**Australia** 0061
**Canada** 001
**Ireland** 00353
**New Zealand** 0064
**UK** 0044
**USA** 001
**South Africa** 0027

### GREEK PHONE PREFIXES

**Local call rate** 0801
**Toll-free/Freefone** 0800

### USEFUL GREEK TELEPHONE NUMBERS

**Ambulance** 166
**Fire brigade, urban** 199
**Forest fire reporting** 191
**Operator** 132 (Domestic)
**Police/Emergency** 100
**Speaking clock** 141
**Tourist police** 171 (Athens); 210 171 (elsewhere) 139 (International)

count on getting anything essential done except from Monday to Friday, between 9.30am and 1pm.

As far as possible, times are quoted through the Guide for **tourist sites,** but these change with exasperating frequency, especially since the economic crisis. Both winter and summer hours are quoted throughout the Guide, but to avoid disappointment either phone ahead, check on the Greek Ministry of Culture website (http://odysseus.culture.gr), or time your visit during the core hours of 9am–2pm. **Monasteries** are generally open from approximately 9am to 1pm and 5 to 8pm (3.30–6.30pm in winter) for limited visits. Again, the opening times given for **restaurants**, **cafés** and **bars** can also be very flexible.

## Phones

Three **mobile phone networks** operate in Greece: Vodafone, Cosmote and Nova. **Coverage** throughout the Peloponnese is good, especially in the main towns, though there are a few "dead" zones in the mountains. There are no roaming charges within the EU so EU nationals pay the same price for calls, texts and data to numbers in their home country as they would at home; UK nationals should check the situation post-Brexit. For calling Greek numbers, however, you can save money by buying a **pay-as-you-go** SIM card from any of the mobile phone outlets. Top-up cards are available at all *períptera* (kiosks). North American users can only use tri-band phones in Greece.

Landlines and public phones are run by OTE who provide phonecards (*tilekártes*), available from kiosks and newsagents. If you plan on making lots of international calls, use a **calling card**, which involves calling a free access number from certain phone boxes or a fixed line (not a mobile) and then entering a twelve-digit code. OTE has its own scheme, but competitors generally prove cheaper. Avoid making calls direct **from hotel rooms**, as a large surcharge will be applied, though you will not be charged to access a free calling card number.

## Photography

You can feel free to snap away at most places in Greece, although some **churches** display "No photography" signs, and museums and archeological sites may require **permits** at least for professional photographers. The main exception is around **airports** or **military installations** (usually clearly indicated with a "No pictures" sign).

## Sports and outdoor pursuits

The north Peloppponese coast is a great place to set sail from. On land, the greatest attraction lies in hiking, through what is one of Europe's more impressive mountain terrains. There's also much potential for **rafting** and **kayaking**. Specialist companies offer sea kayaking (see page 72). As for spectator sports, the twin Greek obsessions are football (soccer) and basketball.

## Time

**Standard Greek time** is two hours ahead of GMT. Along with the rest of Europe, the clocks move forward one hour onto **summer time** between the last Sunday in March and the last Sunday in October. For North America, the difference is usually seven hours for Eastern Standard Time, ten hours for Pacific Standard Time.

## Toilets

**Public toilets** are usually in parks or squares, often subterranean; otherwise try a bus station. Except in tourist areas, public toilets tend to be filthy – it's best to use those in restaurants and bars. Remember that throughout Greece, you drop paper in the adjacent **wastebins**, not the toilet bowl.

## Tourist information

The **National Tourist Organization of Greece** (Ellinikós Organismós Tourismoú, or EOT; Visit Greece, http://visitgreece.gr) maintains offices in several European capitals and major cities around the world. It publishes an array of free, glossy pamphlets, invariably several years out of date, fine for getting a picture of where you want to go, though low on useful facts.

You can often get information from **municipal tourist offices** in larger tourism spots such as Náfplio, Sparti, Kalamata and Olympia including advice on local attractions and public transport, as well as informal advice. In the absence of any of these, you can visit the **Tourist Police**, essentially a division (often just a single room) of the local police. They can sometimes provide you with lists of rooms to let, which they regulate, but they're really the place to go if you have a **serious complaint** about a taxi, accommodation or eating establishment.

### GREEK NATIONAL TOURIST OFFICES ABROAD

**UK & Ireland** 4 Great Portland St, London W1W 8QJ; 020 7495 9300, info@gnto.co.uk.

**USA** 800 3rd Ave, New York, NY 10022; 212 421 5777, info@greektourism.com.

## Travelling with children

**Children** are worshipped and indulged in throughout Greece as a whole, presenting few problems when travelling. They are not segregated from adults at mealtimes, and early on in life are inducted into the typical late-night routine – kids at tavernas are expected to eat (and talk) like adults. Other than certain all-inclusive resorts with children's programmes, however, there are very few amusements specifically for them – certainly nothing like Disneyland Paris. Water parks, tourist sites and other places of interest that are particularly child-friendly are noted throughout the guide.

Luxury hotels are more likely to offer some kind of **babysitting** or **crèche service**. All the same basic baby products that you can find at home are available in Greece, though some may be more expensive, so it can pay to load up on nappies, powders and creams before leaving home.

Most domestic ferry-boat companies and airlines offer child **discounts**, ranging from fifty percent to completely free depending on their age; hotels and rooms won't charge extra for infants, and levy a modest supplement for an extra bed.

# Corinth and around



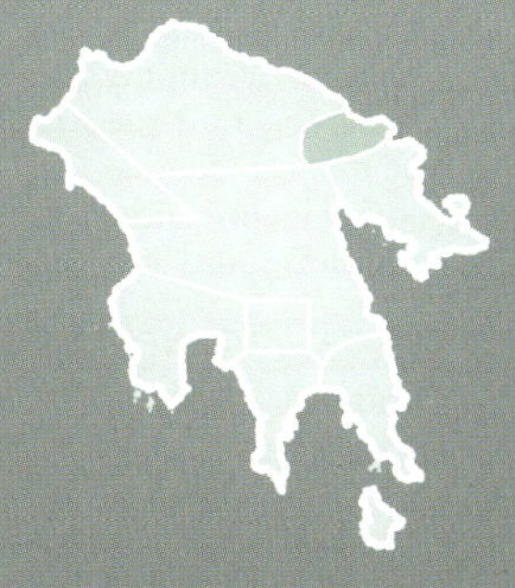

THE CORINTH CANAL

1

# Corinth and around

Throughout Greek history the Isthmus of Corinth, the mainland gateway to the Peloponnese, was strategically important, accounting for the great significance of the city of Corinth in the classical world. In modern times, this small strip of land was further enhanced, at least economically, by the cutting, at long last, of the Corinth Canal–at 8m-deep and rocks on either side reaching up to 76m-high, making it the world's deepest. The modern city of Kórinthos, the capital of its eponymous province, unfortunately fails to live up to its historic hype – now little more than a minor transport hub. By contrast, the archeological site of Ancient Corinth is one of the high points of a visit to the Peloponnese, while the sanctuary of ancient Nemea is also an evocative spot. In this region you'll also find the Loutráki Thermal Spa, the oldest in Greece.

### Brief history

Korinthos' (Corinth) rich history dates back to the Neolithic period. It flourished as a major Greek city-state, known for its wealth and strategic location on the Isthmus of Corinth, connecting mainland Greece with the Peloponnese. The city was famed for its monumental architecture, such as the Temple of Apollo, and its significant role in commerce and culture.

The **Corinth Canal**, completed in 1893, is a vital waterway cutting through the Isthmus of Corinth, linking the Aegean Sea with the Ionian Sea. It significantly shortens maritime travel, bypassing the lengthy route around the Peloponnese.

**Nemea**, located near Corinth, was an important site in ancient Greece, known for the Nemean Games, similar to the Olympics. It also features the Sanctuary of Zeus and is famous for its association with the myth of Hercules and the Nemean Lion. Loutráki, a coastal town near Corinth, is renowned for its therapeutic thermal springs, attracting visitors since ancient times. Today, it is a popular resort destination, known for its beaches, casino, and spa facilities.

## Kórinthos

Like its ancient predecessor, **KÓRINTHOS** (modern Corinth) has been levelled on several occasions by **earthquakes** – most recently in 1981. Repaired and reconstructed with buildings of characterless concrete, it is largely an industrial and agricultural centre, the economy bolstered by the drying and shipping of **currants**, for centuries one of Greece's most successful exports (the word "currant" itself derives from "Corinth"). The modern city has little to offer the outsider, so plan to move on quickly if you come. Having said that, the pedestrianized centre has made what used to be a rather colourless Greek city much more lively and pleasant.

### ARRIVAL AND INFORMATION — KÓRINTHOS

**By bus** The Kórinthos town KTEL bus station is a few blocks east of the centre, at Dimocratías 4 (http://ktelkorinthias.gr).

Destinations Ancient Corinth (every 4 hours; 15min); Athens (1–2 hourly; 55min–1hr 25min); Kiáto (Mon–Fri roughly 2 hourly; 35min); Nemea (4–5 daily; 30min).

**By train** The Proastiakós train station is located about 3km southwest of town (http://trainose.gr) alongside the Néa Ethnikí Odhós expressway; you can then take a taxi into town.

NEMEA'S ARCHAEOLOGICAL TREASURES

# Highlights

❶ **Corinth Canal** The deepest canal in the world with walls of 76m-high, it's an engineering marvel. See page 49

❷ **Ancient Corinth** An extensive site next to the village of the same name, the Temple of Apollo at its core. See page 49

❸ **Loutráki Thermal Spa** Dating back to 1847, this thermal spa is the oldest in Greece and now offers a range of treatments. See page 53

❹ **Ancient Nemea** An ancient sanctuary with the Temple of Nemean Zeus its highlight plus the Stadium once holding over forty thousand spectators. See page 55

HIGHLIGHTS ARE MARKED ON THE MAP ON PAGE 48

1

**Destinations** Athens (hourly; 1hr 5min); Kiáto (hourly; 15min).

**Services** You'll find various banks along northern Ethnikís Andístasis, and the main post office on Adhimándou, on the south side of the park. For car rental try Cars–Hire at Adhimándou 39 (http://cars-hire.gr) near the post office. Their website has a scannable QR code for Smartphone users.

## GETTING AROUND

**By taxi** Cabs wait along the Ethnikís Andístasis side of the park. Try Korinthos Taxi Transfers (http://korinthos-transfers.com/en/) or Radio Taxi Korinthos (27410 73000) at Thrakis 1.

**On foot** The pedestrianized centre revolves around two parallel streets: Kolokotróni and Periándhrou.

## ACCOMMODATION AND EATING

SEE MAP PAGE 50

**Corinthian House Grill** Ethnikis Adistasseos 14, http://corinthianhousegrill.gr/en/. Located in the heart of the town, this place is great for meat lovers with its choice of grills, souvlaiki and gyros. €

**Efeteio** Kolokotróni 24; 27410 21777. Opposite the city courts, this is a 1950s-style ouzerí with a regular clientele of lawyers popping in for lunch. Try its famed kondosoúvli (pieces of chicken on a spit). Closed August. €

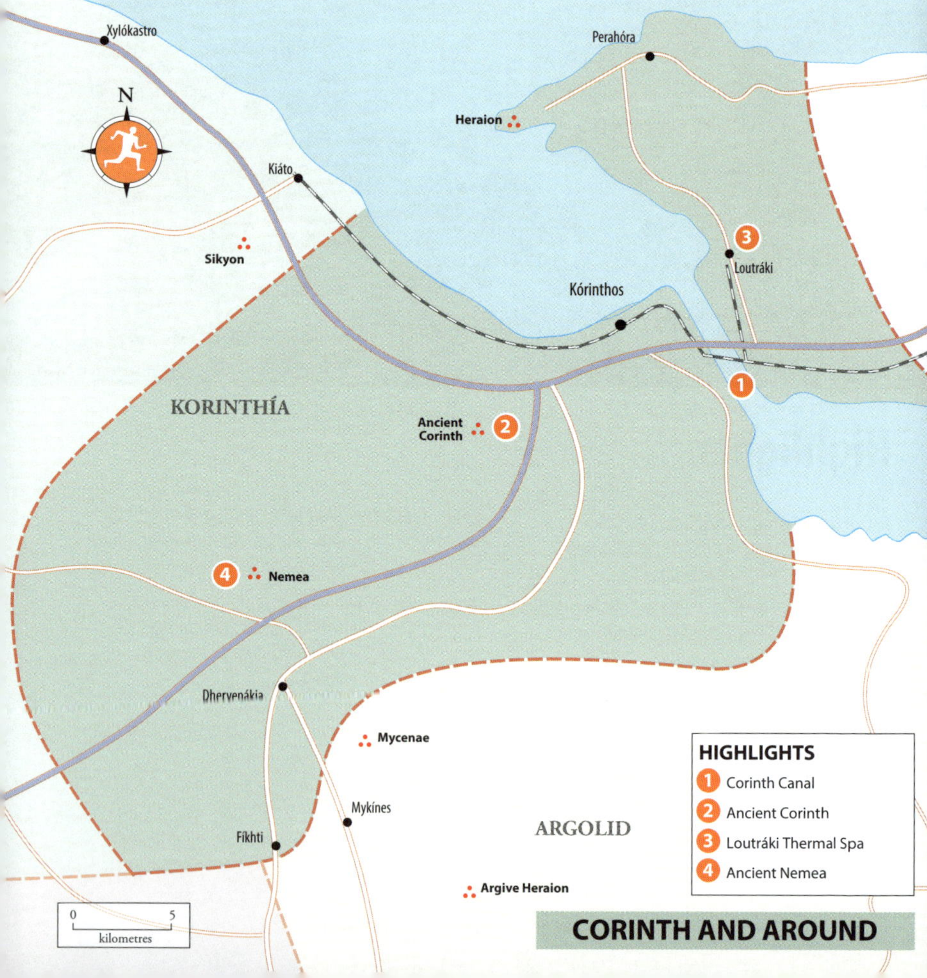


CORINTH AND AROUND

★ **Korinthos** Damaskinou 26, http://korinthoshotel.gr. Just a few metres from the marina, this medium-sized family hotel is plain, clean and very central. Rooms are en suite and have a/c and balconies, some with good views. Parking is available at the public car park behind the hotel. The buffet breakfast costs extra. €

# Corinth Canal

Cutting through the narrow isthmus that joins the Peloponnese to the mainland, the 6km **CORINTH CANAL** seems a very narrow strip of water when viewed from the bridge above, until a huge freighter from Pireás or cruise ship to the Ionian islands suddenly assumes toy-like dimensions as it passes nearly 80m below. Today, super tankers tend to make it something of an anachronism, but it is still used by large vessels and remains a memorable sight. At the western end of the canal, by the old Kórinthos–Loutráki floating bridge, there are remains of the **diolkós**, a paved way along which a wheeled platform used to carry boats across the isthmus. In use from Roman times until the twelfth century, the boats were strapped onto the platform after being temporarily relieved of their cargo.

## Brief history

The idea for a canal providing a short cut and safe passage between the Aegean and Ionian seas harks back at least to Roman times, when **Emperor Nero** himself performed the initial excavations with his little silver shovel, later heavily supplemented by Jewish slave labour. It was only in the 1890s, however, that the technology finally became available for cutting right across the 6km isthmus. Opened in July 1893, the canal, along with its near-contemporary Suez, helped establish Pireás as a **major Mediterranean port** and shipping centre.

### ARRIVAL AND DEPARTURE — CORINTH CANAL

**By car** The national road passes directly over the canal, and the free car park is easy to spot. Look out for the cluster of tourist shops and restaurants, and you'll know you're there.

**By bus** Almost all buses between the Peloponnese and elsewhere stop here.

Destinations Árgos (10–11 daily; 1hr–1hr 25min); Fichti for Mycenae (10–12 daily; 45min); Kalamáta (5 daily; 2hr 25min); Náflpio (10–12 daily; 1hr 15min–1hr 45min); Pátra (hourly; 2hr 30min); Spárti (1 daily; 3hr); Trípoli (1–2 daily; 1hr 30 min).

# Ancient Corinth

The ruins of **ANCIENT CORINTH** (Arhéa Kórinthos), which occupy an extensive site next to the village of the same name and 7km southwest of the modern city, are an essential stop. The site is split into a vast, impressively excavated city with the **Temple of Apollo** at its core, and even more compelling is the stunning acropolis site of **Acrocorinth**, towering 565m above the ancient city. To explore both you need a full day or an overnight stay – a much more agreeable option than staying in Kórinthos itself.

## Brief history

Ancient Corinth was a key centre of the Greek and Roman worlds, whose possession meant the control of trade between northern Greece and the Peloponnese. Not surprisingly, therefore, the area's ancient and medieval history was one of invasions and power struggles that, in Classical times, was dominated by Corinth's **rivalry with Athens**, against whom it sided with Sparta in the Peloponnesian War.

After defeating the Greek city-states of the Achaean League, the Romans **razed** the city in 146 BC, before rebuilding it on a majestic scale in 44 BC under the command of Julius Caesar. Initially it was intended as a colony for veterans, but later became

the **provincial capital**. Once again, Corinth grew rich on trade – with Rome to the west, and Syria and Egypt to the east. The city endured until rocked by two major **earthquakes**, in 375 and 521, which brought down the Roman buildings and again depopulated the site until a brief Byzantine revival in the eleventh century.

## The site

http://odysseus.culture.gr • Various Summer/Winter opening hours, see website • Charge

Entering from the north, you are in the **Roman agora**, an enormous marketplace flanked by the substantial foundations of a huge *stoa*, once a structure of several storeys, with 33 shops on the ground floor. Opposite the *stoa* is a *bema*, a marble platform used by **St Paul** in his defence against the charges brought against him by the Corinthians. At the far end are remains of a **basilica**, while the area behind the *bema* is strewn with the remnants of numerous Roman administrative buildings. Back across the agora, hidden in a swirl of broken marble and shattered architecture, there's a fascinating trace of the Greek city – a grille-covered **sacred spring**, at the base of a narrow flight of steps.

### Fountain of Peirene

More substantial than the spring is the elaborate Roman **Fountain of Peirene**, which stands below the level of the agora, to the side of a wide, excavated stretch of the marble-paved **Lechaion Way** – the main approach to the city. The fountain house was, like many of Athens' Roman public buildings, the gift of the wealthy Athenian

## CORINTHIAN SAINTS AND SINNERS

Roman Corinth's reputation for wealth, fuelled by its trading access to luxury goods, was soon equalled by its appetite for **earthly pleasures** – including sex. Corinthian women were renowned for their beauty and much sought after as *hetairai* (courtesans); over a thousand sacred prostitutes served a temple to Aphrodite/Venus, on the acropolis of Acrocorinth. **St Paul** stayed in Corinth for eighteen months in 51–52 AD, though his attempts to reform the citizens' ways were met with rioting – tribulations recorded in his two **letters to the Corinthians**.

and friend of Emperor Hadrian, Herodes Atticus. Water still flows through the underground cisterns and supplies the modern village.

### Temple of Apollo

Museum same hours as site • Entrance included in site admission

The real focus of the ancient site, though, is a rare survival from the Classical Greek era, the fifth-century BC **Temple of Apollo**, whose seven austere Doric columns stand slightly above the level of the forum, flanked by foundations of another marketplace and baths. Over to the west is the site **museum**, housing a large collection of domestic pieces, some good Greek and Roman mosaics from nearby, a frieze depicting some of the labours of Hercules, and a good number of Roman statues.

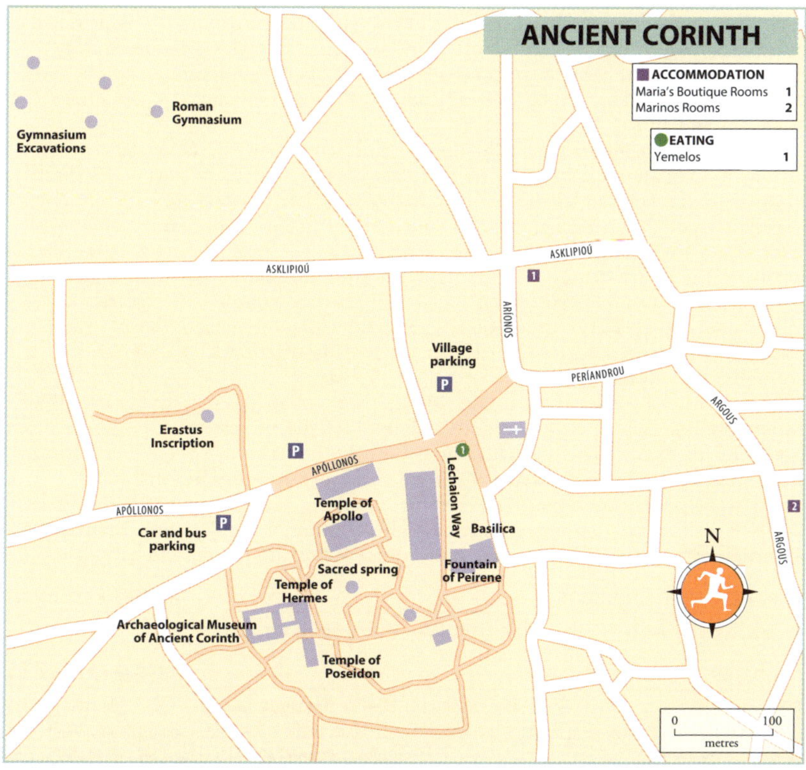

### ANCIENT THERMAL SPAS

**Thermal springs** in Greece date back to ancient times with the Greeks long recognizing their therapeutic benefits for physical and mental well-being. In **Loutráki**, these springs, known as Thermae during antiquity, were dedicated to the gods and believed to possess healing properties. The ancient Greeks built **baths** and **sanctuaries** around these springs, utilising the mineral-rich waters for relaxation and medical treatments. Over the centuries, Loutráki has maintained its reputation as a therapeutic destination attracting visitors worldwide seeking the curative powers of its famed thermal waters.

### Other excavations

A number of miscellaneous smaller excavations surround the main site. To the west, just across the road from the enclosing wire, there are outlines of two **theatres**: a Roman **Odeon** (endowed by Herodes Atticus) and a larger Greek theatre, used by the Romans for gladiatorial battles. To the north are the inaccessible but visible remains of an **Asclepeion** (dedicated to the god of healing).

## Acrocorinth

A hot 4km climb (nearly 1hr) or a 10min drive up from Ancient Corinth • http://odysseus.culture.gr • Various Summer/Winter opening hours, see website • Charge

Rising almost sheer above the lower town and the fertile plains, the medieval fortress of **Acrocorinth** is sited on an imposing mass of rock, still largely encircled by 2km of wall. Despite the long approach, a visit is unreservedly recommended. Looking down over the Saronic Gulf and the Gulf of Kórinthos, you get a real sense of its strategic importance. Amid the extensive remains is a jumble of chapels, mosques, houses and battlements, erected in turn by Greeks, Romans, Byzantines, Frankish crusaders, Venetians and Turks.

The Turkish remains are unusually substantial. Elsewhere in Greece, evidence of the Ottoman occupation has been removed or defaced, but here, at the start of the climb to the entrance, you can see the still-used **fountain of Hatzi Mustafa**, Christianized by the addition of great carved crosses. The outer of the citadel's **triple gates** is also largely Turkish; the middle is a combination of Venetian and Frankish; the inner, Byzantine, incorporating fourth-century BC towers. Within the citadel, the first summit (to the right) is enclosed by a **Frankish keep** – as striking as they come – which last saw action in 1828 during the War of Independence. Keeping along the track to the left, you pass some interesting (if perilous) cisterns, the remains of a Turkish bathhouse, and crumbling Byzantine chapels.

In the southeast corner of the citadel, hidden away in the lower ground, is the **upper Peirene spring**. This is not easy to find: look out for a narrow, overgrown entrance, from which a flight of iron stairs leads down some 5m to a metal screen. Here, broad stone steps descend into the dark depths, where a fourth-century BC arch stands guard over a **pool** of (non-potable) water that has never been known to dry up. To the north of the fountain, on the second and higher summit, is the site of the **Temple of Aphrodite**; after its days as a brothel, it saw use as a church, mosque and belvedere.

### ARRIVAL AND DEPARTURE — ANCIENT CORINTH

**By bus** Buses to Arhéa Kórinthos village leave from Kórinthos every 4 hours (15min).

### ACCOMMODATION AND EATING

SEE MAP PAGE 51

There are a scattering of rooms to rent in Arhéa Kórinthos village and plenty of tavernas along the fence that encloses the site.

**Maria's Boutique Rooms** 27410 31304. You couldn't get nearer to the ancient site if you tried: only 600m away, walking distance. All rooms come with a small kitchenette.

Breakfast included. €€

★ **Marinos Rooms** http://marinos-rooms.gr. A perennial Rough Guides favourite, this is a long-standing family-run hotel with huge rooms and a view of Acrocorinth. Breakfast included. There's great food in the taverna below too – try their three-course menu (€). €

**Yemelos** 27410 31325. Large taverna with quirky, kitsch Greek decor and a panoramic roof terrace overlooking the Temple of Apollo. Excellent meals feature the likes of grilled chicken, home-made pitta bread and fat juicy olives. €

# Loutráki

A mere 8km northeast of Corinth lies the appealing seaside town of **LOUTRÁKI** with its thermal springs. Located on the Gulf of Corinth, Loutráki has been a popular destination since ancient times, celebrated for its healing mineral waters. The **Loutráki Thermal Spa** attracts visitors seeking wellness and relaxation, offering a range of therapeutic treatments.

Beyond this, Loutráki is famous for its beautiful beaches. The town is also home to one of Europe's largest casinos, the **Club Hotel Casino Loutráki**, a five-star resort drawing tourists seeking entertainment and nightlife with a whole host of cultural events in the summer ranging from film festivals and ballet with the Corinth Canal is only a 15min drive away.

One of the best websites for more information on the area is http://visitloutraki.com/en.

## Thermae Spa

Various opening times, check website • Charge • http://www.loutrakispa.gr/en/page/facilities

With three indoor pools, two heated and one cool water for rehabilitation purposes, one outdoor pool with water mushroom, hydro massaging and pool bar plus a whole host of treatments ranging from sauna room, hamam, steam room and therapeutic mud therapies and massage, you'll

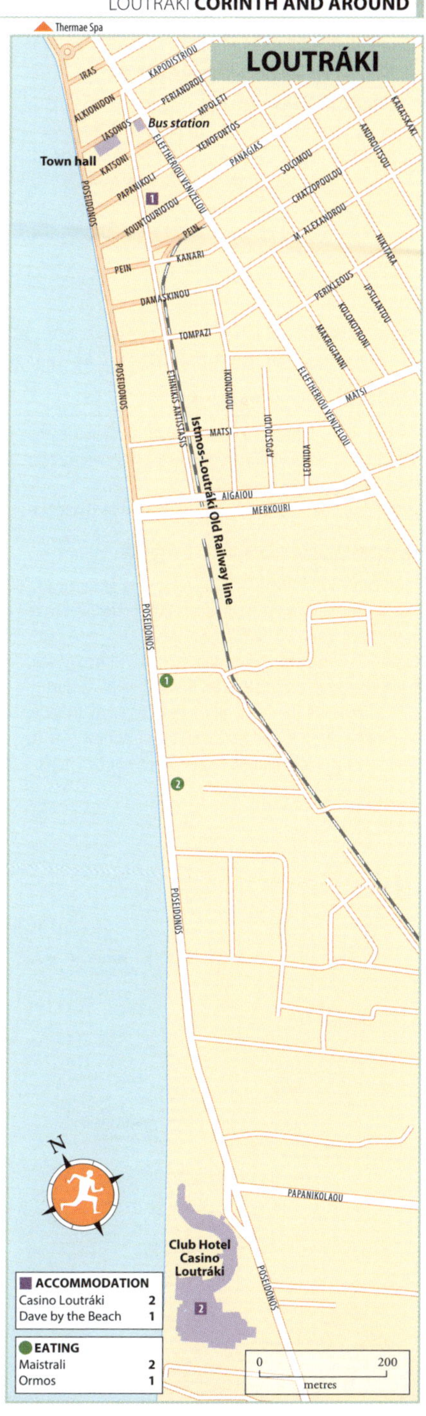

1

## WINE ROUTES OF NEMEA

**Greek Mythology** had its own God of Wine, Dionysos, and it's thought that the rolling plains around Nemea are the most fertile for cultivating vineyards. The climate and soil is perfect for growing the unique *agiorgitiko*, a grape that has been designated PDO (Protected Designation of Origin) status and which in turn produces some of Greece's most celebrated red and rosé wines. To explore the wine routes of Nemea will take you around some 38 wineries, all PDO statues' themselves. http://venikos.gr will give you the whole list of these.

truly be spoilt for choice. Loutráki is, after all, famed for its thermal treatments and is the place to come for an alternative away from the beach.

### ARRIVAL AND DEPARTURE — LOUTRÁKI

**By bus** The Loutráki KTEL bus station is opposite the Town Hall, at Eleftheriou Venizelou & Matsi (27440 22262; https://www.ktelkorinthias.gr/).

Destinations Athens (8–10 daily; 1hr 15 min change in Corinth); Corinth (hourly; 20 min).

**By train** Train to Corinth then taxi.

Destination Athens (hourly; 1hr 15 min).

### ACCOMMODATION AND EATING — SEE MAP PAGE 53

Most places are located along the main 'drag' of the beach, Poseidonos Ave. A selection of some of the better ones have been picked here.

**Casino Loutráki** Poseidonos 48, http://www.clubhotelloutraki.gr/hotel/. The 5-star beachside luxury hotel attached to the Casino of Loutráki. As you'd imagine, nothing has been spared here and it's the perfect base to thoroughly indulge yourself, if only for one or two nights. €€–€€€

**Dave by the Beach** Ethnikis Antistasis 9, http://brownhotels.com/loutraki/dave. This beachside hotel, part of a small chain around the country, is actually in Loutráki and is a good base if you're looking for a seaside break. With only 39 sea facing rooms, expect hip vibes and cocktails on their room terrace. Basic breakfast included. €€

**Maistrali** Poseidonos 81, http://maistraliloutraki.gr/. A

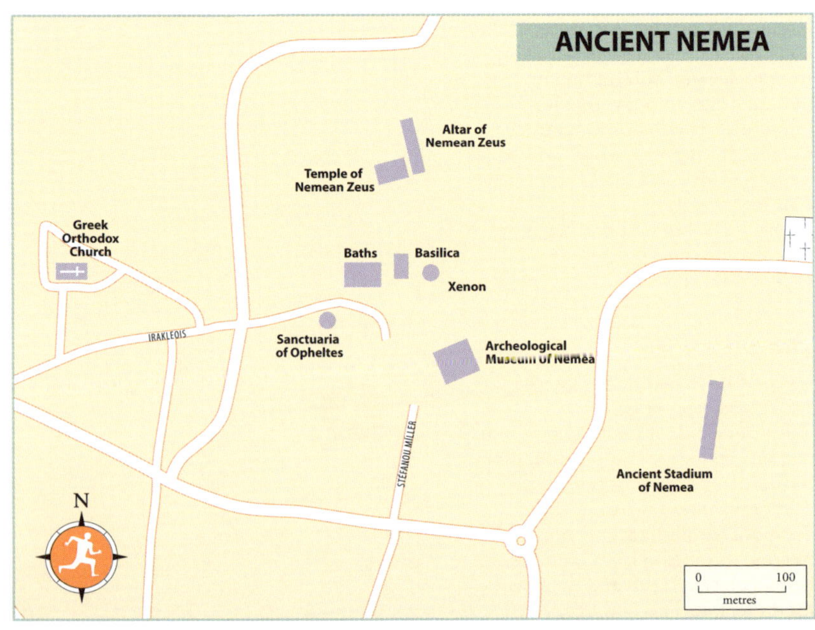

family run taverna for upwards of twenty years, expect meat and seafood delights such as crab meatballs and fresh squid or octopus rounded off with a glass of white or red wine. €

**Ormos** Poseidonos 69, http://ormos-loutraki.gr/. Popular restaurant overlooking the Gulf of Corinth with a strong connection to using local Greek produce and traditional flavours in their dishes. Expect any manner of dishes to cater to all tastes including vegetarian options. Their medley of sharing dishes such as pumpkin 'meatballs', homemade tzatziki and fried aubergines are a favourite. €

# Nemea

http://odysseus.culture.gr • Various Summer/Winter opening hours, see website • Charge, including museum • Bus runs from Kórinthos to Nemea (4 daily; 30min); ask to be dropped at Arhéa Neméa, a small village 300m west of the ruins

**NEMEA** – home to the Lion of Hercules' (Herakles) first labour – is just 31km southwest of Kórinthos, off the road to Mycenae and Árgos. Like Olympia (see page 148), Nemea held athletic games for the Greek world from the sixth century BC, until these were transferred to Árgos in 270 BC.

A sanctuary rather than a town, the principal remains at the **site** are of the **Temple of Nemean Zeus**, currently three slender Doric columns surrounded by other fallen and broken drums, but slowly being reassembled. Nearby are a **palaestra** with **baths** and a Christian **basilica**, built with blocks from the temple. There is also an excellent **museum**, with contextual models, displays relating to the biennial games and items from the area.

Outside the site, 500m east, is the **stadium**, which once seated forty thousand spectators. The vaulted entrance tunnel, now reconstructed, and complete with the graffiti of ancient athletes, is the oldest known. There is a guide available, written by archeologist Stephen Miller, who organized the (now quadrennial) **New Nemean Games** in 1996 as a non-commercial alternative to the Olympics; anyone can enter if they run barefoot and wear traditional tunics (http://nemeangames.org). It is held every two years.

# Argolid

NÁFPLIO HARBOUR

# Argolid



The region that you enter to the south and southeast of Corinth was once known as the Argolid (Argolídha in modern Greek), after the city of Árgos, which held sway here in the Pre-Classical era. This compact peninsula, its western boundary delineated by the main road south from Kórinthos, contains the greatest concentration of ancient sites in Greece. Within less than an hour's drive of each other are Agamemnon's fortress at Mycenae, the great theatre of Epidaurus (see page 70), plus the magnificent hill fort at Tiryns and ancient Árgos.

In peak season, you may want to see the sites early or late in the day to realize their magic. When ruin-hopping palls, you can enjoy the urban pleasures of elegant **Náfplio** (see page 65), and a handful of **beach resorts**.

### Brief history

The Mycenae-Árgos region is one of the longest occupied in Greece, with evidence of Neolithic settlements from around 3000 BC. But it is to the period from around 1550 to 1200 BC that the citadel of Mycenae and its associated drama belong. This period is known as **Mycenaean**, a term that covers not just the Mycenae region but a whole **Bronze Age civilization** that flourished in southern Greece at the time, referred to in Homer's epics.

Náfplio's past stretches back to prehistory, and parts of the Akronafplía wall bear witness to that fact, though little else remains dating to earlier than the Byzantine era. From the thirteenth century down to the early nineteenth, it, as with the rest of the region, became an object of contention among invading forces. Finally came the Greek War of Independence, and the city was named the first capital, from 1829 to 1834. It was also in Náfplio that the first president, Kapodhistrias, was assassinated by vengeful Maniot clansmen, and here, too, that the young Bavarian Prince Otho, put forward by the European powers to be (briefly) the first king of Greece, had his initial royal residence from 1833 to 1834. He is now commemorated by a locally unpopular statue.

The **archeological remains** of Mycenae fit remarkably easily with the tales, at least if it is taken as a poetic rendering of dynastic struggles, or, as most scholars now believe it to be, a merging of stories from various periods. The buildings unearthed by Schliemann show signs of occupation from around 1950 BC, as well as two periods of intense disruption, around 1200 BC and again in 1100 BC – at which stage the town, though still prosperous, was **abandoned**.

No coherent explanation has been put forward for these events, but it seems that **war** among the rival kingdoms was a major factor in the Mycenaean decline. These struggles appear to have escalated as the civilization developed in the thirteenth century BC: excavations at Troy revealed the sacking of that city, quite possibly by forces led by a king from Mycenae, in 1240 BC. The Mycenae citadel seems to have been replanned, and heavily **fortified**, during this period.

# Mycenae

Tucked into a fold of the hills just east of the road from Kórinthos to Árgos, Agamemnon's citadel at **MYCENAE** (Mykínes) fits the legend better than any other place in Greece. It was uncovered in 1874 by the German archeologist **Heinrich Schliemann** (who also excavated the site of Troy), impelled by his single-minded belief that there was a factual

LÁRISSA CASTLE

# Highlights

❶ **Mycenae** Important archaeological site of the region tucked into the hills between Kórinthos and Árgos. See page 58

❷ **Lion's Gate** Entrance to the ancient site of Mycenae with huge sloping gateposts holding up walls either side. The heads of the two Lion's have now worn off, only the bodies are seen. See page 60

❸ **Tomb of Agamemnon** 400 metres from Mycenae Archaeological site is said to be where Agamemnon, the King of Mycenae is buried. See page 63

❹ **Castle of Lárissa** Above the Agora in Argos. This hugely walled Frankish medieval castle, built on sixth-century BC foundations has wonderful views across the Aegean – a reward for the tough walk to get here. See page 64

❺ **Boúrtzi Fort** On the islet of Áyios Theódhoros just off the coast of Náfplio, this Venetian fortress was once the Residence of the Executioner of Prisoners. Can now be visited by boat trip from Náfplio harbour. See page 67

❻ **Epidaurus Theatre** Stunning ancient theatre, built around 330–320 BC with extraordinary acoustics. The Athens and Epidaurus Festival is held here yearly. See page 70

HIGHLIGHTS ARE MARKED ON THE MAPS ON PAGES 60 AND 62

basis to Homer's epics. Schliemann's finds of brilliantly crafted gold and sophisticated tomb architecture bore out the accuracy of Homer's epithets of "well-built Mycenae, rich in gold". And with the accompaniment of the sound of bells drifting down from goats grazing on the hillsides, a stroll around the ramparts is still evocative of earlier times.

## The Citadel

Daily: summer 8am–8pm; winter 8am–3pm • Charge, including the museum & Treasury of Atreus. Note that this site was previously accessible for those with mobility requirements, however recent renovations have left only the museum and the way to Lion's Gate fully accessible

**The Citadel** of Mycenae is entered through the famous **Lion Gate**, whose huge sloping gateposts bolster walls dubbed "**Cyclopean**" by later Greeks, in bewildered attribution

### MYCENAEAN MURDERS

According to legend, the city of Mycenae was founded by Perseus, the slayer of Medusa the Gorgon, before it fell into the bloodied hands of the House of Atreus. **Atreus,** in an act of vengeance for his wife's seduction by his brother Thyestes, murdered Thyestes' sons, and fed them to their father. Not surprisingly, this incurred the wrath of the gods: Thyestes' daughter, Pelopia, subsequently bore her father a son, Aegisthus, who later murdered Atreus and restored Thyestes to the throne.

The next generation saw the gods' curse fall upon Atreus' son **Agamemnon**. On his return to Mycenae after commanding the Greek forces in the Trojan War – a role in which he had earlier consented to the sacrifice of his own daughter, Iphigeneia – he was killed in his bath by his wife Klytemnestra and her lover, Aegisthus, who had also killed his father. The tragic cycle was completed by Agamemnon's son, Orestes, who, egged on by his sister Elektra, took revenge by murdering his mother, Klytemnestra, and was pursued by the Furies until Athena finally lifted the curse on the dynasty.

to the only beings deemed capable of their construction. Above them, a graceful carved relief stands out in confident assertion: at its height, Mycenae led a confederation of Argolid towns (Tiryns, Árgos, Assine, Hermione – present-day Ermióni), dominated the Peloponnese and exerted influence throughout the Aegean. The motif seen here of a pillar supported by two muscular lions was probably the symbol of the Mycenaean royal house – a seal found on the site bears a similar device. There's also a small but interesting site **museum**.

### Royal graves

Inside the walls to the right is **Grave Circle A**, the royal cemetery excavated by Schliemann, who believed it contained the bodies of Agamemnon and his followers, murdered on their triumphant return from Troy. Opening one of the graves, he found a tightly fitting and magnificent **gold mask** that had somehow preserved the flesh of a Mycenaean noble; "I have gazed upon the face of Agamemnon," he exclaimed in an excited cable to the king of Greece. For a time it seemed that this provided irrefutable evidence of the truth of Homer's tale. In fact, the burials date from about three centuries before the Trojan War, though given Homer's possible combining of several earlier sagas, there's no reason why they should not have been connected with a Mycenaean king Agamemnon. They were certainly royal graves, for the finds, which are now displayed in the National Archeological Museum in Athens, are among the richest that archeology has yet unearthed.

### Royal Palace

Schliemann took the extensive **South House**, beyond the grave circle, to be the Palace of Agamemnon. However, a building much grander and more likely to be the **Royal Palace** was later discovered near the summit of the acropolis. Rebuilt in the thirteenth century BC, this is an impressively elaborate and evocative building complex; although the ruins are only at ground level, the different rooms are easily discernible. Like all Mycenaean palaces, it is centred around a **great court**: on the south side, a staircase would have led via an anteroom to the big rectangular **throne room**; on the east, a double porch gave access to the **megaron**, the grand reception hall with its traditional circular hearth. The small rooms to the north are believed to have been **royal apartments**, and in one of them the remains of a **red stuccoed bath** have led to its fanciful identification as the scene of Agamemnon's murder.

### The secret cistern and merchants' houses

A salutary reminder of the nature of life in Mycenaean times is the **secret cistern** at the eastern end of the ramparts, created around 1225 BC. Whether it was designed

2

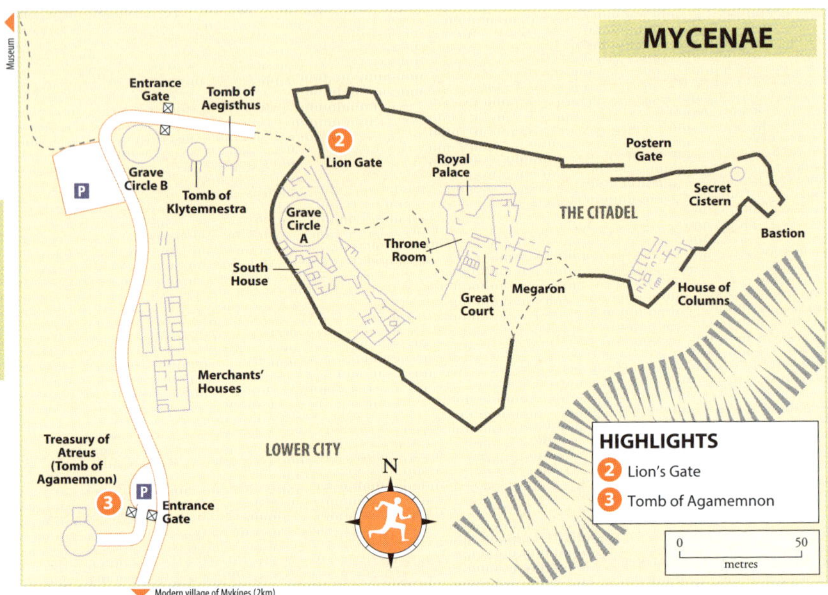


to enable the citadel's occupants to withstand siege from outsiders, rival Mycenaeans or even an increasingly alienated peasantry is not known. Steps lead down to a deep underground spring; it's still possible to descend the whole way, though you'll need to have a torch and be sure-footed, since there's a drop to the water at the final turn of the twisting passageways. Nearby is the **House of Columns**, a large and stately building with the base of a stairway that once led to an upper storey.

Only the ruling Mycenaean elite could live within the citadel itself. Hence the main part of town lay outside the walls and, in fact, extensive remains of **merchants' houses** have been uncovered near to the road. Their contents included **inscribed tablets** (in Linear B, an early form of Greek), which detailed the spices used to scent oils, suggesting that the early Mycenaeans may have dabbled in the **perfume trade**. The discovery of the tablets has also shown that, here at least, writing was not limited to government scribes working in the royal palaces, as had previously been thought, and that around the citadel there may have been a commercial city of some size and wealth.

### Tholos tombs

Alongside the merchants' houses are the remains of **Grave Circle B**, from around 1650 BC and possibly of an earlier, rival dynasty to those kings buried in Grave Circle A, and two **tholos** (circular chamber-type) **tombs**, identified by Schliemann as the **tombs of "Aegisthus" and "Klytemnestra"**. The former, closer to the Lion Gate, dates from around 1500 BC and has now collapsed, so is roped off; the latter dates from some two centuries later – thus corresponding with the Trojan timescale – and can still be entered.

## Treasury of Atreus

Included in the Citadel ticket

Four hundred metres down the road from the Citadel site is another, far more breathtaking **tholos**, known as the **Treasury of Atreus** or – the currently preferred official name – "**Tomb of Agamemnon**". This was certainly a royal burial vault at a late stage in Mycenae's history, contemporary with the "Tomb of Klytemnestra", so the attribution to Agamemnon is as good as any – if the king were indeed the historic leader of the Trojan expedition. Whoever it belonged to, this beehive-like structure, built without the use of mortar, is an impressive monument to Mycenaean building skills. Entering the tomb along a majestic 15m corridor, you arrive at the chamber doorway, above which is a great lintel formed by two immense slabs of stone – one of which, a staggering 9m-long, is estimated to weigh 118 tonnes.



# Mykínes

Unless you have your own transport, you might want to stay at the modern village of **MYKÍNES**, 2km from the main Kórinthos–Árgos road and the small train station at Fíkhti. It can be busy enough during the day, but the place quietens down once the site has closed and the tour buses depart. The archeological site is a 2km walk uphill from Mykínes centre.

### ARRIVAL AND DEPARTURE — MYKÍNES

**By bus** Buses from Athens drop passengers at Fíkhti rather than at Mykínes village, then take an inexpensive taxi; local buses from Árgos or Náfplio do serve the village and the site, but they're unreliable at the best of times.

Destinations Athens (10–13 daily; 1hr 40min); Árgos (9 daily; 15min); Náfplio (10–13 daily; 40min).

### ACCOMMODATION

There are very few places to stay in Mykínes but what's listed can be found along the village's single street.

**Atreus Camping** atreus@otenet.gr. Friendly family-run site to your left as you enter the town from Fíkhti. Good facilities including washing machines. Great home cooking is on offer, too, at the restaurant (mains €6). Tents to rent if needed. Open all year. €

**Le Petite Planète** http://petite-planet.gr. At the top end of the village, this recently refurbished hotel is the nearest to the site, with a/c rooms, great views and a swimming pool. Dinner, which features organic produce, is available at the on-site restaurant. Breakfast included. April–Oct. €

### EATING

**Electra** 27510 76447. Very welcoming, despite its bland decor and overweening size. The food (typical Greek fare) is all home-made and there's a very good three-course set menu. €

**Melina's Taverna** 27510 76955. Popular with groups who come for their sizable dishes such as the usual moussaka and also lamb with yogurt sauce. Caters to vegetarians too. €–€€

# Árgos

**ÁRGOS**, 12km south of the Mykínes junction, is said to be the oldest continuously inhabited town in Greece (c.5000 years), although you wouldn't think it from first impressions. However, this busy trading centre has some pleasant squares and Neoclassical buildings, and a brief stop is worthwhile for the excellent **museum** and mainly **Roman ruins**.

## Archeological Museum of Árgos

Platía Ayíou Pétrou • Currently closed for renovations: call 27510 68819 to check re-opening times

The modern **Archeological Museum of Árgos** makes an interesting detour after Mycenae, with a good collection of Mycenaean tomb objects and armour as well as extensive pottery finds. The region's Roman occupation is well represented here, in sculpture and mosaics.

## Agora

Daily 8.30am–3.30pm • Free • 10min walk down the Trípoli road from Árgos

Before leaving Árgos, visit the town's ancient **Agora**; from the market square take Fidhónos, then Theátrou. The **site** is surprisingly extensive and excavations are ongoing. The Classical Greek **theatre**, adapted by the Romans, looks oddly narrow from the road, but climb up to the top and it feels immense. Estimated to have held twenty thousand spectators – six thousand more than Epidaurus – it is matched on the Greek mainland only by the theatres at Megalopolis and Dodóna. Alongside are the remains of an **Odeon** and **Roman baths**.

## Castle of Lárissa

Free • http://kastra.eu/castlegr.php?kastro=argos • A steep walk up indistinct trails from the Agora, or via a winding uphill road from the village

Above the Agora looms the ancient **acropolis**, on a conical hill capped by the largely Frankish medieval **castle of Lárissa**, built on sixth-century BC foundations and later augmented by the Venetians and Turks. Massively walled, cisterned and guttered, the sprawling ruins offer wonderful views – a reward for the tough walk to get here.

### ARRIVAL AND DEPARTURE — ÁRGOS

**By bus** The station is at the eastern end of the city at the beginning of the Náfplio highway, about 1.5km from the centre.

**Destinations** Athens via Fíkhti for Mykínes (10–13 daily; 2hr); Náfplio (10–13 daily; 30min).

### ACCOMMODATION

**Apollon Hotel** 27510 68065. Basic one-star hotel, yet clean and very well located to the Castle of Lárissa by car–about a 3.5km drive. Parking on site and breakfast included. €

**Hotel Theoxenia** http://hoteltheoxenia.webnode.gr/. Two-star hotel in Argos, again with basic, clean facilities plus balconies. Less than 1km to the Theátrou. €

### EATING

**Kata Kouzina** 27513 06865. Right in the heart of the town offering hearty dishes such as the usual souvlaki and gyros, grills and vegetarian dishes to boot. €

**Mezedokipos** 27510 66368. Vegetarians will love the array of dips such as spicy cheese, or try the fried feta with honey. €

# Tiryns

8km southeast of Argos • Charge • http://visitworldheritage.com/en/eu/the-archaeological-site-of-tiryns/2413784a-f003-4bf6-a528-ab8b52c45d49

In Mycenaean times, the impressive fortress of **TIRYNS** (Tíryntha) stood by the sea, commanding the coastal approaches to Árgos and Mycenae. The Aegean shore gradually receded, leaving it stranded on a low hillock, surrounded by citrus groves. History buffs consider it a better Mycenaean site than Mycenae, though the setting is not as enchanting – which in part explains why this highly accessible, substantial site is undeservedly neglected and relatively empty of visitors. After the crowds at Mycenae, however, the opportunity to wander about Homer's "wall-girt Tiryns" in near-solitude is worth taking.

## The site

The entrance to **the site** is on the far side of the fortress from the road, from where you can explore a restricted number of passages, staircases and parts of the palace. The walls, 750m long and up to 7m thick, formed of huge Cyclopean stones, dominate the site; the Roman guidebook writer Pausanias found them "more amazing than the Pyramids" – a claim that seems a little exaggerated today. Despite this, the sophistication and defensive function of the citadel are evident as soon as you climb the **entrance ramp**. Wide enough to allow access to chariots, the ramp is angled to leave the right-hand, unshielded side of any invading force exposed for the entire ascent. The **gateways**, too, constitute a formidable barrier; the outer one would have been similar in design to Mycenae's Lion Gate.

Of the **palace** itself, only the limestone foundations survive, but the fact that they occupy a level site gives you a clearer idea of its structure than at hilly, boulder-strewn Mycenae. The walls would have been of sun-dried brick, stucco-covered and decorated with frescoes, fragments of which are now in the Náfplio museum. From the forecourt, one enters a spacious **colonnaded court** with a round sacrificial altar in the middle. A typically Mycenaean double porch leads directly ahead to the **megaron** (great hall), where the base of a throne was found – it's now in the National Archeological Museum in Athens. Sometime in the sixth century BC, part of the palace became the site of a **temple to Hera**, a structure whose column bases now pepper the ground. **Royal apartments** lead off on either side; the women's quarters are thought to have been to the right, while to the left is the bathroom, its floor – a huge, single flat stone – still intact.

A tower further off to the left of the megaron gives access to a **secret staircase**, as at Mycenae, which winds down to an inconspicuous **postern gate**. The walled-in **lower acropolis**, north of the megaron, is the site of two underground vaulted cisterns outside its far end, on the western side. The most stunning part of the site, however, is the stone-vaulted **galleria**, a covered walkway dating from c.1580BC on the eastern side.

# Náfplio and around

**NÁFPLIO** (also sometimes known as Nafplia or Náfplion) is a rarity among Greek towns. A lively, beautifully situated place, it exudes a grand, occasionally slightly faded elegance, inherited from the days when it was the fledgling capital of modern Greece. The town is a popular year-round weekend retreat for Athenians being only a couple of hours from there, and remains by far the most attractive base for exploring the Argolid region.

There's ample pleasure to be had in just strolling and looking around the town's harbour, walking the coastal circuit and, when you're feeling energetic, exploring the great twin fortresses of **Palamídhi** and **Akronafplía**. Náfplio also offers some of the peninsula's best **restaurants** and shops, plus facilities, including car rental. In the town itself there are a few minor sights, mainly part of its Turkish heritage, and some good **museums**.

**Platía Syndágmatos**, the main square of the old town, is the focus of most interest with its fountains, cafes and plane tree where, in 1862 Georgios Gennadios, the 'teacher of Greece' gave an extremely powerful and moving speech to encourage donations for the Greek rebellion against the Ottoman forces.

The nearest good **beach** is at **Karathónas**, and closer to the town is **Arvanitiá**, see page 67.

## Brief history

The town's past certainly stretches back to prehistory, and parts of the **Akronafplía wall** bear witness to that fact, though little else remains dating to earlier than the Byzantine era. From the thirteenth century down to the early nineteenth, Náfplio, along with the rest of the region, became an object of contention among **invading forces**. Finally came the **Greek War of Independence**, and the city was named the **first capital**, from 1829 to 1834. It was also in Náfplio that the first president, Kapodhístrias, was assassinated by vengeful Maniot clansmen, and here, too, that the young Bavarian Prince Otto (Óthon), put forward by the

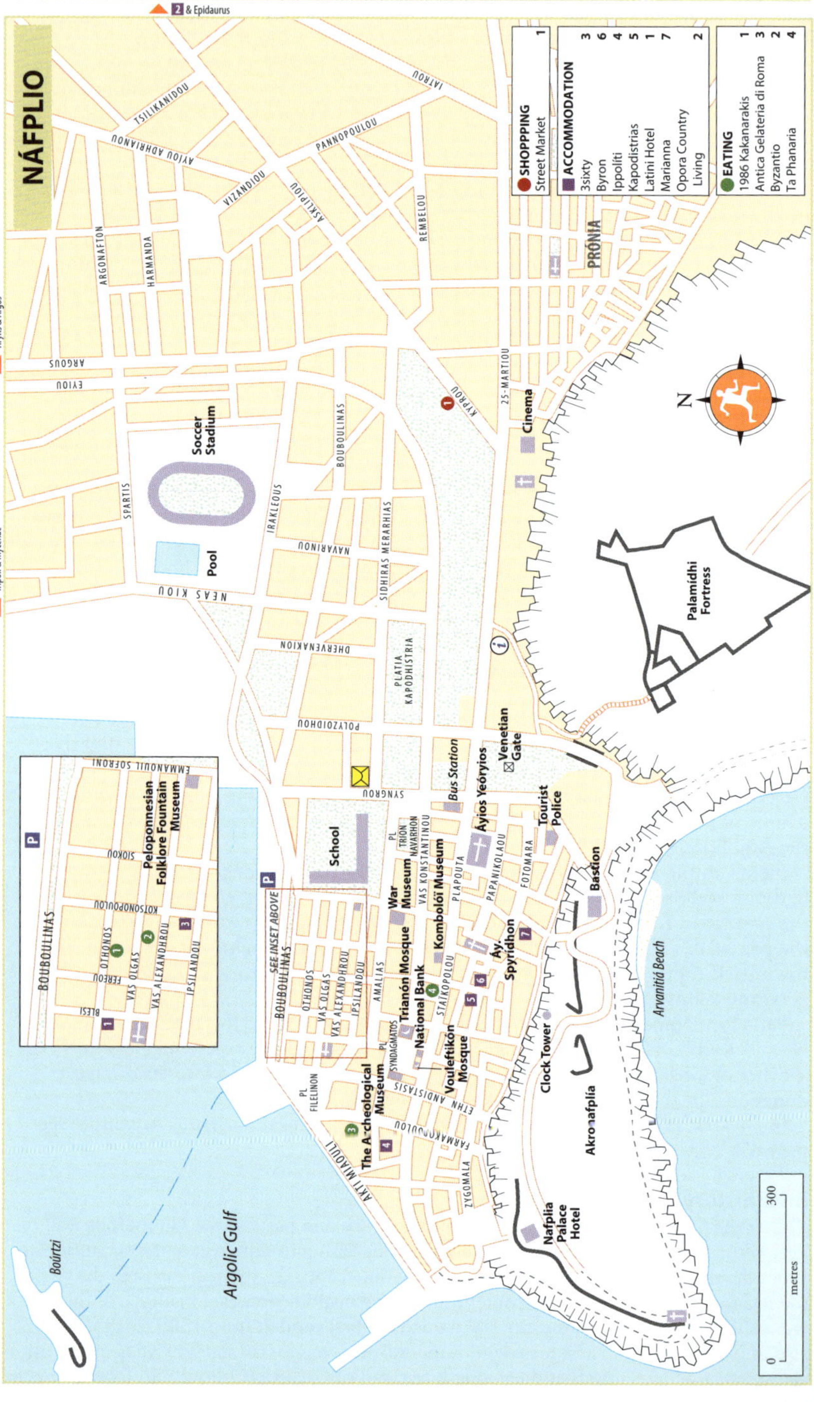

# NÁFPLIO

**SHOPPPING**

| | |
|---|---|
| Street Market | 1 |

**ACCOMMODATION**

| | |
|---|---|
| 3sixty | 3 |
| Byron | 6 |
| Ippolíti | 4 |
| Kapodistrias | 5 |
| Latini Hotel | 1 |
| Marianna | 7 |
| Opora Country Living | 2 |

**EATING**

| | |
|---|---|
| 1986 Kakanarakis | 1 |
| Antica Gelateria di Roma | 3 |
| Byzantio | 2 |
| Ta Phanaria | 4 |

### PALAMEDES – CLEVEREST OF THE GREEKS

Palamídhi fortress takes its name from Náfplio's most famous and brilliant legendary son, **Palamedes**. According to mythology, he was responsible for a range of inventions including dice, lighthouses, measuring scales, an early form of chess and military formations for soldiers. The Greeks at Troy killed him on charges of treachery trumped up by Odysseus, who regarded himself as the cleverest of the Greeks.



European powers to be crowned as the first king of Greece, had his initial **royal residence** from 1833 to 1834. A locally unpopular statue now commemorates him.

## Palamídhi

Various opening times, check website • Charge • http://odysseus.culture.gr • The most direct approach is from the end of Polyzoïdhou street, beside a Venetian bastion from where it's a very steep climb up roughly 890 stone-hewn steps (in shade early morning); there is also a circuitous approach by car directly to the gate – follow the signs from the southeast end of town

The **Palamídhi**, Náfplio's principal **fort**, was a key military flashpoint of the War of Independence. The Greek commander Kolokotronis – of whom there's a majestically bewhiskered statue at Platía Kapodhístria – laid siege for over a year before finally gaining control. After independence, he was imprisoned in the same fortress by the new Greek government; wary of their attempts to curtail his powers, he had kidnapped four members of the parliament.

If coming via the somewhat challenging steep steps approach, as you reach the 216m summit you're confronted with a bewilderingly vast **complex**. Within the outer walls there are three self-contained castles, all of them built by the

Venetians between 1711 and 1714, which accounts for the appearance of that city's symbol – the Lion of St Mark – above the various gateways. The middle fort, San Niccolo (Miltiádhes), was the one where Kolokotronis was incarcerated; it became a notorious **prison** during the 1947–51 civil war.

## Akronafplía

24hr • Free

The **Akronafplía**, to the west of the Palamídhi, is the oldest part of the town and a **fort** occupying the ancient acropolis, whose walls were adapted by three successive medieval restorers – hence the name. The fortifications are today far less complete than those of the Palamídhi, and the most intact section, the lower Torrione castle, was adapted to house hotels.

## Arvanitiá beach

A fork in the access road to Akronafplía brings you down to the small **Arvanitiá beach**, an enjoyable spot to cool off in the shelter of the forts. Be warned that it does get crowded in peak season and is more pleasant in the early evening when there are only a few swimmers. Continue along the path from just past the beach entrance for a few minutes, and you can take steps down to some small stone platforms by the sea, or take the attractive paved route around the western end of Akronafplía, to the main town harbour. A dirt road to the southeast of Arvanitiá leads to Karathónas beach, a 45-minute walk.

## Boúrtzi

Daily every 30 min 8am–sunset • Small charge for return boat trip, from the northeastern end of Aktí Miaoúli

The town's third **fort**, the much-photographed **Boúrtzi**, occupies the islet of Áyios Theódhoros, offshore from the harbour in the Gulf of Árgolis. Built in 1473 by the Venetians to control the shipping lane to the town and to much of Árgos bay, the castle has seen various uses in modern times – from the nineteenth-century home of the town's public executioner to a luxury hotel in the early twentieth century. In her autobiography *I Was Born Greek*, the actress and politician Melina Mercouri claimed to have consummated her first marriage there.

## Ottoman sights

Near Platía Syndágmatos, three converted **Ottoman mosques** survive: one, the **Trianón**, in the southeast corner of the square, is an occasional theatre and cinema; another, the **Vouleftikón**, just off the southwest corner, was the modern Greek state's original Voulí (parliament building). A third, fronting nearby Plapoúta, was reconsecrated as the cathedral of **Áyios Yeóryios**, having started life as a Venetian Catholic church. Worth a quick look are a pair of handsome **Turkish fountains** – one abutting the south wall of the theatre-mosque, the other on Kapodhístria, opposite the church of Áyios Spyrídhon. On the steps of the latter, president **Ioannis Kapodhístrias** was assassinated by two members of the Mavromihális clan from the Máni in September 1831; there is a scar left in the stone by one of the bullets.

## The Archeological Museum

Platia Syndágmatos • closed Tues • Charge • http://nafplio.gr

**The Archeological Museum** in Náfplio occupies a dignified Venetian mansion at the western end of Syndágmatos. It has some good collections, as you'd expect in a town near the Argolid sites, including a unique and more or less complete suit of **Mycenaean armour**, the Dendra panoply from around 1400 BC, wonderful, birdlike Mycenaean **female figurines**, and reconstructed **frescoes** from Tiryns.

## Peloponnesian Folklore Museum

Vassiléos Alexándhrou 1 • Various opening times; check website • Charge • http://pli.gr

The fine **Peloponnesian Folklore Museum** features gorgeous embroideries, costumes and traditional household items from all over Greece. There are also entire period rooms, re-created down to the last detail.

## War Museum

Amalías 22 • Various opening times; check website • Charge • http://nafplio.gr

The **War Museum** has weaponry, uniforms, illustrations and other military memorabilia from the War of Independence to the civil war, including a series of portraits of the heroes of the War of Independence, enabling you to put faces to all those familiar Greek street names.

## Kombolóï Museum

Staïkopoúlou 25 • Various opening times; check website • Charge • http://komboloi.gr

The private labour of love that is the quirky **Kombolóï Museum** is unmissable. Its large collection of worry beads and rosaries dating from the mid-sixteenth century to the 1950s have been sourced across Greece, the Middle and Far East as well as Western Europe and are displayed across four halls. A comprehensive, entertaining and well-researched collection. Museum shop on site, too.

## Karathónas beach

4 morning bus services from Náfplio run daily in season

The closest proper beach to Náfplio is at **Karathónas**, a fishing hamlet just over the headland beyond the Palamídhi fortress, reached by a short spur off the drive going up to the ramparts. A more direct dirt road, theoretically closed to traffic, around the base of the intervening cliffs makes for a pleasant 45-minute walk; however solo female travellers can occasionally be pestered by local scooter drivers. The narrow **sandy beach** stretches for a couple of kilometres, and there's a summer taverna at its far end.

### ARRIVAL AND DEPARTURE — NÁFPLIO

**By bus** The KTEL bus station (http://ktelargolida.gr) is at Syngroú 8, just south of the inter-locking squares, Platía Trión Navárhon and Platía Kapodhistría.

Destinations Árgos (hourly; 30min); Athens (10–13 daily; 2hr 5min); Epidaurus (5 weekly, more during Epidaurus Festival; 50min); Fichti for Mycenae (5 weekly; 45min); Kalamáta (2 weekly; 2 hrs); Pátra (1 weekly; 3hr 15 min); Tiryns (hourly; 10 min); Trípoli (2–4 daily; 1hr 20 min).

**By car** Finding a parking space near the old town is very difficult in summer – your best chance may be on the harbour front, or if you're staying up near the Akronafplía, there are good options on top.

### INFORMATION AND ACTIVITIES

**Tourist office** The tourist office is just by the free car park at the port (Place Trion Niavarchon; Various opening times; 27520 24444), and there's a useful website at http://all-about-nafplio.com.

**Tourist police** The helpful tourist police is on Koundourióti (daily 7.30am–9pm; 27520 98728).

**Watersports** Náfplio Diving Center, http://nafpliodiving center.gr.

### GETTING AROUND

**By bike** Sellis Bike, at Argous 54, rents and maintains various bicycles and helmets for all the family. Also in Argos. (http://www.sellisbike.gr/).

**By car and scooter** Euro Rent A Car, on Polizoidi, rent cars and mopeds (http://www.eurorentacar.eu/).

**By taxi** Taxi Náfplio (698 184 2389; http://taxi-nafplio.com/en/).

**Hop On Hop Off Bus** (http://www.nafplioguide.com/nafplio-hop-on-hop-off-bus-tour/). Hourly until about 5pm, starts at the tourist office (see above) where tickets can be bought and takes in sites such as Palamidi Castle, Akronafplia Castle, The Lion of Bavaria and Platía Syndágmatos.

### ACCOMMODATION — SEE MAP PAGE 66

Accommodation in Náfplio is generally expensive, particularly in the Old Town, though out of season during the week most hotels drop their prices significantly.

**3sixty** Kolétti & Papanikoláou 26; http://3sixtyhotel.gr. The original 1880s spiral staircase and contemporary silver sculptures at reception cry out "boutique", and the overall design – Versace sheets, mirrors turning into giant TV screens and real fireplaces – is exceptional. Its fine dining restaurant, open to all, is surprisingly affordable (€). Breakfast included. €€€

**Byron** Plátonos 2; http://byronhotel.gr. A beautifully restored old mansion up steep steps above Áyios Spyrídhon church, which has expanded into a second neoclassical building. The cheaper rooms don't have views, but up your budget a little and you'll get either a balcony or a decent view. Breakfast included. €

**Ippolíti** Ilía Miniáti & Aristídou 9; http://ippoliti.gr. The only hotel in the old town with a pool and gym, this is a comfortable place that succeeds in being luxurious without sacrificing the sought-after Náfplio atmosphere. Choose between a jacuzzi or a personal hammam cabin in your room. Breakfast included. €€

**Kapodistrias** Kokkínou 20; http://hotelkapodistrias nafplio.gr. Boutique hotel with individually decorated rooms, in a 200-year-old house just 50m from where Kapodhístrias met his end. Breakfast not included. €

**Latini Hotel** Óthonos 47; http://latinihotel.gr. A friendly, recently refurbished family-run hotel, with a nautical theme and spacious rooms right in the centre of the old town. Ask for a top-floor room for great views of Bourtzi. Breakfast not included. €

**Marianna** Potamiánou 9; http://hotelmarianna.gr. Restored house up by the Akronafplía fortress walls, with some of the best views in town from the terrace, where an organic breakfast is served – extra charge, but very good value. There are new maisonettes and apartments on a courtyard below. Parking nearby. €€

★ **Opora Country Living** Pyrgiotika, Nafplio; http://oporacountryliving.com. On the road to Epidaurus, just outside Nafplio, you'll find this rustic luxury 30-acre farmhouse with a small smattering of cottages, large outdoor pool and the chance to become involved in their activities such as olive harvesting. Gastronomy classes often held, or simply relax the day away in nature. Homegrown breakfast included. €€€

## EATING

SEE MAP PAGE 66

2

The waterfront of Bouboulínas is lined with cafés, popular with Athens weekenders. A cosier place to start menu-gazing is Staïkopoúlou, where there are many enjoyable, if touristy, tavernas.

**1986 Kakanarakis** Vassilísis Ólgas 18; 27520 25371. A lively, stylishly refurbished local favourite, serving a variety of appetisers plus dishes such as *kokkinistó* (meat simmered in tomato sauce). €

**Antica Gelateria di Roma** Farmakopoúlon 3 & Komninoú; 27520 23520. Real home-made Italian ice cream pulls the crowds here and has done so since 1870. They offer a full range of other Italian sweets, as well, including soft *torrone* and almond *cantucci*, and some tempting coffee concoctions. €

★ **Byzantio** Vassiléos Alexándhrou 15; http://taverna-byzantio.gr. This excellent taverna is on a quiet corner of a beautiful street, under a cloud of pink and purple bougainvillea. Specialities include home-made sausages, its own organic wine and an unfinishable meat meze platter. €€€

**Ta Phanaria** Staikopoúlou 13; http://fanaria.gr. The place to try good seasonal cooking featuring local veg like aubergine baked with cheese filling and lots of grilled meat options, too. Choose cosy seating indoors, or eat in the bougainvillea-covered courtyard. €

## SHOPPING

SEE MAP PAGE 66

**Street Market** Along Kyprou, on the park side, up to 25 Martiou. Mostly food produce but also clothes, housewares, ceramics and jewellery. Wed & Sat morning.

## DIRECTORY

**Banks** These are concentrated around Platía Syndágmatos and along Amalías; most have ATMs.

**Post office** The main branch (Mon–Fri 7.30am–8.30pm) is on the northwest corner of Platía Kapodhistría.

# Epidaurus

**Site** Daily: summer 8am–8pm, winter 8am–5pm • Charge, including theatre, museum and Asclepian Sanctuary • **Athens Festival performances** Fri & Sat evenings from June till the last weekend in Aug • Various prices; available in advance online (http://greekfestival.gr) or sometimes at the site during the festival

**EPIDAURUS** is a major Greek site visited for its stunning **ancient theatre**, built around 330–320 BC. With its extraordinary acoustics, this has become a very popular venue for the annual **Athens Festival** productions on summer evenings. The works range from the ancient tragedies of Sophocles, Euripides and Aeschylus to operas and guest appearances by foreign theatre groups. Note that subsidies have been drastically cut with the crisis, meaning that fewer and fewer performances are taking place.

The theatre is just one component of what was one of the most important sanctuaries in the ancient world, dedicated to **Asclepios** (god of healing) and a site of pilgrimage for half a millennium, from the sixth century BC into Roman times. In addition to its medical activities, the sanctuary hosted a quadrennial festival, which followed the Isthmian Games.

## The ancient theatre

Epidaurus's **ancient theatre** is the primary sight. With its backdrop of rolling hills, this 14,000-seat semicircle merges perfectly into the landscape, so well, in fact, that it was rediscovered and unearthed only in the nineteenth century. Constructed with mathematical precision, it has an extraordinary equilibrium and, as guides on the stage are forever demonstrating, near-perfect natural **acoustics** – such that you can hear coins, or even matches, dropped in the circular orchestra from the highest of the 54 tiers of seats. Constructed of white limestone (red for the dignitaries in the front rows),

### SNAKES ALIVE: HEALING IN ANCIENT GREECE

Temples to **Asclepios**, god of medicine, were once found across ancient Greece, and his symbol, the **staff and serpent**, is still seen today on everything from ambulances to the logo of the World Health Organization. Although quite advanced surgical instruments have been found at Epidaurus, healing methods were far from conventional. Harmless **snakes** are believed to have been kept in the building and released at night to bestow a divinely curative forked-tongue lick. In other cases, snakes might have been used as a primitive kind of shock therapy for the mentally ill. The afflicted would have crawled in darkness through the maze-like Tholos (see page 71) guided by a crack of light towards the middle, where they would find themselves surrounded by writhing reptiles.



the tiered seats have been repaired, though the beaten-earth stage has been retained, as in ancient times.

## The museum

Most of the ruins visible today are just foundations – the sanctuary was looted by the Romans in 86 BC – but a visit to the **museum** helps identify some of the former buildings. The finds displayed show the progression of medical skills and cures used at the Asclepeion.

## Asclepian Sanctuary

The **Asclepian sanctuary**, as large a site as Olympia or Delphi, holds considerable fascination, for the ruins are all of buildings with identifiable functions: hospitals for the sick, dwellings for the priest-physicians, and hotels and amusements for the fashionable visitors to the spa. The setting, a wooded valley thick with the scent of thyme and pine, is clearly that of a health farm.

The reasonably well-labelled **site** begins just past the museum, where there are remains of **Greek baths** and a huge **gymnasium** with scores of rooms leading off a great colonnaded court; in its centre the Romans built an **odeon**. To the southwest is the **stadium** used for the ancient games, while to the northeast, a small **sanctuary of Egyptian gods** suggests a strong influence on the medicine used at the site.

North of the stadium are the foundations of the **Temple of Asclepios**, and beside it a rectangular building known as the **Ávaton** or **Kimitírion**. Patients would sleep here to await a visitation from the healing god, commonly believed to assume the form of a serpent. The deep significance of the **serpent** at Epidaurus is elaborated in the circular **Tholos**, one of the best-preserved buildings on the site. Its inner foundation walls form a labyrinth, thought to have been used as a snakepit (see box, page 71). Another theory is that the labyrinth was used as an initiation chamber for the priests of Asclepios, who underwent a symbolic death and rebirth, a common theme in ancient religion.

### ARRIVAL AND INFORMATION — EPIDAURUS

**By bus** Most people take in Epidaurus as a day-trip from Athens or Náfplio: there are also special buses to the site from Náfplio and Athens on show days (Athens 21051 34588; Náfplio 27520 27323). Buses only go up to the site June–Sept; the rest of the year they stop at *Café Tzaní*, 1.5km from the site.

**Destinations** Athens (2 daily; 2hr); Náfplio (2–4 daily; 45min).

### ACCOMMODATION AND EATING

★ **Leonidas** Asklipiou 112, Ligourio; 27520 22115. Great traditional taverna serving the standard Greek dishes, with a garden out the back; you'd be wise to book ahead if your visit coincides with a performance at the ancient theatre. Actors eat here after shows, and photos on the wall feature the likes of François Mitterrand and Sir Peter Hall. €

### AN UNDERWATER CITY

There's more to Epidaurus than its famed amphitheater. At **Kalyminos Bay**, 30km east of Nafplio, is a rudimentary sign to the **Sunken City of Epidaurus**. Accidentally discovered in the 1970's from a hot air balloon photo shot (no drones back then), its actually misleadingly named, as it's more of the remains of a second century Roman Villa only 2m below sea level and 45m offshore. Snorkel above it to see the layout of rooms, earthenware pots weighted down to stay in place – but don't tread on it, it's forbidden.

**Tribal Kayak** (www.seakayak-argolida.gr) can organise kayaking tours from Kalyminos Bay with all equipment including snorkels and masks, plus a picnic lunch. Transfers can be arranged from Nafplio if needed. Enquire.

Fans of kayaking should also ensure to explore the Mani Peninsula (see page 115) in this manner, with kayaking trips from Kardamyli. **Explore Messinia** (www.exploremessinia.com) can organise trips with possible pick up from Kalamata.

# Southwest Argolid

The roads across and around the southern tip of the Argolid are sensational scenic rides, though the handful of touristy resorts here, such as **Toló** and **Pórto Héli**, are somewhat lacking in character and are generally overdeveloped. They do, however, serve as perfect bases for those who want to combine a beach holiday with a spot of ancient sightseeing.

## Toló

Some 9km southeast of Náfplio, **TOLÓ** is a functioning fishing village with a long stretch of sandy beach that has made it very popular with package tour groups. Nevertheless, the old marina facing a bay punctuated by three small, pine-clad islands has considerable charm.

### ARRIVAL AND INFORMATION — TOLÓ

**By bus** The bus station is by the harbour, with regular services from Náfplio (9–12 daily; 20min).

### ACCOMMODATION

★ **Minoa Hotel** Aktís 56; http://minoa-hotel.gr/. At the edge of the long beach close to the marina and right by the bus stop and public parking area, this three-star hotel is the best budget option in town. The buffet breakfast (included) and dinner are surprisingly good. Half board extra. **€–€€**

## Pórto Héli

Exclusive, developed **PÓRTO HÉLI** has pretty waterfront views around a roughly circular bay, numerous very expensive accommodation options (although there are some cheaper alternatives to be found), and is popular with yachters exploring the Argo-Saronic islands. It is much easier to come here by ferry from Pireás than by bus from Athens or even bus from Náfplio.

### ARRIVAL AND INFORMATION — PÓRTO HÉLI

**By bus** There are no direct buses from Náfplio to Pórto Héli. You must change buses at Kranídhi (3–4 daily Mon–Sat; 1hr) and then take the local bus to Porto Héli (3–4 daily; 30 min).

**By ferry and hydrofoil** The ferry and hydrofoil departure port is at the centre of the seafront.

Destinations Pireás (3–5 daily; 2hr 30min); Póros (1–3 daily; 2hr); Spétses (3–5 daily; 15min); Ýdhra (3–4 daily; 1hr).

**By water-taxi** Water-taxis run every 10–15min to Spétses, from Costa, 3km south of the port.

## ACCOMMODATION

★ **Nautica Bay** www.nauticabayhotel.gr. This is a well-equipped resort with a bar, a sizeable pool and a variety of activities, including tennis and volleyball courts, table tennis and miniature golf. There are nine buildings in total and most rooms have balconies with sea or pool views. Breakfast included. March–Sept. €€

**Nikki Beach Resort & Spa** http://porto-heli.nikkibeach.com. 5-star resort with a choice of rooms, suites and villas–some with own pools, Nikki Beach is one to treat yourself to. Breakfast included. April–Oct. €€€€

**Rozos** http://hotelrozos.com. Large, beige-coloured hotel with airy, comfortable rooms, all with sea-view balconies (although they also look down on the busy road in front). Breakfast included. April–Oct. €

# The southeast

MONEMVASIÁ'S OLD TOWN

# The southeast

The isolated southeasternmost "finger" of the Peloponnese comprises a dramatic and underpopulated landscape of harsh mountains and poor, dry, rocky soil. The highlight here is the extraordinarily preserved Byzantine enclave of Monemvasiá – an essential visit for any tour of the southern Peloponnese. The rest of this slim peninsula is little visited by tourists, except for the area around Neápoli, the most southerly town in mainland Greece, which offers access to the islet of Elafónissos, just offshore, and to the larger island of Kýthira. This may begin to change now that the new highway is completed, joining the main Kalamata-Kórinthos motorway to Monemvasia and a new fast road from Monemvasiá to Neápoli.



## Monemvasiá

**MONEMVASIÁ**, standing impregnable on a great island-like irruption of rock, was the medieval seaport and commercial centre of the Byzantine Peloponnese. Its modern mainland service town is called **Yéfira**, from which a 1km **causeway** takes visitors out to the medieval site. Divided into the inhabited lower town and the ruined upper town, it's one of the oldest continually inhabited old towns in Europe with a fascinating mix of atmospheric heritage, careful restoration and sympathetic redevelopment.

Fortified on all approaches, it was invariably the last outpost of the Peloponnese to fall to invaders, and was only ever taken through siege. Even today, it differs deeply in character from the nearby mainland.

### Brief history

Founded by the **Byzantines** in the sixth century, Monemvasiá soon became an important port. It later served as the chief commercial port of the Despotate of Mystra and was for all practical purposes the Greek Byzantine capital, with a population of almost sixty thousand. Like Mystra, Monemvasiá had something of a golden age in the thirteenth century, when it was populated by a number of noble Byzantine families and reaped considerable wealth from estates inland, wine production (Malvasia, from which Malmsey wine comes) and from their own roving corsairs who preyed on shipping heading for the East.

When the rest of the Moreas fell to the Turks in 1460, Monemvasiá was able to seal itself off, placing itself first under the control of the papacy, later under the **Venetians**. Only in 1540 did the **Turks** gain control, after the Venetians had abandoned their garrison following the defeat of their navy at Préveza.

Monemvasiá was again thrust to the fore during the **War of Independence**, when, in July 1821, after a terrible siege and wholesale massacre of the Turkish inhabitants, it became the first of the major Turkish fortresses to fall. After the war, there was no longer any need for such strongholds and, with shipping moving to the Corinth Canal, the town drifted into a village existence, its buildings allowed to fall into ruin. By World War II, only eighty families remained. Today it enjoys a renaissance with a permanent population of a thousand, while much restoration work has been done to the houses, walls and many of the churches. Its shape and the fact people still live here have earned it the nickname 'Gibraltar of the East'.

SOFT GOLDEN SAND AT SÍMOS BEACH

# Highlights

❶ **Medieval Town of Monemvasiá** Ancient fortified UNESCO castle town, one of the oldest inhabited in Europe, with labyrinthine cobbled streets, churches, tavernas and boutique shops. Akin to an open-air museum. See page 79

❷ **Submerged ruins of Pavlopétri** A UNESCO-protected Bronze Age city now submerged underwater where it's possible to see, as you snorkel, the old streets and stone foundations. See page 82

❸ **Kastania Cave** A few kilometres north of Neápoli sits a hidden natural wonder over 3 million years old. Come and discover the stalactite and stalagmite formations of Kastania Cave. See page 82

❹ **Símos Beach, Elafónissos island** The rolling sand dunes here are a great place to set up away from the crowds, with a gorgeous sea view back to the mainland. This beach is popular for good reason. See page 83

HIGHLIGHTS ARE MARKED ON THE MAP ON PAGE 78

THE SOUTHEAST
HIGHLIGHTS
1 Medieval Town of Monemvasiá
2 Submerged ruins of Pavlopétri
3 Kastania Cave
4 Símos Beach, Elafónissos island
Leonídhio
Pláka
Poúlithra
Kosmás
PÁRNONAS
Marí
Yeráki
R. Evrótas
Kyparíssi
LAKONÍA
Krokeés
Skála
N
Moláï
Yérakas
Yíthio
Plýtra
Monemvasiá
Arhángelos
Gulf of Lakonía
Doúnda
Kastania Cave
Neápoli
Elafónissos
Pavlopétri
Símos
Cape Maléas
Kýthira
Ayía Pelayía
Potamós
Dhiakofti
Mylopótamos
Avlémonas
Hóra
Kapsáli
0
10
kilometres
Andikýthira (13km)

## The rock: medieval Monemvasiá

From mainland Yéfira nothing can be seen of **medieval Monemvasiá** itself, which is built purely on the seaward face of **the rock**. Nor is anything revealed as you cross the causeway to the **kástro** (castle); but the 1km-long entrance road, used for parking, finally comes to a dead end at castellated walls. Once through the fortified entrance gate, narrow and tactically z-shaped, everything looms into view. In the **lower town**, it's a cluster of houses with tiled roofs and walled gardens, narrow stone streets and distinctively Byzantine churches. High above it, the extensive castle walls protect the **upper town** on the summit.

## Lower town

The **lower town** once numbered forty churches and over eight hundred homes, an incredible mass of building, which may account for the confusing labyrinth of alleys today. The volume of religious buildings can be further explained by the fact that in 1293, Andronikos Komnenos II elevated Monemvasiá's religious status, making it a see, or seat of the bishop, which would have led to significant religious architectural developments on the rock. A single main street – up and slightly to the left from the gateway – is lined with cafés, tavernas, souvenir and boutique shops.

At the end of this street is the lower town's main square, a beautiful public space, with a cannon and a well in its centre, and the setting for the great, vaulted **cathedral** (opening hours erratic: free), built by the Byzantine emperor Andronikos II. The largest medieval cathedral in southern Greece, it is dedicated to Christ in Chains, Khristós Elkómenos. Inside, you can see one of the most important religious paintings in the Peloponnese, a large fourteenth-century icon of the Crucifixion to the right of the iconostasis: it was stolen in 1979, then recovered, damaged, a year later, but only returned to the church in 2011. Across the square is a domed eighteenth-century mosque, which according to local tradition was originally the church of Áyios Pétros. It now houses the small **Archaeological museum** of local finds (https://archaeologicalmuseums.gr; charge). Unusually for Ottoman Greece, the Christian cathedral was allowed to function during the occupation, and did so next door to this mosque.

Access by water is as limited as it is by land. In peaceful times, the town received supplies via the tiny external harbour, **Kourkoúla**, below the road as you approach the entrance gateway. In town heading towards the sea, make for the **Portello**, a small gate in the sea wall where you can **swim** off the rocks.

## Upper town

The climb to the **upper town** is highly rewarding – not least for the solitude, since most day-trippers stay in the lower town – and it is less strenuous than it initially looks (20–30min depending on fitness). Having said that, due to the extreme heat in summer, it's best to ascend in the early morning as there are sheer drops from the rock face, and unfenced cisterns. Likewise, ensure to make the descent before dusk.

The fortifications, like those of the lower town, are substantially intact – even the **entrance gate** retains its iron slats. Within, the site is a ruin, unrestored and deserted, though many structures are still recognizable, and there are information boards on display. The only building that is relatively complete, even though its outbuildings have long since crumbled back to their very foundations, is the beautiful thirteenth century **Ayía Sofía** (usually locked), a short distance up from the gateway. It was founded on the northern rim of the rock as a monastery by Andronikos II.

Beyond the church extend acres of ruins; in medieval times the population here was much greater than that of the lower town. Among the remains are the stumpy bases of Byzantine houses and public buildings, and, perhaps most striking, vast **cisterns** that were used to ensure a water supply in time of siege. Its weak point was its food supply, which had to be entirely imported from the mainland. In the last siege, by Mavromihalis's Maniot army in the War of Independence, the Turks were reduced to eating rats and, so the propagandists claimed, Greek children.

## Yéfira

**Yéfira** (now also labelled "Monemvasia" on road signs, to the consternation of the inhabitants of the rock itself) is little more than a straggle of hotels, rooms and restaurants serving the rock's tourist trade. It has a pebble beach, called Oúga, though for a proper swim, it's best to head 3–4km north along the coast to Porí. Alternatively, take a separate road to the very clean, northern, Kastráki beach, by the Cyclopean walls of ancient **Epidavros Limira**, where snorkellers can see further marble remains from the site, underwater, as well as the wreckage of a sunken German warship.



### ARRIVAL AND INFORMATION — MONEMVASIÁ

**By bus** Buses arrive in the modern mainland village of Yéfira, from where a minibus shuttles across to the rock every 30min at various times throughout the year – check with Malvasia Travel (see below). All buses connect with Spárti, although they are not timed to allow a day-visit from there.

Destinations Athens (1 daily via Spárti; 7hr 45); Corinth (1 daily via Isthmos and Spárti; 5hr 30min); Spárti (3–4 daily; 2hr).

**Tourist information** Travel agent Malvasia Travel (27320 61752) in Yéfira can help with rooms, bus tickets and car or scooter rental (Nov–March Mon–Fri 9am–3pm & 5–7pm; May & Oct Mon–Fri 9am–3pm & 5–7pm; June–Aug 7am–3pm & 5–8.30pm).

**Services** Yéfira has a bank, three ATMs and a post office. There are no ATMs on the Monemvasiá rock itself.

### ACCOMMODATION — SEE MAP PAGE 80

Accommodation on the Monemvasiá rock itself is boutique and expensive, and from June to Sept, you should book months ahead. For cheaper hotel options, check out Yéfira yet there are also some lovely boutique options here too, more specifically in Áyios Stéfanos (see below) with gorgeous sea views of the rock.

#### MONEMVASIÁ ROCK

**Byzantino** http://hotelbyzantino.com. This elegant, historic property features a range of rooms and suites with

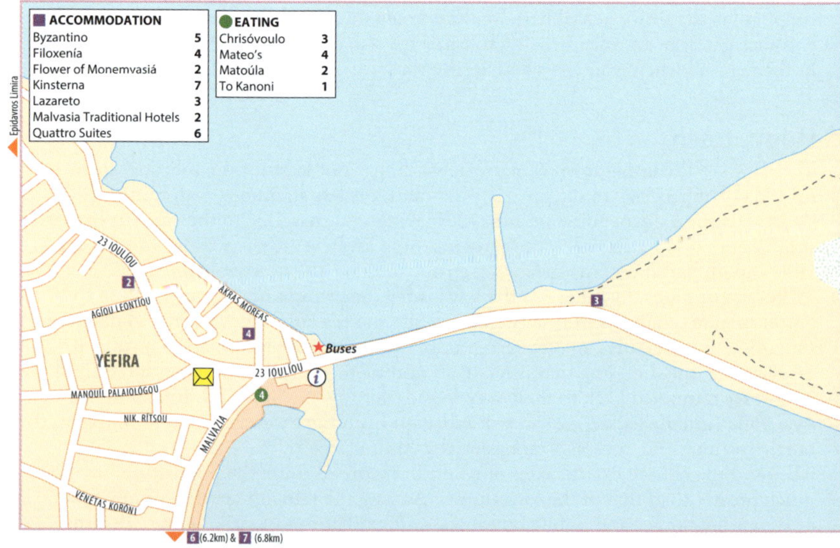

period details, some with balconies and sea views. All rooms come with a/c and vary widely in price depending on the view. Breakfast included. €€–€€€

**Lazareto** http://lazareto.gr. On the rock itself – 800m from the KTEL bus stop and about 1km from the Kastro gate – but in the formidable shadow of the kástro, this is a luxury resort complex with access to the sea, a pool, a spa and parking facilities. It's a collection of traditional stone buildings with comfortable, sleekly modern rooms shaded by mulberry trees. Try to book the suite in the restored Venetian tower. Breakfast included. €€

★ **Malvasia Traditional Hotels** http://malvasiahotel-traditional.gr. This well-appointed complex occupies three separate buildings between the main street and the sea as well as the more modern hotel *Malvasia* at the end of the main commercial road. Call first at the common reception, just after the main gateway and they will direct you to your building. Breakfast included. April–Oct. €€–€€€

### YÉFIRA

**Filoxenía** http://filoxenia-monemvasia.gr. Located just north of the causeway, this modern hotel has comfortable rooms with a/c and large balconies with views of the sea and the rock. Prices almost double in high season. Breakfast included. €€

**Flower of Monemvasiá** http://flower-hotel.gr. Just inland of the road, this pleasant, red-tile-roofed property has self-catering rooms with kitchenette, a/c and balconies with panoramic views. Great shoulder-season offers are available through the hotel website. Breakfast included. €–€€

★ **Kinsterna** Áyios Stéfanos; http://kinsternahotel.gr. One of the finest hotels in the region, this seventeenth-century manor has been converted into a luxury property and spa overlooking the rock, some 8km south of Yéfira. With its freshwater infinity pool, period olive press, open cistern and grape-stomping vat, it's like staying in an open-air museum and well worth the price. Many of their in room toiletries are hand made on site using their organic farm ingredients. Check the many special offers on its website. Breakfast included. €€€

**Quattro Suites** Xifias; http://quattrosuites.gr. This minimalist boutique hideaway in the seaside area of Xifias – some 8km from the rock – has a huge salt-water pool taking centre court, surrounded by rooms and suites on three levels with gorgeous sea views. Walking distance to the small beach of Xifias. Breakfast included. €€

3

## EATING

SEE MAP PAGE 80

**Chrisóvoulo** Kástro; http://chrisovoulo.gr. A snazzy, successful fine-dining place on the Monemvasiá rock, 10m up some steep steps off the main commercial street (signposted). There's creative Greek cooking on the à la carte menu, as well as several four-course menus. April–Oct. €€–€€€

**Mateo's** Yéfira; 27320 61356. A café/snack bar right by the sea, you can pick from a variety of freshly prepared seafood (calamari) and a choice of over 120 premium beers, including Belgium and the Czech Republic. Try the octopus in wine sauce or the local sausage. €

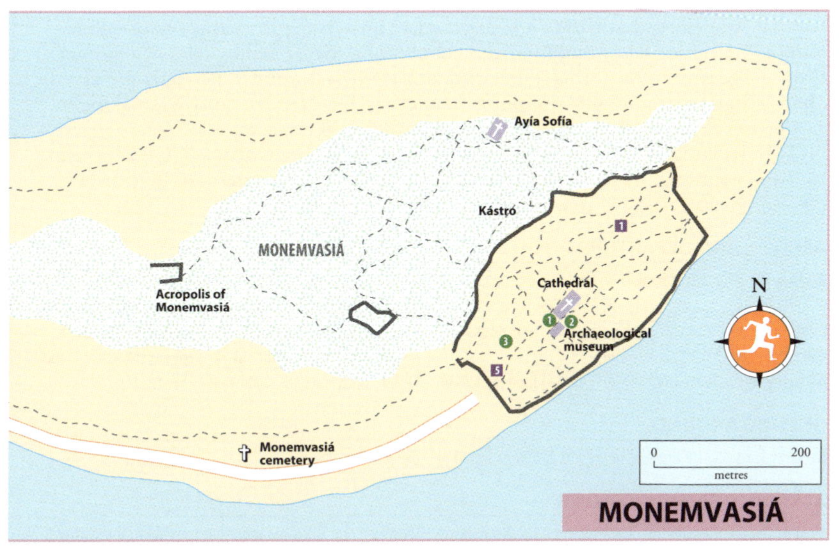

**Matoúla** Kástro; 27320 61660. This family taverna, established in 1950, offers both excellent food and a leafy garden overlooking the sea. Everything, including the plump *dolmádhes* is home-made. €

**To Kanoni** Kástro; http://tokanoni.com. A friendly place in the main square that serves traditional Greek food but is better known for its Italian pizza and pasta dishes. Try to book a table on the balcony overlooking the sea. €–€€

# Neápoli

3

**NEÁPOLI** (full name Neápoli Voïón), 42km south of Monemvasiá, is a mix of old buildings and modern Greek concrete behind a grey-sand beach with views of **Kýthira** and **Elafónissos** islands. The new road from the northeast has cut the journey time from Monemvasiá to Neápoli down to twenty minutes opening up this rarely visited part of Greece. It's really a place not to spend any great length of time, except to see some of the interesting sights as highlighted here.

3km northeast of Neápoli along a winding road, lovers of natural geographical sites will love **Kastania Cave** (http://kastaniacave.gr/en/). Similar to Kapsis Cave (see page 122), Kastania is waiting to be discovered and is not nearly as well frequented by international tourists, simply because it's not so well known. It's a subterranean marvel boasting some of the most intricate and colourful stalactite and stalagmite formations in Greece. As you descend into its depths, you'll be greeted by a stunning array of natural sculptures formed over 3 millions years ago. Each chamber reveals a new tableau of geological artistry, making it a must-see for spelunkers and nature enthusiasts alike. In a country famous for ancient ruins, the uniqueness that Kastania Cave brings to the region promises an unforgettable delve into the Earth's, and Greece's, ancient secrets.

Neápoli's beach extends northwest to Vigláfia village and the little harbour of **Poúnda**, some 12km west of Neápoli, with frequent vehicle ferry crossings over the short strait to Elafónissos island. To left of Pounda ferry docks, and beyond the sand spit, lie the submerged ruins of **Pavlopétri**, an ancient city beneath the waves dating back to around the third millennium B.C., Sometime between 480-650A.D., a series of earthquakes pushed the site down about 3 meters, as well as continuing sea level rises of 1.5 meters since 1500 B.C., immersing it into the Mediterranean and making it the oldest submerged city in the world. It's become a popular snorkeling destination and as you dive into its depths, expect to see stone foundations of long-lost buildings and cobblestone streets, telling tales of a vibrant Bronze Age community. This submerged archaeological wonder, perfectly preserved, offers a unique glimpse into a sophisticated urban life that once thrived, making it an unparalleled destination for history enthusiasts and underwater explorers alike. NOTE: As it's a UNESCO protected site, no scuba diving is allowed, but snorkeling is. Bring your own mask and snorkel, or buy locally. As the waters are so clear here it's also possible to view from the land.

## ARRIVAL AND DEPARTURE — NEÁPOLI

**By bus** The KTEL bus station is on Leofóros Dhimokratías 7 (27340 23222).

Destinations Athens via Spárti (every 4hrs then 2 daily; 5hr 45min); Spárti (2 daily; 2hr 15min).

**By ferry** Ferries leave from the jetty at the junction of Voïon and Ayias Triadhas streets – tickets are available from the office of the Vatika Bay Shipping Agency (http://vatikabay.gr) about 200m after entering the town from the north.

Destinations Andikýthira (May–Sept 2 weekly; 4hr 15min); Kýthira (May–Sept 3–4 daily; 1hr 15min).

## GETTING AROUND

**By taxi** Taxis can be ordered on 27340 22590 or found at the jetty.

## ACCOMMODATION & EATING

Most of the accommodation and eating establishments are located along the main road that runs along the seafront.

**Aïvalí** Akti Voïon 164; http://aivalihotel.gr. This clean, unpretentious hotel is right on the seafront, near the ferry for Kýthira. Rooms have a/c and balconies, all facing the water, though family suites look towards the back. Breakfast included. €

**Glycanisos** Akti Voïon 128; 27340 29180. Great vegetarian and grilled meat dishes served in a simple taverna environment right by the ferry terminal. Try their pumpkin meatballs and grilled chicken with yogurt. €

**Le Farfella** Akti Voïon 170; 27340 22980. Italian restaurant along the waterfront serving great pork tenderloin with cream sauce as well as the ubiquitous pizzas and pasta dishes. €

**Limina Mare** Voïïon 230; http://limiramare.gr. Elegant and comfortable hotel northwest of the waterfront, most of whose beautifully furnished rooms – some with four poster beds – come with views of Elafonissos opposite. Good garden restaurant, free parking and a large buffet breakfast included. €

# Elafónissos

Part of the mainland until 375 AD, when an earthquake separated it, **ELAFÓNISSOS** – also referred to as 'Deer Island' as they bred quite freely here and were hunted in antiquity, even today there are a few herds left – is just 19 square kilometres and gets very busy in the short summer season, when its 700-odd resident population is vastly outnumbered by visitors. The island's eponymous town is largely modern, but has plenty of hotels, plus some good fish tavernas.

3

One of the island's two surfaced roads leads 5km southeast to **Símos**, one of the best **beaches** in this part of Greece – a large double bay with fine pale sand heaped into dunes and views across to Kýthira. To the southwest of town is the small, scattered settlement of Káto Nisí, and **Panayítsa** beach, quieter than Símos but almost as beautiful, with views to the Máni peninsula. There is a petrol station on the Panayítsa road.

## ARRIVAL AND DEPARTURE — ELAFÓNISSOS

**By ferry** Ferries to the island leave from Poúnda docks, 12km west of Neápoli (Jul & Aug; hourly; 15min; http://elafonisosferries.gr/).

## ACCOMMODATION AND EATING — SEE MAP PAGE 84

### ELAFÓNISSOS TOWN

Accommodation in the town is more resort style.

**Antonis Restaurant** 27340 61007. Specialising in seafood and popular with tourists and locals alike, Antonis has a great location along the port with outdoor seating and sea views back to the mainland. Try the lobster pasta or fried calamari. €–€€

★ **Elafónisos Resort** http://elafonisosresort.com/. A combination of 18 rooms and suites over two traditional stone buildings around a pool, and right by the beach, there's a good choice of rooms from Economy on the lower ground level through to suites. Breakfast included. €€

**Konstantinos–Evanghelia** 698 380 3316. The oldest taverna in Elafonissos joining the throng of tavernas by the port, try their grilled sardines and vegetarians/vegans will love the *yemista* (peppers or tomatoes stuffed with rice). €

**Voúla** http://voularesort.gr. A romantic resort with large landscaped garden and a range of rooms from single up to junior suites and apartments. Despite being only 300m from where the ferries dock, it's secluded enough to appeal to couples. Buffet breakfast included. Two nights minimum. May–Sept. €€

### SÍMOS

**Simos Camping and Bungalows** http://simoscamping.gr. Well-equipped campsite, 4km from the harbour, at the western end of the beach. There are bungalows (with a/c and fridges) as well as campsites, plus a minimarket and restaurant. May–Oct. Camping €, bungalow €

# Kýthira

Isolated at the foot of the Peloponnese, the island of **KÝTHIRA** traditionally belongs to the Ionian islands, sharing their history of **Venetian** and, later, **British** rule; under the

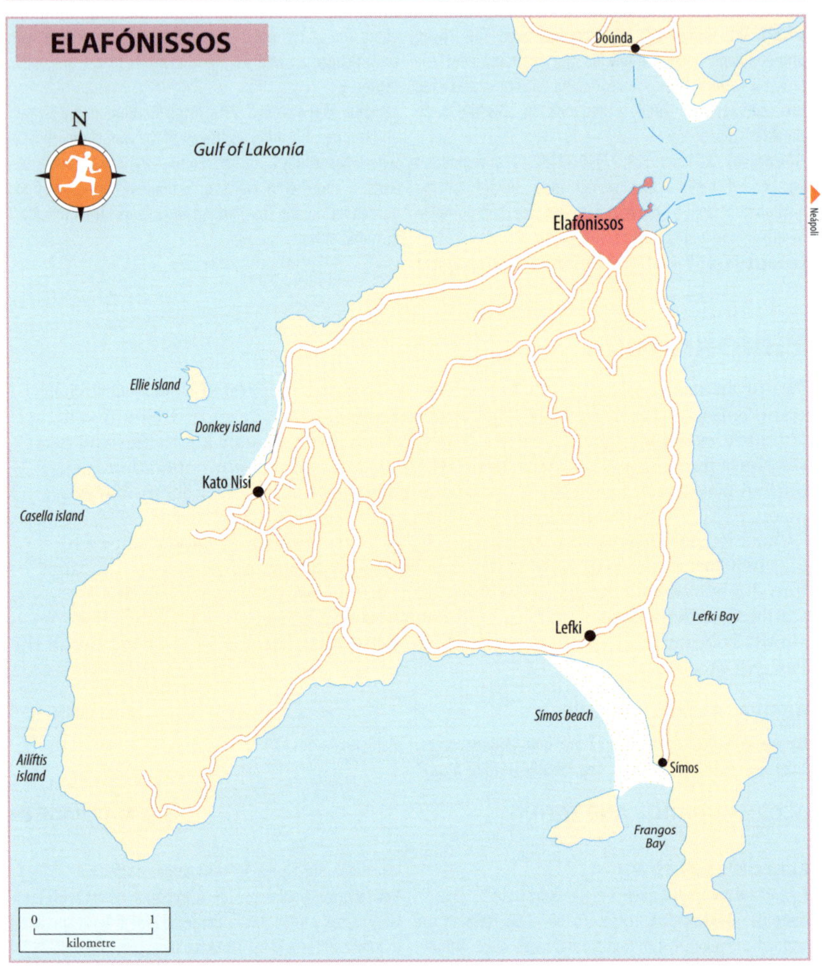


former it was known as Cerigo. For the most part, similarities end there. The island architecture of sugar-cubed whitewashed houses and flat roofs resembles that as seen in the Cyclades. The landscape is different, too: wild scrub- and gorse-covered hills, or moorland sliced by deep valleys and ravines. Though badly affected by **emigration,** tourism has brought some prosperity but most summer visitors are Greeks. For the few foreigners who reach Kýthira, it remains something of a refuge, its undeveloped **beaches** a principal attraction.

## ARRIVAL AND INFORMATION — KÝTHIRA

**By air** Kýthira's Alexander Onassis airport is deep in the interior, 8km southeast of Potamós (http://kythira.info): take a taxi to Livadhi (http://kithera.gr/en/transportation-kythira/kythira-taxi/, http://drakakistours.com).

Destination Athens (1–2 daily Apr–Oct; Nov–Mar Twice weekly; 50 mins).

**By ferry** The huge all-weather harbour at Dhiakófti is the arrival point for Neápoli and Andikýthira ferries (http://drakakistours.com/ferry-tickets/). Dhiakófti has a sandy beach and a few places to stay, but most people move on.

Destinations Andikýthira (high season 4 weekly; 1hr 40min–2hr 30min); Neápoli (June–Sept 4 weekly; 1hr 15min).

**Information and services** http://kythira.info/ is a useful website. Potamós town has tavernas, a bank ATM, a post office and petrol stations. Hóra has a couple of banks with ATMs and a post office on the main square. Drakakis Tours in Livadhi (27360 31160, http://drakakistours.com) and El Greco at Ayía Pelayía (27360 33903, http://elgrecotours.gr) can organize accommodation, ferry and air tickets plus excursions.

### GETTING AROUND

**By bus** The only bus on the island runs from Ayía Pelayía to Hóra (40min) then on to Kapsáli (a further 10min). Check locally for times as they vary, sometimes not running at all.

**By taxi** There are fewer than twenty licensed taxis on the whole of the island, so make sure you have transport to and from your hotel pre-arranged. You can establish a price beforehand with taxis from the port to Kapsáli and Potamós. A list of local drivers and numbers can be found here; http://kithera.gr/en/transportation-kythira/kythira-taxi/.

**By car, motorbike and bike** Panayotis, based in Kapsáli (27360 31600, http://panayotis-rent-a-car.gr), rents cars, motorbikes, mountain bikes and scooters: they also have offices at Dhiakófti, the airport and Ayía Pelayía.

## Potamós and around

3

Inland, northwest of the ferry port, is **POTAMÓS**, Kýthira's largest town. It's a pleasant, unspoilt place, which makes a perfect lunch stop when you're exploring the island. For overnight stops though, it's better to actually stay at one of the towns on or near one of the beaches. The **Sunday market** here (usually around 8am–4pm) is the island's biggest event – local cafés provide live music to coincide (https://visitkythera.com/in/potamos/).

### Paleohóra

About 3km east of Potamós

Few people seem to know about or visit **Paleohóra**, the ruined **medieval capital** of Kýthira (then called Áyios Dhimítrios), despite the fact that these remains constitute one of the best Byzantine sites around and boast a spectacular setting, surrounded by a sheer 100m drop on three sides.

The town was built in the thirteenth century, and when Mystra fell to the Turks, many of its noble families sought refuge here. Despite its seemingly concealed and impregnable position, the site was discovered and **sacked** in 1537 by Barbarossa, commander of the Turkish fleet, and the island's seven thousand inhabitants were killed or sold into slavery. The principal remains are of the surviving **churches**–some still with traces of **frescoes** (but kept firmly locked, so peer in through the windows), and the **castle**.

### Ayía Pelayía

About 4km northeast of Potamós

The resort of **Ayía Pelayía** has a good choice of **rooms** and **tavernas**; the main beaches are cleaner since the ferries stopped coming here, but the beach at Kalamítsa, 2km along a dirt track off to the south, is better – the track continues on to the mouth of the Kakí Langádha gorge which offers excellent hiking.

### Mylopótamos

Head south from Potamós for about 4km, then take the westbound turning for another couple of kilometres

It's worth taking the time to stop off at **Mylopótamos**, a lovely traditional village and a shady oasis in summer, set in a wooded valley with a small stream. Follow the signs from the main square to find a series of old **watermills** and a small **waterfall**, hidden from view by lush vegetation where you can have a refreshing swim.

#### Ayía Sofía cave

A 30min signposted walk from Mylopótamos, or a short drive along a paved road off the Limniónas road; temporarily closed at the time of writing

Most visitors come to Mylopótamos to see the **Ayía Sofía cave**, the largest and most impressive of a number of caverns on the island. The cave's entrance has been used as a **church** and has an iconostasis carved from the rock, with important Byzantine **frescoes** on it. Beyond, the cave system comprises a series of **chambers**, which reach 250m into the mountain, although the guided tour (in Greek and English) only takes in the more interesting outer chambers.

## ANDIKYTHERA MECHANISM

Dating from around 150-100BC, the **Andikythera Mechanism** was discovered in a shipwreck off the island in 1900, but modern scanning techniques have only just revealed its full complexity. It's thought to be an astronomical computer capable of predicting the movement of stars and planets, plus its sophisticated use of gears is unique to say the least. Technologically it was at least 1500 years ahead of its time.

## ACCOMMODATION AND EATING — POTAMÓS AND AROUND

### POTAMÓS

**Kastraki Art Houses** http://kastrakiarthouses.com. About 3km south of Potamós lies the village of Kousounari on a high ridge overlooking the sea. Here you'll find the delightful Kastraki Art Houses – five traditional stone houses each sleeping 2, with custom made furniture. Basic in-room kitchenette facilities are provided to prepare your own breakfast. €€

★ **Panaretos** http://panaretos-kythira.gr. Traditional, lively taverna that dominates the central square with indoor seating in the main restaurant below. Farm-to-table produce all year; try the tenderloin in thyme sauce or aubergines baked with local cheese. €

### AYÍA PELAYÍA

★ **Kaleris** http://kaleris.gr/. Great seaside location and under new management since 2024, the chef here specializes in inventive, original versions of a whole range of Greek and Mediterranean dishes, such as chicken risotto with graviera cream sauce. €

**Venardos** http://venardos-hotels.gr. Extensive hotel complex with hilltop views and just a short walk from the beach. Rooms range from standard doubles to suites and studios, and facilities include parking, a pool and spa, as well as advice on hikes and excursions. Breakfast included. €

### MYLOPÓTAMOS

**Plátanos** 27360 33397. This shady café-taverna above the village spring with a beautifully painted ceiling makes a pleasant stop for a meal. It serves standard Greek main courses, but it's the home-made local sweets such as *avgokalamara* (fried dough wraps in honey) that are the highlight. Very popular with locals. €

3

# Kapsáli and the south

**KAPSÁLI**, on the **south coast**, is largely devoted to summer tourism – in fact, much of it closes down from September to June. Most savvy foreign visitors who come to Kýthira during the summer stay here, and it's a popular port of call for yachts, particularly since it is sheltered from the strong north winds of summer. Set behind double-coved beaches and looked over by a **castle**, as well as the tiny white **monastery** of Áyios Ioánnis Éngremmos perched high on grey cliffs, it is certainly memorable.

## Hóra

**Hóra** (or Kýthira Town), the island's picturesque capital, is a steep 2km haul above Kapsáli, and is quite somnolent in comparison. It enjoys an equally dramatic position, however, with its Cycladic-style houses tiered on the ridge leading to its very own Venetian **castle**. Below the castle are both the remains of older Byzantine walls and, in Mésa Voúrgo, numerous well-signed but securely locked Byzantine churches.

### Archeological Museum

Times are irregular, call first; 27360 39012 • http://archaeologicalmuseums.gr/en • Charge

Reopened with a new permanent exhibition, the modern **Archeological Musuem** has walk-through multimedia displays covering the eras from 9000BC to Hellenistic times. The most interesting finds include the emblematic Lion of Kýthira, an Archaic-era marble lion statue (525–500BC), and those from the Minoan temple at Áyios Yeóryios, whose wealth of bronze statuettes constitutes the biggest such treasure haul outside Crete.

Hóra's castle

Daily 8am–8pm • Free

**Hóra's castle** is a must mostly for the breathtaking 360-degree **panorama** it affords over the entire area. Within the castle walls, most of the buildings are in ruins, except for the paired churches of Panayía Myrtidhiótissa and the smaller Panayía Orfaní (Catholic and Orthodox respectively, under the Venetian occupation). There are spectacular **views** down to Kapsáli and out to sea to the chunk of inaccessible islet known as **Avgó** (Egg), legendary **birthplace of Aphrodite**. On its cliffs grow the endemic yellow-flowered everlasting *sempreviva*, used locally for making small dried flower arrangements (which you see for sale in every shop), symbol of the goddess's eternal beauty.

### ACCOMMODATION AND EATING — KAPSÁLI AND THE SOUTH

In high season, you must book ahead in Kapsáli. Finding a hotel up in Hóra, away from the beach, is easier.

3

**KAPSÁLI**

**Alataria** 27360 31128. This appealing harbourside taverna offers all the best of Greek traditional staples and fish. Expect freshly prepared dishes such as catch of the day or grilled meats. April–Oct. €

**Porto Delfino** http://portodelfino.gr. Individual bungalows in a great location overlooking Kapsáli with both sea and kástro views, an infinity pool, bar, garden and restaurant. Breakfast included. May–Oct. €€

**HÓRA**

**Castello Apartments** http://castelloapts-kythera.gr. This cheerful complex, on the Kapsáli side of town, has a garden setting with great views all around. The nine self-catering studios and one apartment are the epitome of tranquility, some with balconies. €

**★ Margarita** http://hotel-margarita.com. This beautiful, immaculately maintained 1840s mansion just below the main street offers wonderful views of the coast and the castle, and has very friendly and helpful staff. The buffet breakfast is extra. Prices double in August. April–Oct. €–€€

**Zorba's** 27360 31655. By far the best value grill taverna in town, with specialities such as *kondosoúvli* (similar to a chicken kebab), served on a roof terrace. May–Sept. €

## Avlémonas

The prettiest destination on the east coast is **AVLÉMONAS**, on a rocky bay at the top of this coast. It's a small **fishing port** with an end-of-the-world feel as you approach from a distance. It becomes much more attractive once reached, and has a remarkable coordination of colour schemes throughout the village. There is a small **Venetian fortress** and little coves with some of the clearest water around, a fine spot for **swimming**.

### ACCOMMODATION AND EATING — AVLÉMONAS

**Maryianni** http://maryianni.gr. This bright, pleasantly landscaped complex is the closest to the sea. Rooms are fully self-catering (including a washing machine) and offer great views from private terraces to the kastro, the sea or the garden. Book well ahead. €€

**Sotiris** 27360 33722 This taverna, with seating overlooking the sparkling cove, offers a wide selection of fresh, well-prepared and decently priced fish dishes. If you feel in a lavish mood, order the *astakomakaronádha* (lobster spaghetti). €€

# Andikýthira

Thirteen kilometres to the south of Kýthira, the tiny, wind-blown 22-square-kilometre island of **ANDIKÝTHIRA** is linked to its bigger sister by a sporadic ferry service. Rocky and poor, and a site of political exile until 1964, the island only received electricity in 1984, but it has one remarkable claim to fame: the **Andikythera Mechanism** (see page 87). Local attractions include good birdlife (a bird observatory has been built in the old school at Lazianá) and flora, but it's not the place if you want company, with only 45 permanent residents (500 in the summer) divided among a scattering of settlements – mainly in **Potamós**, the harbour, and **Sohória**, the village. Ferries permitting, the **festival of Áyios Mýron** is held here on August 17 – an annual reunion jamboree for the Andikytheran diaspora.

Excavation work above Xeropótamos has revealed the site of ancient **Aigila**, a 75-acre fortress city of the Hellenistic period. At the harbour below are the remains of one of ancient Greece's best-preserved warship slipways, a *neosoikos*, carved out of the rock. The organization Dig Kythera (http://krg.org.au) can arrange volunteer excavation work either at Andikýthira or Kýthira.

## ARRIVAL AND INFORMATION — ANDIKÝTHIRA

**By ferry** Andikýthira has, theoretically, a summer connection 4 times a week with Kýthira (1hr 40min), but landings are often difficult, if not impossible, due to adverse weather such as high winds.

## ACCOMMODATION AND EATING

You can camp in the open anywhere on the island - hardcore campers only as there aren't campsite facilities. There aren't many places to eat, so buy supplies from the village shop at Sohória, but also bring plenty with you.

**Antikythera Rooms** Potamós; 27360 33004. The only official accommodation on the island, this hostel-like set of rooms with shared bathroom is run by the local community. Call, and they may find you rooms rented by villagers, as well. June–Sept. Or try http://destinationkythira.gr/where-to-stay-antikythira/ that lists some rooms and houses to rent with numbers to call. €

# Spárti and around

AGE-OLD FRESCOES IN THE MITRÓPOLIS, MYSTRA

# Spárti and around

The central core of the Peloponnese is the luxuriantly spreading Mount Ménalo, but due south, in the Lakonian Evrótas valley, are Spárti and its Byzantine companion, Mystra, both overlooked and sheltered from the west by the massive and astonishing wall of the Taïyetos mountain ridge. Spárti had a big role in the development of ancient Greece, while Mystra, arrayed in splendour on its own hillside, is one of the country's most compelling historical sites.

## Spárti (Sparta)

Despite lying on the site of the ancient city-state of Sparta, modern **SPÁRTI**, capital of **Lakonía,** has few remaining ancient ruins, and is today merely the administrative centre of a huge agricultural plain. Spárti's appeal for the visitor, however, lies in its very ordinariness – the pedestrianized side streets, café-lined squares and evening *vólta* all make it a pleasant place to come. The obvious reason for coming here though is to see the Byzantine town of **Mystra**, 5km to the west, which once controlled great swaths of the medieval world.



### Brief history

Commanding the Lakonian plain and fertile Evrótas valley from a series of low hills just west of the river, **ancient Sparta** was at the height of its power from the eighth to the fourth century BC, a period when its society was structured according to extremely harsh laws (see box, page 94). The ancient "capital" occupied more or less the site of today's town, though it was in fact less a city than a grouping of villages. **Lykurgos**, architect of the warlike Spartan constitution and society, declared that "it is men not walls that make a city".

The Spartans famously defeated Athens in the **Peloponnesian War** between 431 and 421 BC (see page 178) and later established colonies around the Greek world. They eventually lost hegemony through defeat to Thebes. A second period of prosperity came under the Romans – for whom this was an outpost in the south of Greece, with the Máni never properly subdued. However, from the third century AD Sparta declined, as nearby Mystra became the focus of Byzantine interest.

The annual September **Spartathlon**, a 246km run from Athens to Spárti, commemorates the messenger Pheidippides who ran the same route in 490 BC: the current course record is 20hr25min.

### Acropolis

Daily • Charge

There are a few ruins to be seen to the north of the city. From the bold **Statue of Leonidas**, hero of Thermopylae, at the top of Paleológou follow the track around and behind the modern stadium towards the old **acropolis**, tallest of the Spartan hills. An immense **theatre** here, built into the side of the hill, can be quite clearly traced, even though today most of its masonry has gone – hurriedly adapted for fortification when the Spartans' power declined and, later still, recycled for the building of Byzantine Mystra. Above the theatre, a sign marks a fragment of the **Temple of Athina Halkiakou**, while at the top of the acropolis sit the knee-high ruins of the tenth-century Byzantine church and monastery of **Ósios Níkon**.

THE REMAINS OF SPARTA ACROPOLIS

# Highlights

❶ **Sparta Acropolis** Although not much is left of this once vast ancient site, it's still worth going to see various spots of antiquity that give insight into this once great kingdom. See page 92

❷ **Museum of the Olive and Greek Olive Oil** Situated in a beautiful building, come and learn more about the importance of this fruit to the Greeks' life throughout the ages. See page 95

❸ **Archaeological Site of Mystra** Remarkably intact Byzantine town hugging the side of Taïyetos Mountains. Once home to up to 20,000 inhabitants. See page 96

❹ **Pandánassa convent** Located in the Archaeological Site of Mystra, the church inside this convent was built in 1428 and five nuns still live inside, selling wares they've made to tourists who visit. See page 98

HIGHLIGHTS ARE MARKED ON THE MAPS ON PAGES 94 AND 96

### A SPARTAN UPBRINGING

As the blood-spattered film *300* confirms, the famously tough Spartans can still stir the imagination. In part, this stems from their legendary upbringing. Under a system known as the **agoge**, Spartan boys were rigorously trained by the state to develop physical toughness, loyalty and cunning. Babies judged unlikely to make the grade were left exposed on the slopes of Mount Taïyetos. Other boys were taken from their families at the age of seven to live in barracks. They were habitually underfed, so that they would learn to live off the land. At the age of twelve, they were required to form a sexual bond with a young Spartan soldier, who would act as their mentor. At eighteen, they would become provisional members of the army until the age of thirty, when it would finally be decided if they were worthy of **Spartan citizenship**. At this point they were expected to marry and produce offspring. The system was much admired in the ancient world, and boys from other city-states were sometimes sent here for their education.

## Sanctuary of Artemis Orthia

24hr, though you can't walk inside the actual site • Free

Out on the Trípoli road (Ton 118, just past the junction with Orthias Artémidhos), a track leads to the remains of the **Sanctuary of Artemis Orthia**. This was where Spartan boys underwent gruelling tests by flogging. The Roman geographer and travel writer **Pausanias** records that young men often perished under the lash, and the altar had to be splashed with blood before the goddess was satisfied. The Romans, addicts of morbid blood sports, revived the custom here – the main ruins are of the spectators' grandstand they built.



## Archeological Museum

Cnr Lykoúrgou & Ayíoy Níkonos • Closed Tues • Charge • https://archaeologicalmuseums.gr/en

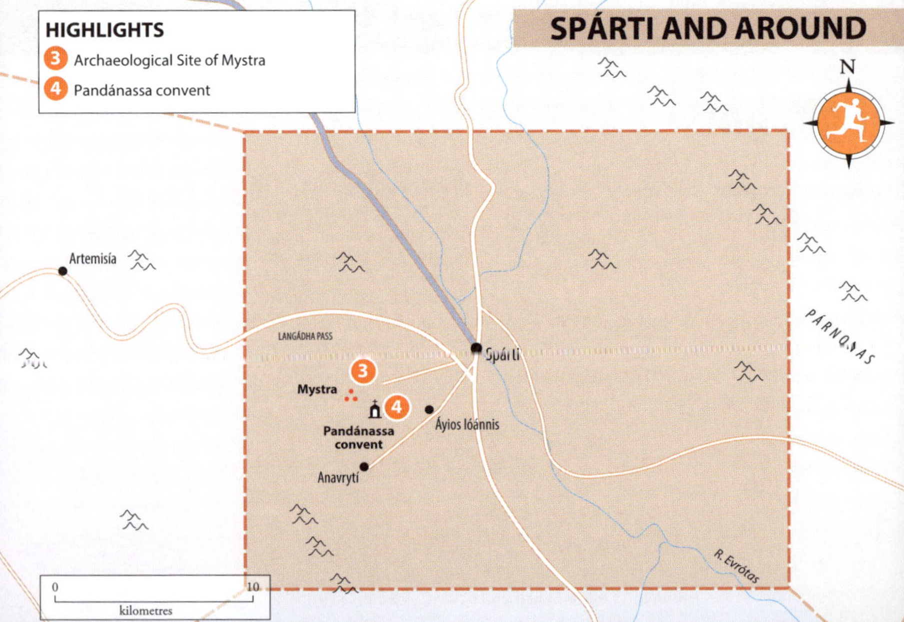

All Spárti's moveable artefacts and mosaics have been transferred to the town's small **Archeological Museum**. Among its more interesting exhibits are a number of votive offerings found on the sanctuary site – sickles set in stone that were presented as prizes to the Spartan youths and solemnly rededicated to the goddess – and a fifth-century BC marble bust of a running Spartan hoplite, found on the acropolis and said to be Leonidas. There is a dramatic late sixth-century BC stele, with relief carvings on both sides, possibly of Menelaus with Helen and Agamemnon with Klytemnestra; the ends have carved snakes. Look out, too, for fragments of Hellenistic and Roman mosaics, and numerous small lead figurines, clay masks and bronze idols from the Artemis Orthia site.

## Museum of the Olive and Greek Olive Oil

Óthonos–Amalías 129 • Wed–Mon • Charge • http://piop.gr

In the southwest corner of town, the informative **Museum of the Olive and Greek Olive Oil**, situated in a beautifully designed building with café downstairs, is worth a visit for its insight into the love affair of the Greeks with the olive tree that has provided them with food, heat, soap and medicines for thousands of years. Of most interest are the olive tree fossils from fifty thousand years ago, as well as a fully functioning olive press from the nearby village of Xerokambi.

### ARRIVAL AND DEPARTURE — SPÁRTI AND AROUND

**By bus**The main bus terminal is on the eastern edge of town, at the far end of Lykoúrgou, though to reach the centre, get off earlier, near the Archeological Museum. For bus info call 27310 26441; http://ktel-lakonias.gr/

Destinations Areópoli (3 daily; 2hr); Athens (7–8 daily; 3hr 30min); Kalamáta (2 weekly; 1hr 50min); Monemvasiá (1 daily; 2hr); Neápoli (2 daily; 2hr 15min); Trípoli (2 weekly; 1hr 50min); Pátra (4 weekly; 4hr); Yeroliménas (2–3 daily; 2hr 45min); Yíthio (2 daily to Krokeés then taxi; 1hr).

### ACCOMMODATION — SEE MAP PAGE 96

There are usually enough hotels to go around, many of them on the main avenue, Paleológou, though noise can be a problem here.

**Dioscouri** Lycourgou 182 & Atreidon; http://dioscouri.gr. The best budget option in town, in a good location with no lack of comfort. There's lots of space, art on the walls, large comfortable beds and parking possibilities – on top of that, the home-made buffet breakfast (included) is fantastic. €–€€

**Lakonia Hotel** Paleológou 89; http://lakoniahotel.gr/. Across the street from the Archeological Museum, this rather business like but nonetheless comfortable hotel has good facilities, balconies in all rooms and delicious buffet breakfast included. €–€€

**Maniatis** Paleológou 72–76; 27310 22665. Another one across the street from the Archeological Museum, this modern hotel – all glass and metal with blond wood trim – has good facilities: four lounge areas, a bar and two restaurants. Rooms have spotless decor, a/c and some have views of the countryside. Buffet breakfast included. €–€€

★ **Menelaïon** Paleológou 91; http://menelaion.gr. Housed in a restored Neoclassical property this is a sleek, modern eco-friendly hotel with a bar, restaurant and swimming pool. All rooms come with high ceilings, double-glazing to prevent street noise and solar-powered hot water. Buffet breakfast included. €€

### EATING AND DRINKING — SEE MAP PAGE 96

★ **Diethnes** Paleológou 105; 27310 28636. Long-established and reliably good, with an extensive menu of traditional Greek dishes. There's plenty of atmosphere inside, with photographs of old Sparta on the walls, but you're best to head straight for the delightful garden filled with orange and lemon trees, and home to ten or so terrapins roaming free. €

**En Hatipi** Hrysikou 27; 27310 26677. A local taverna where quality meat is grilled on hot coals, service is friendly and relaxed, and the food tastes fantastic. Try as many dishes as you can, especially their burgers. €

**Kápari** Gkortsologou 77; 27313 00520. Behind the Old Town Hall in the main square, sit outside at a pavement table and watch life go by as you enjoy traditional Greek staples homemade every day such as *pastitsio* (Greek style lasagna). €

**Ministry** Palaiologou 84; 27313 81288. Set in a former supermarket, this is a café, restaurant and cocktail bar all in one, depending on the time of day. It has a convincing Moulin Rouge decor inside, while music in the evenings attract the Spartan youth. €–€€

4

## DIRECTORY

**Banks** Most of the banks are on Paleológou.

**Bookshop** Dorikon Bookstore (http://dorikonbookstore.gr/) at Paleológou 34 has a good selection of books and maps.

# Mystra

Daily: note a lack of staff may mean earlier closing times, so it's best to call first and check • Charge • 27310 83377

**MYSTRA** is one of the most exciting and dramatic sites in the Peloponnese – a glorious, airy place, hugging a very steep, 280m foothill of Taïyetos. Winding up the lushly vegetated hillside is a remarkably intact Byzantine town that once sheltered a population of some twenty thousand, and through which you can now wander. Snaking alleys lead through monumental gates, past medieval houses and palaces, and above all into the **churches**, several of which yield superb if faded frescoes. The overall effect is of straying into a massive unearthing of architecture, painting and sculpture – and into a different age with a dramatically different mentality.

### ACROSS THE LANGÁDHA PASS

The remote and wild **Langádha pass**, the 60km road over the **Taïyetos** mountain range from Spárti to Kalamáta, is a worthwhile scenic drive. With long uninhabited sections, it unveils a constant drama of peaks and precipitous drops, magnificent at all times but startling at sunrise; the pine forests suffered extensive damage in recent fires, but are showing signs of a comeback. This was the route Telemachus took in the *Odyssey* on his way from Nestor's palace near Pýlos (see page 141) to that of Menelaus at Sparta; his journey, by chariot, lasted a day. The road climbs steeply into the mountains and enters the **Gorge of Langádha**, a wild sequence of hairpins. The rock of Keádhas, high above the southern side of the road a short distance from the village, is where the Spartans used to leave their sick or puny babies to die. Above Keádhas is a **climbing park** with marked routes for rock climbers. At the **pass**, tracks and paths head north and south along the mountain ridge – peaks up to 1900m are accessible in a day's outing. On the Kalamáta side you enter the **Nédhondas Gorge** for the final zigzagging descent.

### Brief history

In 1249, Guillaume II de Villehardouin, fourth **Frankish** prince of the Moreas, built a castle here – one of a trio of fortresses (the others at Monemvasiá and the Máni) designed to garrison his domain. The Franks, however, were driven out of Mystra by the **Byzantines** in 1262, and by the mid-fourteenth century this isolated triangle of land in the southeastern Peloponnese, which encompassed the old Spartan territories, became the **Despotate of Mystra**. This was the last province of the Greek Byzantine empire and, with Constantinople in terminal decay, its virtual capital.



During the next two centuries, Mystra was the focus of a defiant rebirth of Byzantine power before eventual subjugation by the Turks in 1460, seven years after the fall of Constantinople. Mystra remained in Turkish hands until 1687 when it was captured, briefly, by the **Venetians**. Decline set in with a second stage of Turkish control, from 1715 onwards, culminating in the destruction that accompanied the **War of Independence**; the site was evacuated after fires in 1770 and 1825. **Restoration**, begun in the first decades of the twentieth century, was interrupted by the civil war – during which it was, for a while, a battle site – and renewed in earnest in the 1950s when the last inhabitants were relocated.

## The kástro and Upper Town

The **kástro**, in the **Upper Town**, reached by a path direct from the upper gate, maintains the Frankish design of its original thirteenth-century construction. There is a walkway around most of the keep, with views of an intricate panorama of the town below. The castle itself was the court of Guillaume II de Villehardouin but in later years was used primarily as a citadel.

### Ayía Sofía

Following a course downhill from the kástro, the first identifiable building you come to is the church of **Ayía Sofía** (1350). The chapel's finest feature is its floor, made from polychrome marble. Its frescoes, notably a *Pandokrátor* (Christ in Majesty) and *Nativity of the Virgin*, have survived reasonably well, protected until recent years by coatings of whitewash applied by the Turks, who adapted the building as a mosque.

### Palatáki and the Despot's Palace

Heading down from Ayía Sofía, you have a choice of routes. The right fork winds past ruins of a Byzantine mansion, one of the oldest houses on the site, the **Palatáki** ("Small Palace"; 1250–1300), and **Áyios Nikólaos**, a large seventeenth-century building decorated with unsophisticated paintings. The left fork is more interesting, passing the fortified **Náfplio Gate**, which was the principal entrance to the upper town, and the vast, multistorey, Gothic-looking complex of the **Despots' Palace** (1249–1400). Most prominent among its numerous rooms is a great vaulted audience hall, built at right angles to the line of the building; its ostentatious windows regally dominate the skyline, and it was once heated by eight great fireplaces. Flanking one side of a square, used by the Turks as a marketplace, are the remains of a **mosque**.

## Lower Town

At the **Monemvasiá Gate**, there is a further choice of routes down to the **Lower Town**: right to the Pandánassa and Perivléptos monasteries or left to the **Vrondohíou** monastery and cathedral, all very clearly signed. If you have a car, you may find it easier to go back to the upper gate, then drive down to and park by the Lower Gate and continue your visit from there (keep your ticket).

### Pandánassa convent

When excavations were resumed in 1952, the last thirty or so families who still lived in the lower town were moved out to Néos Mystrás. Only five nuns of the **Pandánassa** ("Queen of the World") **convent** remain today; they have a reception room where they sell their own handicrafts and sometimes offer fresh juice to visitors. The convent's church, built in 1428, is perhaps the finest surviving in Mystra, perfectly proportioned in its blend of Byzantine and Gothic. The **frescoes** date from various centuries, with some superb fifteenth-century work, including one in the gallery that depicts scenes from the life of Christ. Other frescoes were painted between 1687 and 1715, when Mystra was held by the Venetians.



### Perívleptos monastery

The diminutive **Perívleptos monastery** (1310), a single-domed church, partially carved out of the rock, contains Mystra's most complete cycle of frescoes, almost

## THE MYSTRA RENAISSANCE

Throughout the fourteenth century and the first decades of the fifteenth, Mystra was the principal **cultural and intellectual centre** of the Byzantine world. It attracted the finest Byzantine scholars and theologians and sponsored a **renaissance** in the arts. Most notable of the court scholars was the humanist philosopher **Gemisthus Plethon**, who revived and reinterpreted Plato's ideas, using them to support his own brand of revolutionary teachings, which included the assertions that land should be redistributed among labourers and that reason should be placed on a par with religion. Although his beliefs had limited impact in Mystra itself – whose monks excommunicated him – his followers, who taught in Italy after the fall of Mystra, exercised wide influence in Renaissance Florence and Rome.

More tangibly, Mystra also was home to the final flourish of **Byzantine architecture**, with the building of a magnificent palace for the despots and a perfect sequence of multi-domed and brilliantly frescoed churches.

all of which date from the fourteenth century. They are in some ways finer than those of the Pandánassa; they blend an easy humanism with the spirituality of the Byzantine icon traditions. The position of each figure depended upon its sanctity, and so upon the dome the image of heaven is the *Pandokrátor* (the all-powerful Christ in glory after the Ascension); on the apse is the Virgin; and the higher expanses of wall portray scenes from the life of Christ. Prophets and saints could only appear on the lower walls, decreasing in importance according to their distance from the sanctuary.



### Laskaris House

Along the path leading from Perívleptos to the lower gate are a couple of minor, much-restored churches, and, just above them, the **Laskaris House**, a mansion thought to have belonged to relatives of the emperors. Like the House of Frangopoulos, it is balconied; its ground floor probably served as stables. Close by, beside the path, is the old Marmara Turkish Fountain.

### Mitrópolis

The **Mitrópolis** or cathedral, immediately beyond the gateway, is the oldest of Mystra's churches, built between 1270 and 1292. A marble slab set in its floor is carved with the double-headed eagle of Byzantium, commemorating the 1448 coronation of Constantine XI Paleologos, the last Eastern emperor; he was soon to perish, with his empire, in the Turkish sacking of Constantinople in 1453. A stone with red stains is said to mark where Bishop Ananias Lambadheris was murdered in 1760. Of the church's frescoes, the earliest, in the northeast aisle, depict the torture and burial of Áyios Dhimítrios, the saint to whom the church is dedicated. Opposite are frescoes illustrating the miracles of Christ and the life of the Virgin; more intimate and lighter of touch, they date from the last great years before Mystra's fall. Adjacent to the cathedral, a small **museum** contains various fragments of sculpture and pottery.

### Vrondohíou monastery

The **Vrondohíou monastery**, a short way uphill, was the centre of cultural and intellectual life in the fifteenth-century town – the cells of the monastery can still be discerned – and was also the burial place of the despots. Of its two attached churches, the furthest one, **Odhiyítria** (Afendikó; 1310), has been beautifully restored, revealing startlingly bold, fourteenth-century frescoes similar to those of Perívleptos.

## Néos Mystrás

The pleasant roadside community of Néos Mystrás has a small square with several tavernas. It's crowded with tour buses by day but low-key at night, except at the end of August when the place buzzes with live music during the week-long annual *paniyíri* (fête).

### ARRIVAL AND DEPARTURE — MYSTRA

**By bus** Buses run from Spárti to the *Xenia* café near the lower Mystra site entrance (6 daily; 30min); they stop en route at the modern village of Néos Mystrás, 500m from the lower entrance.

### GETTING AROUND

**Orientation** The site of the Byzantine city comprises three main parts: the Káto Hóra (lower town), with the city's most important churches; the Áno Hóra (upper town), grouped around the vast shell of a royal palace; and the kástro (castle). There are two entrances to the site: one is at the base of the lower town: the other is 2km away, up near the kástro. A road loops up from the modern village of Néos Mystrás passing near both upper and lower entrances. Once inside, the site is well signposted.

### ACCOMMODATION AND EATING

There are no accommodation or catering facilities at the site itself, so it's best to base yourself at nearby Néos Mystrás – a better, though more expensive option than Spárti, just for the relative quiet setting and easy access to the site. The nearest eating option is the *Xenia* café/restaurant, 250 metres or so outside the lower site entrance towards the town. You will need to book ahead, or arrive early in the day, to find somewhere to stay.

4

#### NÉOS MYSTRÁS

**Castle View Camping** 27310 83303. Laidback campsite 300m from the main square on the Sparta road, shaded by olive and mulberry trees. Facilities include a pool, restaurant (€) and stone bungalows for 2 or 4 people with ensuite facilities. Cooked breakfast available at a charge. Camping €, bungalow €

**Euphoria Hotel & Spa** http://euphoriaretreat.com. If you're looking to really treat yourself, then this spa retreat is right up your street. Just relax in their facilities with pool and massage treatments, or take up one of their specially planned packages to help you de-stress. It's expensive, but completely worth it. Food included, depending on the package you choose. €€€€

**Mystras Inn** http://mystrasinn.gr. A delightful guesthouse with only fourteen rooms in the square of this traditional town, décor harmonized with the environment using local stone and wood, giving it a warm, rustic feel. €€

**O Ellinas** http://mystrasrestaurant.com. A good quality taverna and café just off the main square with a leafy terrace on the side. The food is reliably good; for something a bit different, try the beef in red sauce or fried cod fillet with garlic aioli, both house specialities. €

**To Kastro** 27310 83774. The simple Greek food such as souvlaiki and Greek salads is offset by the gorgeous setting just off the main square, with garden seating. €

# Máni

THE LIGHTHOUSE AT CAPE TÉNARO

# Máni

The southernmost peninsula of Greece, the Máni stretches from Yíthio in the east to Kardhamýli in the west and terminates at Cape Ténaro. It is a wild landscape, an arid Mediterranean counterpart to Cornwall or the Scottish Highlands, with a wildly idiosyncratic culture and history to match. Perhaps because of this independent spirit, the sense of hospitality is, like nearby Crete, as strong as anywhere in Greece.

The peninsula's spine, negotiated by road at just a few points, is the vast grey mass of **Mount Taïyetos** and its southern extension, **Sangiás**. The **Mésa Máni** – the part of the peninsula south of a line drawn between Ítylo and Vathý bay – is classic Máni territory, its jagged coast relieved only by the occasional cove, and its land a mass of rocks. Attractions include the coastal villages, like **Yeroliménas** on the west coast, or **Kótronas** on the east, as well as the remarkable caves at **Pýrgos Dhiroú**, but the pleasure is mainly in exploring the region's distinctive **tower-houses** and **churches**, and the solitude. The **Éxo Máni** – the somewhat more verdant coast up from Areópoli to Kalamáta, mostly in Messinía province – sees the emphasis shift to walking and beaches. **Stoúpa** and **Kardhamýli** are both attractive resorts, developed but far from spoilt. The road itself is an experience, threading up into the foothills of Taïyetos before looping back down to the sea. Patrick Leigh Fermor's classic *Mani: Travels in the Southern Peloponnese* (see page 190) is the definitive travelogue of the area.

You need at least three days to do the Máni justice, preferably with your own vehicle. Possible bases include Areópoli, or Yíthio, though the latter isn't typical of the region. Otherwise, pick a beach resort, such as Kardhamýli or, better yet, remote Yeroliménas.

## Brief history

The **mountains** offer the key to Maniot history. Formidable natural barriers, they provided a refuge from, and bastion of resistance to, every occupying force of the last two millennia. **Christianity** did not take root in the interior until the ninth century (some five hundred years after the establishment of Byzantium) and the region was ruled by intense and violent internal tribalism, seen at its most extreme in the elaborate tradition of **blood feuds** (see box, page 107).

The Turks, wisely, opted to control the Máni by granting a level of local **autonomy**, thus investing power in one or another clan whose leader they designated "bey" of the region. This system worked well until the nineteenth-century appointment of **Petrobey Mavromihalis**. With a power base at Liméni, he united the clans in revolution in March 1821, and his **Maniot army** was to prove vital to the success of the **War of Independence**. Mavromihalis swiftly fell out with the first president of the nation, Kapodhístrias, and, with other members of the clan, was imprisoned by the president at Náfplio – an act leading to the Kapodhístrias' **assassination** at the hands of Mavromihalis' brother and son. The monarchy fared little better until one of the king's German officers was sent to the Máni to enlist soldiers in a special Maniot militia.

In the twentieth century, ignored by the central government in Athens, this backwater area slipped into decline, with drastic and persistent **depopulation** of the villages. In places like Váthia and Kítta, which once held populations in the hundreds, the numbers are now down to single figures. Recently, there has been an influx of money, partly due to increased tourism, partly to membership in the EU. The result has been considerable refurbishment, with many postwar concrete houses acquiring "traditional" stone facings.

TEMPLE OF POSEIDON AT CAPE TÉNARO

# Highlights

❶ **Marathoníssi** Tiny islet off the shore of Yíthio with swimming off the rocks. See page 107

❷ **Dhiroú caves** Opened to visitors in 1967, these thousands-of-years-old caves have caverns of stalactites and underground waterways. Popular tourist attraction. See page 110

❸ **Cape Ténaro/Cape Matapan** The southernmost point of continental Europe thought to be where the underwater cave of the Entrance to Hell/Hades is locates. See page 111

❹ **Home of Patrick Leigh Fermor** Renowned British writer and war hero made his home in Kardhamýli with his wife, Joan. In 1996 they donated it to the Benaki Museum. Scenes from *Before Midnight* were filmed here. See page 115

❺ **Hike the Výros Gorge** Dramatic gorge that plunges down from the summit ridge of Taïyetos to meet the sea just north of Kardhamýli. See page 114

HIGHLIGHTS ARE MARKED ON THE MAP ON PAGE 106

MÁNI
Kalamáta
Výros Gorge
Kardhamýli
Saïdhóna
Stoúpa
Áyios Nikólaos
Milía
Kastaniá
Plátsa
MOUNT TAÏYETOS
Árna
Spárti
Krokeés
ÉXO MÁNI
Nomitsís
Thalámes
Lagkada
Trahíla
Yerakí, Moláï & Monemvasiá
Selinítza
Yíthio
Marathoníssi
Mavrovoúni
Passavá
Ítylo
Kelefá
Karyoúpoli
Vathý Bay
Karavostási
Néo Ítylo
Ayéranos
Liméni
Areópoli
Skoutári
Gulf of Messíni
Gulf of Lakonía
Pýrgos Dhiroú
Flomohóri
Kótronas
Sangias (1218m)
Haroúdha
Tsópakas
Dhrýalos
MÉSA MÁNI
Angiadháki
Nýfi
Érimos
Mézapos Bay
Mína
Kiónia
Tigáni
Maina
Mézapos
Stavrí
Kokkála
Kítta
Nómia
Moundanístika
Boulari
Yerolíménas
Láyia
Álika
Váthia
Kypárissos
Korogoniánika
Pórto Káyio
Marmári
Páliros
Poseidon Shrine
Cape Ténaro
Stérnes
N
0
5
kilometres
HIGHLIGHTS
1 Marathoníssi
2 Dhiroú caves
3 Cape Ténaro/Cape Matapan
4 Home of Patrick Leigh Fermor
5 Hike the Výros Gorge

## GETTING AROUND

MÁNI

**By bus** Note that as this is a very remote region, there are very sparse services in operation. In the Éxo Máni, the Kalamáta–Ítylo bus serves coastal towns (2–4 daily; 1hr 30min). For detailed information check http://ktelmessinias.gr.

**By car and motorbike** Given the sporadic public transport, you really should consider renting a car or motorbike at Kalamáta, Yíthio or Stoúpa.

**By taxi** There are only a handful of taxis serving the region, generally negotiable, at Areópoli, Yeroliménas, Kótronas and Yíthio. West Mani Taxis are your best bet (www.westmanitaxi.gr)

## INFORMATION AND DIRECTORY

**Tourist information** The best website for planning your trip is http://everythingmani.com/.

**Maps** A good, large-scale map is invaluable for navigating among the innumerable tiny settlements of the Mésa Máni. You can buy detailed walking maps in Kalamáta or Yíthio. A number of walking routes are signposted around Máni with useful map boards at the starting points.

**Services** There are banks with ATMs.

**Shopping** Well-stocked supermarkets in Areópoli, Kalamáta, Kardhamýli, Stoúpa and Yíthio, plus smaller markets in Pýrgos, Dhiroú and Yeroliménas.

# Yíthio

**YÍTHIO** (Gythion) is the eastern gateway to the Máni peninsula, and one of the south's most attractive seaside towns in its own right. Its somewhat low-key harbour, with occasional ferries to Pireás and Kýthira, gives onto a graceful nineteenth-century waterside of tiled-roof houses – some of them now showing their age. In the bay, tethered by a long, narrow jetty, is the picturesque islet of **Marathoníssi**, with the long, sandy Mavrovoúni beach, some 4km south.

## Marathoníssi

**MARATHONÍSSI** islet is Yíthio's main attraction, with swimming possible off the rocks towards the lighthouse. Called **Kranae** in antiquity, it is here that Paris of Troy, having abducted Helen from Menelaus's palace at Sparta, dropped anchor, and the lovers spent their first night. Paris left his helmet there, from which the name Kranae derives. Amid the island's trees and scrub stands the restored **Tzanetákis** tower-fortress, built in around 1810 by the Turkish-appointed Bey of the Máni, to guard the harbour against his lawless countrymen.

### BLOOD FEUDS IN THE MÁNI

**Blood feuds** were the result of an intricate feudal society that seems to have developed across the Máni in the fourteenth century. After the arrival of refugee Byzantine families, the various clans developed **strongholds** in the tightly clustered villages. From these local forts, often marble-roofed towers, the clans conducted **vendettas** according to strict rules. The object was to destroy the tower and kill the male members of the opposing clan. The favoured method of attack was to smash the prestigious tower roofs; the forts consequently rose to four and five storeys.

Feuds would customarily be signalled by the ringing of **church bells**, and from this moment the adversaries would confine themselves to their towers, firing at each other with all available weaponry. The battles could last for years, even decades, with women (who were safe from attack) shuttling in food, ammunition and supplies. Truces were declared at harvest times; then, with business completed, the battle would recommence. The feuds lasted until either one side was annihilated or through **ritual surrender**, whereby a whole clan would file out to kiss the hands of enemy parents who had lost children in the feud; the victors would then dictate strict terms by which the vanquished could remain in the village.

5

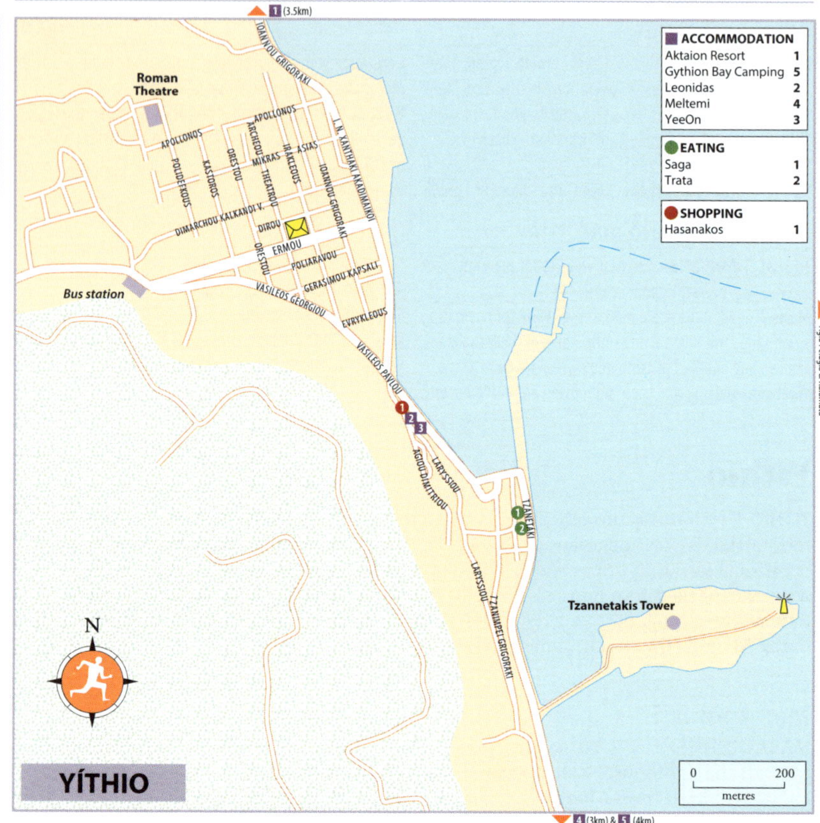


## Roman theatre

Open access • Free • Follow the road past the post office for about 300m until you reach the army barracks – the site stands just to the left, inside the outer gate

There are some impressive remains of a **Roman theatre** at the northeast end of the town. With most of its stone seats intact, and 50m in diameter, the theatre illustrates perfectly how buildings in Greece take on different guises through the ages: to one side is a Byzantine **church** (now ruined) which, in turn, functions as an outer wall of the **barracks**.

## ARRIVAL AND INFORMATION — YÍTHIO

**By bus** The bus station (27330 22228) is close to the centre of town; with your back to it, the main waterfront street, Vassiléos Pávlou, lies ahead of you.

Destinations Athens (5 daily; 4hr via Corinth); Kalamáta (Taxi to Miliá; 50min then bus; 2 weekly; 1hr); Spárti (Taxi to Krokées; 20 mins then bus; 2 daily; 40min).

**Taxi** 24-hr service 27330 23400.

**Travel Agent** Rozakis Travel Agency on the waterfront (27330 22207/22650; http://rozakistravel.gr) rents out cars and can help with accommodation.

## ACCOMMODATION — SEE MAP PAGE 108

Finding accommodation shouldn't be hard, with a fair range in town – most hotels are along the waterfront, though some suffer from late-night noise from the many bars.

**Aktaion Resort** Selinitsa beach, 3.5km north of the centre; http://aktaion-resort.com. Rooms and stone-built bungalows in a spacious luxury resort in the middle of a large fruit grove. There are two pools, a pool bar and great beach, plus sea views from balconies throughout. Breakfast included. June–Sept. Double €€, bungalow. €€

**Gythion Bay Camping** near Yíthio; https://gythiocamping.gr/. A very pleasant campground, Gythion Bay offers a range of amenities, including a pool, beach bar, restaurant, a nice children's play area and access to a sandy beach. Bike rental available. €

**Leonidas** Vassiléos Pávlou 38; 27330 22389 This unassuming hotel has an Art-Deco-style entrance and spartan rooms, which nevertheless have a/c: most also have balconies with sea views. A great comfortable and cheaper alternative. €

**Meltemi** Mavrovoúni beach, 3km from Yíthio; http://campingmeltemi.gr. Nestled in a 25-acre olive grove, this large campsite faces a broad swathe of beach and clean sea. Facilities include a pool, minimarket, restaurant, washing machines and dryers, plus free wi-fi. April–Nov. €

**YeeOn** Vassiléos Pávlou 33; http://yeeonhotel.com/. A fine old (1864) building, now a bespoke boutique hotel with period decorated rooms, even the unique Cave Room with direct access to the indoor pool. All rooms have sea views, there's a hammam and the all-day bistro –where breakfast (extra cost) is made using locally sourced produce. €€€

### EATING

SEE MAP PAGE 108

**Saga** Tzanetáki; 27330 21358. Above-average (and pricey) fish taverna overlooking the Marathoníssi islet. Run by a friendly, knowledgeable French–Greek family, choose your fish from the ice bucket knowing it arrived the same day, and be sure to try the fish soup as a starter. €€

**Trata** Tzanetáki; 27330 24429. Located along the seafront with outdoor seating, expect local Maniot dishes such as spaghetti with *mizithra* (a whey cheese from sheep or goats) and all products are sourced locally. €–€€

### SHOPPING

SEE MAP PAGE 108

**Hasanakos** Larissiou 2; 27330 29128; http://hassanakos.gr. This extensive bookshop is worth scouring for books on the area and has an exhibition of Greek shadow puppets on the first floor (free).

### DIRECTORY

**Banks** There are several banks and ATMs on Vassiléos Pávlou.

# Yíthio to Areópoli

The **road from Yíthio** into the Máni runs slightly inland of the coast and the sandy, Blue-Flag **Mavrovoúni beach**, one of Greece's undiscovered delights. The route begins amid a fertile and gentle wooded landscape, running through tracts of citrus and olive groves and between hilltop towers, until, about 12km beyond Yíthio, the Máni suddenly asserts itself as the road enters a valley below the **Castle of Passavás**. Shortly after, a turning to the left leads down to an attractive long sandy beach at **Vathý Bay** (Vathý Ayéranou), which is popular with German tourists.

As you continue **towards Areópoli** from Passavás castle, the landscape remains fertile until the wild, scrubby mass of Mount Kouskoúni signals the final approach to the Mésa Máni. You enter another pass, with the **Castle of Kelefá** (see page 113) above to the north, and beyond it several southerly peaks of the Taïyetos ridge. Areópoli, as you wind down from the hills, inspires a real sense of arrival.

## Areópoli and the west coast

An initially austere-looking town, **AREÓPOLI** (Aerópoli) sets an immediate mood for the region. Until the nineteenth century, it was secondary to Ítylo, 11km north and the western gateway to the Mésa Máni, but the modern road has made Areópoli, to all intents, the region's centre, and many of the stone buildings have now undergone renovation. Formerly Tsímova, its present name, meaning "town of Ares" (the god of war), was bestowed for its efforts during the War of Independence. It was here that Mavromihalis (commemorated by a statue in the main platía) declared the uprising.

The town's sights are archetypically Maniot in their anachronisms. The **Áyii Taxiárhes** cathedral, for example, has primitive reliefs above its doors that look twelfth century until you notice their date: 1798. Similarly, the tower-houses could readily be described as medieval, though most of them were built in the early 1800s. On its own, in a little platía, is the church of **Áyios Ioánnis**, the Mavromihalis' family church; the interior is lined with frescoes. Facing, there's a tiny but fascinating **Byzantine museum** (Various opening times, check site; Charge; http://manisbyzantinemuseum.blogspot.com/) in the Pikoulakis tower.

### Dhiroú caves

5km beyond the village of Pýrgos Dhiroú, set beside the sea and a separate beach • Various opening hours, check website • Charge; buy a ticket as soon as possible on arrival at the caves to give you a priority number for the tours – on mid-season weekends, you can wait 1hr or more for tickets, so arrive as early as possible in the day. Limited number of advance daily e-tickets available online • http://diros-caves.gr • Taxis from Areópoli will take you to the caves, then wait and take you back

Some 8km south of Areópoli, the road forks off to the **Dhiroú caves** – the Máni's major tourist attraction. Often referred to simply as "Spílea", they are very much a packaged attraction but worth a visit, especially on weekday afternoons when the wait is shorter. A visit consists of a thirty-minute punt around the underground waterways of the **Glyfádha (Vlyhádha) caves**, well-lit and crammed with stalactites, whose reflections are a remarkable sight in the up to 20m deep water. You are then permitted a brief tour, on foot, of the **Alepótrypa caves** – huge chambers (one of them 100m by 60m) in which excavation has unearthed evidence of prehistoric occupation, one of the largest Neolithic burial sites in Europe. Bring swimming gear to make the most of the adjacent beach.

The nearby **museum** (Tues–Sun 8.30am–3pm; Charge), on a bend of the road, contains interesting Neolithic finds from both caves.

#### ARRIVAL AND INFORMATION — AREÓPOLI

**By bus** Buses arrive and depart from the main square, Platía Athánatos.

Destinations Athens (3 daily via Corinth; 2hr 30min then hourly; 55min); Corinth (3 daily; 3hrs 20min); Kalamáta (taxi to Ag. Nikonas; 20 min then 2 daily; 1hr); Spárti (3 daily via Corinth; 2hr 30 min then every 4 hours; 3hrs 30min).

#### ACCOMMODATION

**Ariá Estate Suites & Spa** http://aria-estate.com/en/. 4km from Areópoli, on the way to the Dhiroú caves lies this gorgeous traditional Maniot manor house turned hotel and spa with 16 suites, cleverly built amphitheatrically overlooking the Bay. With its outdoor and indoor pool and restaurant on the terrace, it's a perfect romantic base. Breakfast included. €€€

**Trapela** http://trapela.eu/. By the entrance to the city, this small boutique hotel is furnished in the traditional Maniot style – a typical Areópoli mix of austere and cosy with its stone walls. It also has a garden and its own bar. Breakfast included. €€

#### EATING

**Barba Petros** http://barbapetros.gr/. Oldest taverna in the area running since the 1930's in a spot off the cobbled street towards Áyii Taxiárhes, with lots of perfectly simmered vegetable dishes such as eggplant potatoes and stews to choose from. €

**Lithostroto** http://lithostroto.blogspot.com. Lithostroto translates to 'alley with the paved cobblestones' and this is exactly where you'll find the taverna; in the Old Town–March 17th square. Offers oven-roasted kid as a speciality, plus traditional Mani cuisine such as lip-smacking pork dishes. €

#### DIRECTORY

**Money** On the main platía is a bank with an ATM and the post office.

**Supermarket** On the main road behind the square is a large supermarket for supplies (especially useful if heading on south).

## Yeroliménas and the south

After the journey from Areópoli, **YEROLIMÉNAS** feels like a village in limbo, but it does make a good base for exploring the southern extremities of the Máni. There are a few

**shops**, a **post office**, a couple of **cafés** and several **hotels**. It all feels very remote: the petrol station just by town is the southernmost of the peninsula.

South from Yeroliménas, the scenery becomes browner, treeless and more arid; a good road (and the bus) continues to **Álika**, where it divides. One fork leads east through the mountains to Láyia (see page 112), and the other continues southwards to **Váthia** and across the **Marmári isthmus** towards **Cape Ténaro**. Between Álika and Váthia there are good coves for swimming. One of the best is **Kypárissos**, reached by following a dry riverbed about midway to Váthia. On the headland above are scattered Roman remains of ancient Kaenipolis including (amid the walled fields) the excavated ruins of a sixth-century basilica.

## Váthia

**VÁTHIA**, a photogenic group of tower-houses set uncompromisingly on a high hillside outcrop, is one of the most dramatic villages in the Mésa Máni. It features in Colonel Leake's account of his travels, one of the best sources on Greece in the early nineteenth century. He was warned to avoid going through the village in 1805, as a feud had been running between two families for the previous forty years. Today, it is the closest thing to a ghost town you are likely to find in Greece, mainly because the restored inn, which occupies a dozen tower houses, has been bankrupt and inactive for several years.

## Pórto Káyio

From Váthia, the road south to the cape edges around the mountain, before slowly descending to a couple of junctions. Left at the second one brings you steeply down to the beach and laidback hamlet of **PÓRTO KÁYIO** ("Bay of Quails"), 6km from Váthia. A pleasant short walk goes out to the **Áyios Nikólaos** chapel (usually closed) on the southeastern headland of the bay, while across the bay on the north side are the spectacular ruins of a **Turkish fortress** (open access; free) contemporary with Kelefá and the monastery of Korogoniánika.

## Marmári

Above Pórto Káyio, the right branch of the road goes south along the headland, which is capped by the Grigorákis tower, to the pleasant, sandy **beaches** at the double bay of **MARMÁRI**. The picturesque hamlet itself straddles a promontory between the two bays and amounts to little more than a collection of accommodation options, some of them quite luxurious for such a desolate and stony spot.

## On to Cape Ténaro

Starting from the left fork before Marmári, follow the surfaced road and signs for the fish taverna; pass a turning for Páliros and make your way along the final barren peninsula to Stérnes (Kokkinóyia). The road ends at a knoll crowned with the squat **Chapel of Asómati** (usually closed), constructed largely of materials from an ancient **temple of Poseidon**.

To the left (east) as you face the chapel is the little pebbly **Asómati Bay**; on the shore is a small **cave**, another addition to the list of mythical entrances to the underworld. To the right (west) of Asómati, the marked main path continues along the edge of another cove and through the metre-high foundations of a **Roman town** that grew up around the Poseidon shrine; there is even a mosaic in one structure. From here the old trail, which existed before the road was bulldozed, reappears as a walled path, allowing 180-degree views of the sea on its 25-minute course to the lighthouse on **Cape Ténaro**, also known as Cape Matapan, the southernmost point of Greece and second southernmost in continental Europe after Gavdos in Crete. The barren landscape of

Cape Ténaro has been important throughout Greek history for thousands of years, reputed to be the entry to Hades (Hell) in an underwater sea cave guarded by the three-headed dog Cerberus, as depicted in the film and video game *Clash of the Titans*.

### ACCOMMODATION AND EATING — YEROLIMÉNAS AND THE SOUTH

The tip of the peninsula is so rocky and extreme that coming across any sign of civilization is almost a shock. Yet, somewhat surprisingly, there are enchanting places to stay and eat – usually one and the same as it's such a remote area.

**YEROLIMÉNAS**

**Akroyiali** http://gerolimenas-hotels.com. An accommodation complex with rooms on the beach plus self-catering apartments (200m from the village) in traditional stone-built edifices. It also has its own excellent restaurant where the baked fish in lemon juice and olive oil takes some beating. Breakfast included. €€

★ **Kyrimai** http://kyrimai.gr. Ensconced at the southeastern end of the bay is this castle-like "country chic elegant" property in a restored 1870 trade centre, with a Maniot memorabilia library, a pool and very stylish rooms. Breakfast included. €€€

**PÓRTO KÁYIO**

**Akrotiri** http://porto-kagio.com/. An attractive hotel with adjoining taverna that has an end-of-the-world feel about it, but is very welcoming. The food is simple and good, while each room is different and warmly inviting; all have a/c and some sea views. Breakfast included. €–€€

**MARMÁRI**

**Marmari Paradise** http://marmariparadise.com. A wonderful, traditional stone property with garden terraces, featuring stone rooms with sea views and a panoramic restaurant that serves Máni recipes. Breakfast and beach sunbeds included. Easter–Oct. €

# East coast

The landscape of the **east coast**, the "sunward coast", is different from the western "shadow coast", and it's far less developed, though it offers some of the region's most spectacular views. It works best as a **scenic drive**, rather than a place to stay. There are few **beaches** and less coastal plain, but larger, more scattered and picturesque **villages** hanging on the hillsides. Road signs are fewer than in the west.

### GETTING AROUND — EAST COAST

**By bus** The east coast of the Mésa Máni is most easily approached from Areópoli, where there's a daily bus through Kótronas to Láyia.

**By car or motorbike** If you have your own transport, or you're prepared to walk and hitch, there's satisfaction in doing a full loop of the peninsula, crossing over to Láyia from Yeroliménas (Álika) or Pórto Káyio. Although the Mani is small enough to be considered relatively safe, solo female travellers hitch at your own risk.

## Láyia

From the fork at Álika (see page 111), it's 10km by road to **LÁYIA**, one of the highest villages (400m) in the Mésa Máni. A turning off the road, not far above Álika, takes you to **Moundanístika,** the Máni's highest village – recommended for spectacular views. Láyia itself is a multi-towered village that perfectly exemplifies the feudal setup of the old Máni. Four families lived here, and their four independently sited settlements, each with its own church, survive. One of the taller towers, so the locals claim, was built overnight by four hundred men who hoped to gain an advantage at sunrise. Today, a municipality-owned café faces the main church, and the village shows healthy signs of revival, with the ongoing refurbishment of a number of houses.

## Flomohóri and around

Some 30km northwards, passing views, towered hamlets and modest beaches, you reach **FLOMOHÓRI**. The land below is relatively fertile, and the village has maintained a reasonable population as well as an imposing group of tower-houses, one reckoned by some to be the Máni's highest. The way of life here survives as a bit of a time warp: the deeply traditional black dress of perpetual mourning is usual, and the locals are liable to regard you with an odd mix of amusement and bravado – as if you just stepped off a spaceship. You might feel the same.

**Kótronas**, a few kilometres downhill, feels less harsh than the rest of the Máni. It is still a working fishing village, and there's a sandy beach if you feel like a dip in the sea.

## The Éxo (Outer) Máni Areópoli to Kalamáta

The 40km of road into Messinía, between Areópoli (see page 109) and Kalamáta (see page 134), are as dramatic and beautiful as any in Greece, almost a corniche route between the **Taïyetos** ridge and the **Gulf of Messinía**. The first few settlements en route are classic Máni villages, their towers packed against the hillside. As you move north, with the road dropping to near sea level, there are several small appealing and popular resorts. For walkers, there is a reasonably well-preserved *kalderími* (cobbled footpath) running parallel to much of the paved route, with superb **gorge hikes** just east of Kardhamýli, a good base for local exploration and touring.

### Liméni

The less austere Éxo Máni begins at **LIMÉNI**, Areópoli's tiny traditional port, which lies 3km to the north, in a dramatic location on the coast. Liméni consists of a handful of houses on a curve of sparkling sea, dominated by the restored **tower-house** of Petrobey Mavromihalis, now a luxury **hotel** (see below), though it resembles nothing so much as an English country parish church.

#### ACCOMMODATION AND EATING — LIMÉNI

**O Takis** 27330 51327. A well-regarded fish taverna next to *Pirgos Mavromichali* (below). It's perfect for a blowout meal, but you can also opt for more affordable taverna dishes. €€

★ **Pirgos Mavromichali** http://pirgosmavromichali.gr. A luxury hotel in the refurbished historic tower-house of the legendary clan. It's a magical setting: white stone archways, secret stairways, glistening turquoise waters below, all enhanced at night by imaginative lighting. Bedrooms and suites are coolly sophisticated and perfectly appointed, and breakfast on the terrace is included. The terraced restaurant takes pride in its local produce gastronomy and local wines. €€€

# Ítylo and around

The village of **ÍTYLO** (Oítylo), 8km farther along the main road after the Liméni turn-off, has been experiencing a resurgence in fortunes, with many crumbling old houses now restored. In earlier times, Ítylo was the **capital** of the Máni, and from the sixteenth to the eighteenth centuries it was the region's most notorious base for **piracy** and **slave trading**. The Maniots traded efficiently in slaves; they sold Turks to Venetians, Venetians to Turks, and, at times of feud, the women of each other's clans to both. Irritated by the piracy and hoping to control the important pass to the north, the Turks built the sprawling **Castle of Kelefá** in 1670 (open access; http://kastra.eu/castleen.php?kastro=kelefa; free). It is just a 1km walk from Ítylo across a gorge, and its walls and bastions, built for a garrison of five hundred, are substantially intact. Also worth exploring is the **monastery of Dhekoúlou** down towards the coast; its setting is beautiful and there are some fine eighteenth-century frescoes in the chapel.

#### ACCOMMODATION AND EATING — ÍTYLO

There is not much choice of accommodation in Ítylo, so it's best to head down to the tiny hamlet of Néo Ítylo, where you'll find rooms to rent and a hotel on the beach: it's just round the bay from Ítylo's port, Karavostási.

**Ítylo** Néo Ítylo; http://hotelitilo.gr. This luxury stone-and-iron hotel is right on the beach and comes complete with

5

a restaurant and a playground for kids. Breakfast included; special offers for longer stays. March–Oct. €€€

## Stoúpa

Some 20km north of Ítylo, **STOÚPA** is a first-rate resort and very popular with British holiday makers and holiday-home owners. It has possibly the best sands along this coast, with two glorious **beaches** (Stoúpa and the smaller, deeper Kalogriá) separated by a headland, each sloping into the sea and superb for children. Submarine freshwater springs gush into the bay, keeping it unusually clean. A ten-minute walk to the north of Kalogriá beach is the delightful and often deserted cove of Dhelfíni. A further 600m brings you to the pebble beach of Fonéa, wrapped around a rock outcrop and tucked into a corner of the hillside. Stoúpa was home in 1917–18 to the wandering Cretan writer, Nikos Kazantzakis, who is said to have based the title character in *Zorba the Greek* on a worker at the lignite mine in nearby Pástrova.

Out of peak season, Stoúpa is certainly recommended, though in July and August, and any summer weekend, you may find the crowds overwhelming and space at a premium.

### ARRIVAL AND DEAPRTURE — STOÚPA

**By bus** The Kalamáta–Ítylo bus stops at the junctions at each end of town, but does not go in.

Destinations Ítylo (2 daily; 1hr); Kalamáta (2 daily to Kardhamýli; 35min then taxi; 10min).

**By car** If driving up from the south, you'll find that the main access road to town is well signed; it forks off about 1km away from the centre.

### GETTING AROUND

**By car** Doufexis Travel (27210 77677, http://doufexis.com) can organize car rental and find accommodation.

**By taxi** Stoúpa Taxi is on 697 472 3673, http://taxistoupa.com.

### ACCOMMODATION AND EATING

**Akroyiali** Southern end of main beach; 27210 77335. This taverna at the end of the beach not only serves well-prepared food, including seafood, but also has magical views after dark of the lights of the mountain villages above Stoúpa. Also serves EZA brewery beer. €

**Kastro** Middle of main beach; http://hotel-kastro.gr. The best-located hotel in Stoúpa, right on the beach with twelve tastefully decorated rooms around an internal patio complete with a fountain. It's worth paying extra for the sea-facing balconies. Beach umbrellas for guests, charge. Continental breakfast is included; cooked English breakfasts cost extra. May–Oct. €

★ **Lefktron** In the middle of town, 50m from the beach; http://lefktron-hotel.gr. Friendly and comfortable, this

### HIKING THE VÝROS GORGE

The giant **Výros Gorge** plunges down from the summit ridge of Taïyetos to meet the sea just north of Kardhamýli. Tracks penetrate the gorge from various directions and are well worth a day or two's exploration. From Kardhamýli, the *kalderími* from the citadel continues to the church and village of Ayía Sofía, and then proceeds on a mixture of tracks and lanes either across the plateau up to the hamlet of **Exohóri**, or down into the gorge, where **monasteries** nestle deep at the base of dramatic cliffs. An hour or so inland along the canyon, more cobbled ways lead up to either Tséria on the north bank (there's a taverna, but no accommodation) or back towards Exohóri on the south flank, about 10km from Kardhamýli. If you reach Exohóri, pay a visit to the church of **Áyios Nikólaos** (always closed), where the urn containing the ashes of writer Bruce Chatwin is buried outside, to the right of the sanctuary (unmarked). When he lived in Kardhamýli (see page 115), he used to walk 5km up to Exohóri and back down almost every day.

family-run hotel has rooms with a/c, fridges and balconies facing the pool. There's a well-stocked bar, three patios on different levels, parking spaces and foreign exchange facilities. Breakfast included. April–Oct. €

### DIRECTORY

**Money** There are five ATMs along the waterfront.

# Kardhamýli

**KARDHAMÝLI**, 8km north of Stoúpa, is a major resort by Peloponnese standards and suffers from the busy main road that splits it. The **beach** is good, though not sandy – a long pebble strip north of the village, backed by olive trees. This is where the author Patrick Leigh Fermor chose to make his home, and it's certainly one of the greenest and loveliest of places around – an excellent base for walkers (see box, page 115).

Inland from the platía, there's a nice walk up to "**Old Kardhamýli**", a partly restored citadel of nineteenth-century houses, gathered about the church of **Áyios Spyrídhon** with its unusual multistorey bell tower. Here in the church courtyard, Maniot chieftains Kolokotronis and Mourtzinos played human chess with their troops during the War of Independence. Further back, on the path up to Ayía Sofía, is a pair of ancient tombs, said to be of the **Dioskoúri** (the Gemini twins).

### ARRIVAL AND DEPARTURE — KARDHAMÝLI

**By bus** The bus station is by the central square at the northern end of town.

Destinations Athens (every 3 hrs to Kalamáta, then change); Kalamáta (2 daily; 35hr).

**By car** Driving up from the south, the main road passes through town, just 2 blocks inland.

### GETTING AROUND

**By car** To rent a car, try MyCarRentals at Kardhamýli (27210 64150, http://mycarrentals.gr) Also at Kalamáta airport.

**By taxi** Taxis are on 698 599 9464; http://westmanitaxi.gr.

### ACCOMMODATION

**Anniska** On the seafront; http://anniska-liakoto.com. With easy sea access to a secluded rocky promontory, this property, belonging to an Australian-Greek, offers self-catering studios and apartments. Amenities include concierge service, wi-fi, panoramic terrace coffee bar and a garden patio. April–Oct. €€

**Elies** Ritsá beach, 2km north of town; http://elieshotel.gr. A complex of spacious self-catering stone studios,

### THE FERMOR HOUSE

**Patrick Leigh Fermor**, renowned British writer and war hero, followed his heart to Greece, his second home. Born in London in 1915, Fermor had an adventurous spirit from a young age. He crossed Europe on foot at eighteen, an epic journey detailed in his books *A Time of Gifts* and *Between the Woods and the Water* (see page 190).

Fluent in modern Greek and a tireless traveller, during WWII Fermor joined the Irish Guards, later aiding the Greek resistance. Disguised as a shepherd, he led a daring mission to capture German General Heinrich Kreipe in 1944, earning him the Distinguished Service Order.

Post-war, Fermor settled in Greece's Peloponnese region with his partner Joan Eyres Monsell. Their home in Kardhamýli became a haven for creatives. Fermor continued writing and exploring until his death in 2011, leaving a lasting legacy of bravery and literary brilliance. In 1996 they donated their home in Kardhamýli to the Benaki Museum with the express desire that the house remain open to the public and host researchers. To this day the **Fermor house** operates residences, educational activities with partner universities and scheduled visits (Mon only; 12pm–1pm; Charge; http://.benaki.org/index.php?option=com_buildings&view=building&id=45&Itemid=1080&lang=en).

5

apartments and maisonettes in the middle of a 20-acre olive grove facing a gravel beach. It also has a fabulous restaurant where all the vegetables served are grown in its own garden. €€

★ **Kalamitsi** 1km south of town; www.kalamitsi-hotel.gr. Apart from its great location, set among the orange groves just outside Kardhamýli, this hotel is famous for its connection with British writers Patrick Leigh Fermor, whose house was in the adjoining property, and Bruce Chatwin, who wrote *Songlines* in what is now Room 1 in the annexe. Breakfast included. €€

**Liakoto** On the seafront; http://anniska-liakoto.com. Belonging to the same owner as *Anniska* (see above), this hotel is easily accessible from the main road with parking spaces and a pebble beach in front. The self-catering apartments, in dark wood and white marble, are arranged around the pool and all have at least partial sea views. April–Oct. €€

**Notos** http://notoshotel.gr. Tranquil and tastefully decorated, the two-person self-catering studios here come with all amenities you'd expect. The stone buildings are clustered in a hilly garden enclave, with wonderful views over the whole area. Three-night minimum for best rate. No breakfast. €€

## EATING

**Dioskouri** Beach; 27210 73236. Great little place along the seafront, rated highly for its fabulous sea views and seafood such as calamari and octopus, washed down with house rosé. €

**Kiki** Beach; 27210 73148. This is one of the finest of the traditional tavernas you could hope to find, and serves genuine Maniot dishes created from the freshest local produce. Stick to the dish of the day and you won't be disappointed. March–Nov. €

**Lela's Taverna** Next to Notos Hotel (see above); http://lelastaverna.com/. All home-cooked dishes using locally sourced meats and cheeses. Try their xerosfeli fried cheese with mulberry jam or the seabass. Best to ask to see their dishes as they change daily, depending on produce. €

## DIRECTORY

**Banks** On the main road south of the platía, you'll find a post office (Mon–Fri 7.30am–2pm). There is an ATM at the bank, next to the bridge.

# Arcadia

PRODRHOMÚ MONASTERY

# Arcadia

6

Arcadia (Arkadhía), the heartland province of the Peloponnese, contains some of the most beautiful alpine landscapes in Greece. Dramatic hills are crowned by a string of medieval towns, and the occasional Classical antiquity. Beautiful Karítena is a picture-postcard hill town, but the best area of all is around Stemnítsa and Dhimitsána, where walkers are rewarded with the luxuriant Loúsios Gorge. Another hill town, Andhrítsena, attracts archeology buffs with the nearby Temple of Bassae, which is still spectacular though tented for restoration. The main transport hub of the region is Trípoli, a lively, if rather nondescript, town. A series of Wild fires have severely damaged the area's oak and fir woodland, though recovery is evident and the legendary beauty still holds, especially in spring, when the slopes are bright yellow with masses of broom plants.

### Brief history

Arcadia is also known for its mythological significance. Named after the mythic figure Arcas, a son of Zeus and Callisto, Arcadia has been emblematic of pastoral beauty and idyllic simplicity since antiquity.

During the classical period, Arcadia comprised several small, independent city-states. Its mountainous terrain fostered a sense of isolation and autonomy among its inhabitants. Despite this, the Arcadians were known for their unique dialect and shared cultural practices, including their distinctive musical traditions.

In the fourth century BCE, Arcadia saw a brief period of political unity with the establishment of the Arcadian League, centred in the newly founded city of Megalopolis. This federation was an attempt to counter the power of Sparta and other regional powers.

Trípoli, originally known as Trípolis, meaning "three cities," emerged as a significant urban centre much later, during the Ottoman period. By the eighteenth century, Trípoli became an administrative and commercial hub for the region. The city played a crucial role during the Greek War of Independence; in 1821, the Siege of Tripoli ended in a decisive victory for the Greek revolutionaries against the Ottoman forces.

Today, Trípoli serves as the capital of the Arcadia regional unit, blending its historical legacy with modern administrative functions. The town and its surrounding landscapes continue to captivate visitors with their rich history and natural beauty. Drivers should be aware that Arcadia's highways, some of the broadest and emptiest in the Peloponnese, are shared with sheep- and goat-herds moving their flocks.

# Trípoli

**TRÍPOLI** is a major crossroads of the Peloponnese and is the Arcadian capital. Set in a huge upland plain and surrounded by spectacular mountains, Trípoli is a large, modern town, and home to one of the country's biggest army barracks. Its altitude of 665m means an often markedly cooler summer climate and harsh winters. Medieval Tripolitsá was destroyed during the War of Independence, when the Greek forces, led by Kolokotronis, massacred the town's Turkish population in one of their worst atrocities.

THE OPEN-AIR WATER-POWER MUSEUM

# Highlights

❶ **Kapsia Cave** This ancient cave is one of the ten most important ones in Greece dating back to the Neolithic period (4th millennium BC) with amazing stalactite and stalagmite formations. See page 122

❷ **Prodhrómou Monastery** Ancient Monastery in Loúsios Gorge where five monks still live and can show you around. See page 124

❸ **Church of Ayía Theodora** Twelfth-century church near village of Vasta with seventeen trees growing from its roof. The roof is intact, rendering the church the 'Miracle Church' – it's in the Guinness Book of Records. See page 124

❹ **Ancient Gortys** A remote ancient site strewn across the hillside 8km southeast of Stemnítsa with a huge excavation containing the remains of a temple to Asclepios. See page 126

❺ **Open-Air Water-Power Museum** Award-winning Open-Air Water-Power Museum just outside Dhimitsána with reconstructed watermill, tannery and gunpowder mill. See page 127

❻ **Temple of Apollo Epikourios at Bassae** One of the best-preserved classical monuments in the country, the Temple is thought to have been designed by Iktinos, architect of the Parthenon and the Hephaisteion (Thisseion) in Athens. See page 127

HIGHLIGHTS ARE MARKED ON THE MAP ON PAGE 122

The city doesn't pander to tourism and has few obvious attractions, but its youthful Greek exuberance is hard to match anywhere else in the Peloponnese, and there are far worse places to get stranded by bus schedules for the night. The traffic here can be chaotic, so you may wish to escape to the quiet greenery of **Platía Áreos** or **Kendrikí Platía**, whose shops and cafés seem frozen in the 1960s.

6

## Panarcadic Archeological Museum

Evangelistrías 8 & Spiliopoulou • summer & winter 8.30am–3.30pm, closed Tues • Charge

Housed in a Neoclassical building designed by Ernst Ziller with a beautiful rose garden, the **Panarcadic Archeological Museum** is perhaps Trípoli's most interesting attraction. Its collection includes finds from all over Arcadia, from the Neolithic era to Roman times.

## Kapsia Cave

Mantineia, Arkadia • http://spilaiokapsia.gr/en/main-home/ • Closed Tues • Charge

15km north of Tripoli, nestled just outside the small village of **Kapsia** lies one of the ten most remarkable **caves** in the country. When a Greek-French expedition in

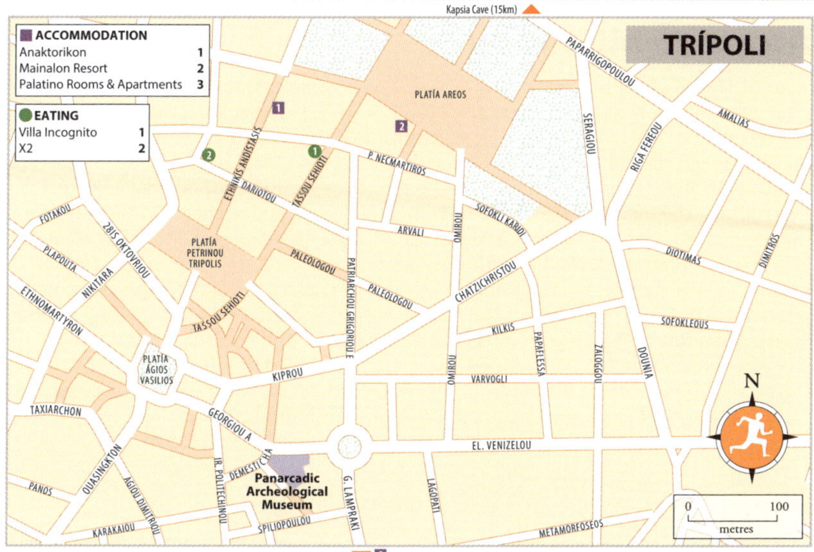


6

1892, traces of numerous fragments of human bones were discovered, plus skulls covered by mud and lamps that probably dated back to the late Greek period (fourth & fifth century AD), all proof that the cave was used for living in. Today it makes fascinating viewing for its stalactite and stalagmites in its chambers formed over millions of years.

## ARRIVAL AND DEPARTURE — TRÍPOLI

**By bus** The main bus terminal is at the top of Nafplíou St (2710 222 560, http://ktelarkadias.gr).

**Destinations** Andhrítsena (Hourly bus to Megalopolis, then taxi; 1hr 30min); Athens (hourly daily; 3hr 15min); Dhimitsána (hourly bus to Megalopolis, then taxi; 1hr 20min); Gortyna (Hourly bus to Megalopolis, then taxi; 1hr 15min); Kalamata (5 daily; 1hr 30min–2hr 45min); Monemvasia (taxi to Spárti, then one bus daily; 2hr 50min); Náfplio (4 daily; 1hr 20min); Pátra (4 weekly; 3hr); Spárti (1 daily. Bus to Kalamata and change; 5hr 55min inc. stop in Kalamata); Stemnítsa (hourly bus to Megalopolis, then taxi; 1hr 20 min); Yíthio (5 daily; 1h 30min).

## ACCOMMODATION — SEE MAP PAGE 123

In Trípoli itself there isn't much choice, but we've listed what there is.

**Anaktorikon** Ethnikís Andístasis 48; http://anaktorikon.gr. Trípoli's only four-star boutique hotel incorporates a spa. Each room has individual furnishings and decor, although room 32 with its black marble bathroom is hard to beat. Breakfast included. €-€€

**Mainalon Resort** Platía Areos; http://mainalonhotel.gr. Unashamedly decorated in carmine red, this 1936 hotel boasts sumptuous fin-de-siècle French cornices. It's worth paying the extra for a room looking over Platia Areos. Breakfast and parking included. €-€€

**Palatino Rooms & Apartments** Polyviou 2; http://www.palatino-tripolis.gr/english/. Right in the town centre, this spacious and welcoming hotel offers single, double, family rooms and suites–most with terraces, some with a kitchenette and spa bath. Expect traditional trimmings such as wooden floors and real fireplaces. €€

## EATING AND DRINKING — SEE MAP PAGE 123

Tripoli's nightlife is at its buzziest in the pedestrianized streets around the small church of St Paul.

**Villa Incognito** Delligianni & Tassou Sehioti 43; https://villaincognito.gr/; 2710 222 111. The "in" place in Trípoli – the massive lighting rigs, large mirrors and wooden tables and chairs almost distract from the very good international cuisine. Booking recommended. €-€€

**X2** Dariotou 18; 2710 226 010. This mezedhopolío attracts a thirty-something clientele, and serves the usual Greek staples, plus massive salads, *mezédhes* featuring six kinds of local cheese and selected local wines by the glass. €

# Arcadian hill towns

West of Trípoli you'll find the best of Arcadia, with minor roads curling through a series of lush valleys and below the area's most exquisite **medieval hill towns**. The obvious first stop is lofty **Karítena**. Then the route to the northwest winds farther up around the edge of the Ménalo mountains to the delightful towns of **Stemnítsa** and **Dhimitsána**, a 12.5km section between the two which is a popular day hike for those hiking the **Menalon Trail**. Either of which you can explore the **Loúsios Gorge**, the remote site of **ancient Gortys** and the stunning eleventh-century **Monastery Ayíou Ioánnou Prodhrómou**, as well as additional ancient monasteries up on the gorge. Further west is the hill town of **Andhrítsena** and the nearby ancient **Temple of Bassae**, plus a further 45km south brings you to the unique eleventh or twelfth century **Church of Ayía Theodora** with its many trees growing atop its roof. Not to be missed is the tiny **Abeliona Village** with its restored main square, cobbled streets, mini springs and surrounded by fir forests,10km east of the Temple of Bassae and a good exploring base.



The hill towns offer plenty of great places to stay and, unlike other Greek resorts, are cheaper in the summer, as they cater mostly for the domestic ski tourism.

## Karítena

In a picturesque setting watching over the strategic Megalópoli–Andhrítsena, **KARÍTENA** provides one of the signature Arcadian images. Like many of the hill towns hereabouts, its history has Frankish, Byzantine and Turkish contributions. It was founded by the Byzantines in the seventh century and had attained a population of some twenty thousand when the Franks took it in 1209. Under their century-long rule, Karítena was the capital of a large barony under Geoffroy de Bruyères, the paragon of chivalry in the medieval ballad *The Chronicle of the Morea*, and probably the only well-liked Frankish overlord.

These days the village has a population of just a couple of hundred, but as recently as the beginning of the nineteenth century, there were at least ten times that figure.

### Froúrio

Open access • Free

Up steps off the platía is the **FROÚRIO**, the castle built in 1245 by the Franks, with added Turkish towers. It was repaired by Theodhoros Kolokotronis and it was here that he held out against Ibrahim Pasha in 1826 and turned the tide of the War of Independence.

### Medieval bridge and the River Alfiós

Don't miss Karítena's **medieval bridge** over the River Alfiós (Alpheus). To find it, stop on the south side of the modern bridge and follow a short track down, almost underneath the new span. The old structure is missing the central section, but is an intriguing sight nonetheless, with a small Byzantine chapel built into one of the central pillars. **Whitewater rafting** is organized near the bridge (see page 127).

## Stemnítsa and around

Some 16km north of Karítena, the winter resort of **STEMNÍTSA** (Ypsoús on many maps) lies at an altitude of 1050m. It's divided by ravines into three distinct quarters: the **kástro** (the ancient acropolis hill, worth the walk up for the views), **Ayía Paraskeví** (east of the stream) and **Áyios Ioánnis** (west of the stream). For centuries, it was one of the premier **goldworking centres** of the Balkans.

Although much depopulated, Stemnítsa remains a fascinating town with a small **folklore museum** and several quietly magnificent medieval churches: the seventeenth-

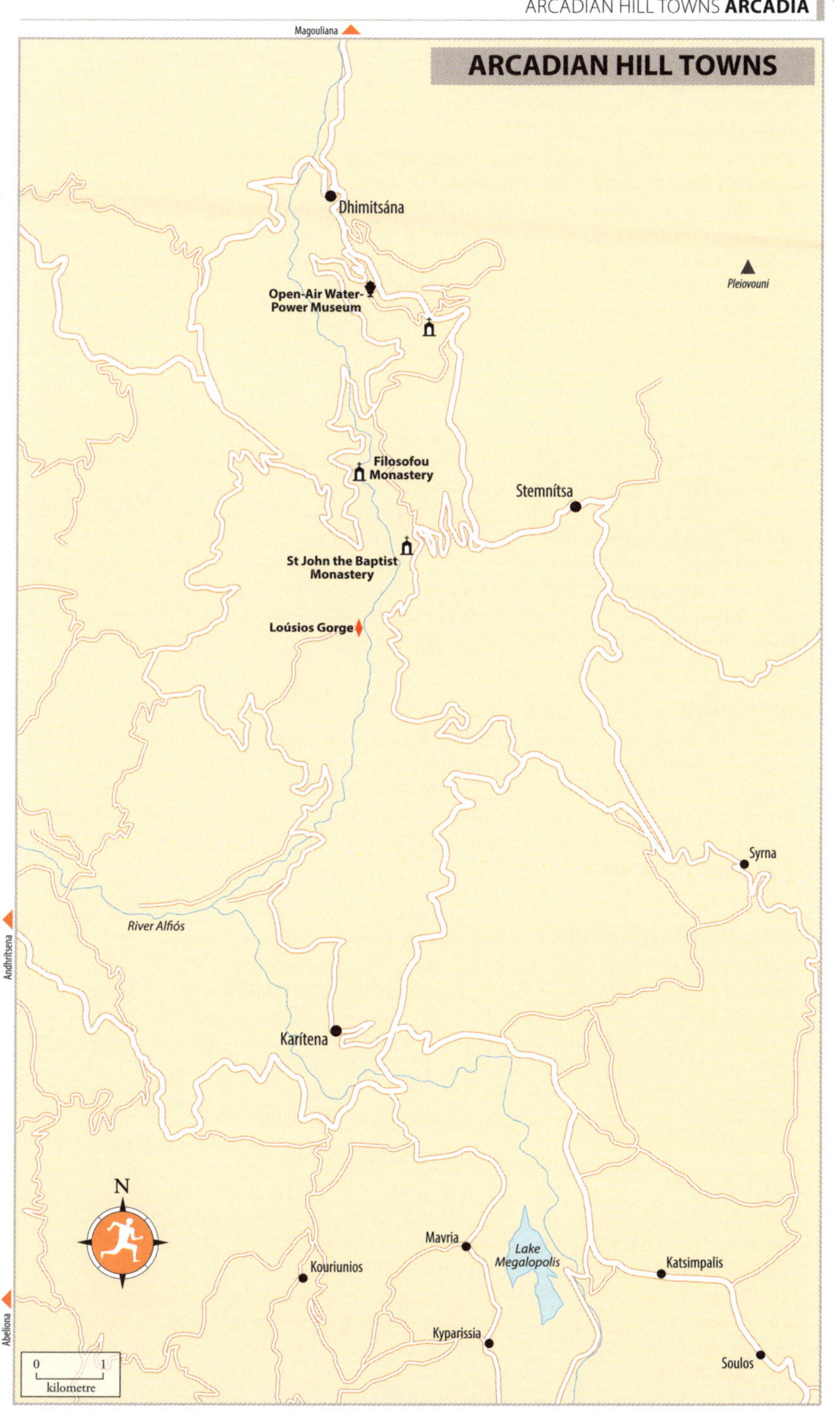
ARCADIAN HILL TOWNS
Magouliana
Dhimitsána
Open-Air Water-Power Museum
Pleiovouni
Filosofou Monastery
Stemnítsa
St John the Baptist Monastery
Loúsios Gorge
Syrna
River Alfiós
Andhritsena
Karítena
N
Mavria
Lake Megalopolis
Kouriunios
Katsimpalis
Abeliona
Kyparissia
Soulos
0 1 kilometre

century **basilica of Trión Ierarhón**, across the way from the museum, is the most accessible of them.

### Folklore Museum

Just off the main road in Ayía Paraskeví • Currently closed for maintenance • Charge • http://stemnitsamuseum.gr

The ground floor of the **Folklore Museum** is devoted to mock-ups of the workshops of indigenous crafts such as candle-making, bell-casting, shoe-making and jewellery. The next floor up features re-creations of the salon of a well-to-do family and a humbler cottage. The top storey is taken up by the rather random collections of the Savopoulos family: plates by Avramides (a refugee from Asia Minor and ceramics master), textiles and costumes from all over Greece, weapons, copperware and eighteenth- and nineteenth-century icons.



## Ancient Gortys

8km southeast of Stemnítsa • Open access • Free

**ANCIENT GORTYS** is a charming site, set beside the rushing river known in ancient times as the Gortynios. The remains are widely strewn over the hillside on the west bank of the stream, but the main attraction, below contemporary ground level and not at all obvious until well to the west of the little Byzantine chapel of Áyios Andhréas (by the old bridge), is the huge excavation containing the remains of a **temple to Asclepios** and an adjoining **bath**, both dating from the fourth century BC. The most curious feature of the site is a circular **portico** enclosing round-backed seats, which most certainly would have been part of the therapeutic centre.

## Dhimitsána

Some 11km north of Stemnítsa, **DHIMITSÁNA** has an immediately seductive appearance, its cobbled streets and tottering houses straddling a twin hillside overlooking the Loúsios River. Views from the village are stunning, and though quite a small resort, it has an excellent accommodation selection, as well as the best choice of tavernas in the area, making Dhimitsána a prime base for exploring this region of the Peloponnese.

### HIKING NEAR ANCIENT GORTYS

The farmland surrounding ancient Gortys belongs to the monks of the nearby **Prodhrómou Monastery** who have carved a path along the **Loúsios Gorge** between Áyios Andhréas and the monastery. It's about a forty-minute walk up a well-graded trail following the stream. The monastery, stuck on to the cliff like a swallow's nest, is plainly visible a couple of hundred metres above the path. There are no more than five monks here, and one of them may show visitors the tiny, frescoed *katholikón*. Strict dress rules apply, with blanket-like clothing provided if necessary. The monastery is also accessible by an asphalt road that makes a circuitous 7km descent from the Stemnítsa–Dhimitsána road to a parking lot and newish chapel, and then it's a further 1km descent on foot along a steep path.

Beyond Prodhrómou, the path continues clearly to the outlying, well-signed monasteries of **Paleá** and then **Néa Filosófou** on the opposite side of the valley. The older (Paleá), dating from the tenth century, is merely a ruin and blends into the cliff against which it is flattened. The newer monastery (Néa, seventeenth-century) has been restored and recently expanded considerably, but retains frescoes from 1663 inside; there is a permanent caretaker monk. From here, paths follow the west then east banks of the river, to reach Dhimitsána via Paleohóri in under two hours.

In the town, a half-dozen churches with tall, squarish belfries recall the extended Frankish, and especially Norman, tenure in this part of the Moreas during the thirteenth century. Yet no one should dispute the deep-dyed Greekness of Dhimitsána. It was the birthplace of **Archbishop Yermanos**, who first raised the flag of rebellion at Kalávryta in 1821, and of the hapless patriarch, **Grigoris V,** hanged in Constantinople upon the sultan's receiving news of the insurrection.



### Open-Air Water-Power Museum

2km east of Dhimitsána • Closed Tues • Charge • 27950 31630 • https://piop.gr/en/diktuo-mouseiwn/Mouseio-Ydrokinisis/to-mouseio.aspx

The award-winning **Open-Air Water-Power Museum** highlights the importance of waterpower in traditional society, looking at pre-industrial techniques. You'll find a reconstructed watermill, tannery and gunpowder mill, with exhibitions on the pre-industrial processes involved.

## Andhrítsena and around

**ANDHRÍTSENA**, 28km west of Karítena along a beautiful route, is a traditional hill town and the base from which to visit the **Temple of Apollo Epikourios** at **Bassae** up in the mountains to the south. Though very much a roadside settlement today, Andhrítsena was a major urban centre during the years of Turkish occupation and the first century of independent Greece.

### Temple of Apollo Epikourios

Summer daily 8am–8pm • Winter daily until 3pm• Charge • 26260 22275 • https://apollotemple.ilia-olympia.org/

Some 14km into the mountains south of Andhrítsena and well signposted stands a **World Heritage Site**, the fifth-century BC **Temple of Apollo Epikourios** at **Bassae** (Vásses), which occupies one of the remotest, highest (1131m) and arguably most spectacular **sites** in Greece. One of the best-preserved Classical monuments in the country, it is thought to have been designed by Iktinos, architect of the Parthenon and the Hephaisteion (Thisseion) in Athens.

Unfortunately, to protect it from the elements during its complicated **restoration**, the magnificent temple is currently swathed in a gigantic marquee suspended from metal girders. The work, recounted in a video on site, is badly needed to keep the whole thing from tumbling, stone by stone, into the valley below and the marquee is quite a sight in itself. However, you may feel a bit disappointed at first sight, until you enter the tent and are awestruck by the sheer scale and majesty of the structure. Even with its scaffolding, the temple is worth all the narrow, precipitous mountain roads it takes to get here.

### GETTING AROUND — ARCADIAN HILL TOWNS

**By car and bus** Having your own transport is essential here, though there are limited buses from Trípoli (see page 123).

**By taxi** Taxis are not that expensive for travelling between towns, if you use a local one for the outward journey: try Taxi Tripolis (http://tripolisarcadiataxi.gr, 6978 18 9724); Taxaki Tripoli (http://tripoli.taxaki.com, 2710 300 300) – they also have a downloadable App.

### ACTIVITIES

**Whitewater rafting** Xreme Greece (http://xtremegreece.gr) organizes rafting trips down the River Alfiós.

### ACCOMMODATION

**KARÍTENA**

**Vrenthi** http://vrenthi.gr. Located on the right just before the main square, this good-value café has rooms to rent at their nearby homely stone-built guesthouse that can sleep up to seven people. **€**

## BASSAE'S MISSING METOPES

Many of the Temple of Apollo Epikourios's stunning **metopes**, the marble frieze sculptures, as well as other fine pieces, were removed and installed in London's **British Museum** in 1814–15. Reportedly, an English archeologist bribed the local Ottoman pasha, who evidently did not consider preservation of the works of any importance. The metopes powerfully depict the battles of the Amazons, Lapiths and Centaurs, and they are on display in a special room with the controversial **Elgin Marbles** which, under similar circumstances, were boxed up and shipped to Britain in 1812.

### STEMNÍTSA

★ **Mpelleiko** http://mpelleiko.gr. High above the town, overlooking the whole mountainous area, stands a marvellous stone mansion, beautifully converted into this unique guesthouse. The rooms are all different and cosy and come with a fireplace. Hearty buffet breakfast included. €€

**Trikolonion** http://trikolonioncountry.gr. Just to the east of town is this very comfortable luxury resort in a converted nineteenth-century boarding school. The rooms have every amenity, and there's a gym/spa and free parking. Horse-riding and rafting trips arranged. Buffet breakfast included. €€

### DHIMITSÁNA

**Amanites** http://amanites.gr. This beautiful stone building stands prominently just above the main road and has very comfortable rooms with spectacular views over the town and valley. The lovely owners are always ready to help, and the breakfast (included) features home-made treats. €–€€

★ **En Dimitsani** http://en-dimitsani.gr. Traditionally built in stone and wood, yet modern and luxurious, this Arcadian hotel manages to combine cosy rooms with functioning fireplaces (free wood) and great views over the Lusios gorge. There's parking – a rarity in Dhimitsána – and a great home-made breakfast included. €–€€

**Xenonas Kazakou** http://xenonaskazakou.gr. It's a steep schlep up from the main road, winding around past the old church, to this magnificent property, which is unbeatable for spacious comfort, friendliness and especially the breakfast cooked to order (included). €–€€

### MAGOULIANA

★ **Manna Arcadia** http://mannaarcadia.gr/. Don't let this gorgeous retreat's remote location put you off. Once a sanitarium in the 1920s for soldiers recovering from TB in the war – the largest in the Balkans – it's now been lovingly converted to house a mixture of just 32 rooms and suites, all in original stone. The spa has a cave pool and it's a beautiful mountain escape. Breakfast included. €€€

### ABELIONA

**Abeliona Retreat** http://abeliona-retreat.com. A gorgeous hillside retreat in the village of the same name, suite accommodation is in a scattering of houses across the hillside with their own gardens providing herbs and vegetables for dinner. €€

## EATING

### STEMNÍTSA

**I Stemnitsa** http://touristorama.com/en/stemnitsa-tavern. The town's eponymous taverna turns out dishes in keeping with its wild mountain setting, with plenty of fresh produce, as well as game – try the country sausage or goat. €

### DHIMITSÁNA

**Sto Kioupi** http://stokioupi.gr. This very central and amiable restaurant has some tables with views down the valley, and an extensive menu featuring both meat and game dishes such as rabbit in garlic sauce: there are also vegetarian specialities, including its signature vegetable pie. €

★ **Tefthis** 27950 31514. Near the main square, this elegant, rustic spot, with a functioning fireplace and friendly service, specializes in pork dishes – try the salt pork omelette, a local staple, or pork in a pot with mustard sauce. €

**To Steki tis Gefsis** http://tostekitisgefsis.gr. With rifle displays on the walls, this "corner of taste", as it dubs itself, has gone for the full Greek Independence revolutionary chic. It fits well with the menu of coal-grilled meats and pork stews that the old warriors would have loved. €

### MAGOULIANA

**Taverna Iosif** 27950 82359. About 3km from Manna Arcadia Resort, this small family taverna serves up locally sourced grilled meat and fresh vegetable dishes throughout the year. Try the chicken wings and their own feta. €

# Messinía and Kalamáta

AERIAL VIEW OF KALAMÁTA

# Messinía and Kalamáta

The province of Messinía stretches from the western flank of the Taïyetos ridge across the plain of Kalamáta (see page 134) to include the hilly southwesternmost "finger" of the Peloponnese. Green, fertile and luxuriant for the most part, it is ringed with a series of well-preserved castles overlooking some of the area's most expansive beaches. The towns of Koróni, Methóni and Finikoúnda and their beaches draw the crowds, while the pale curve of fine sand at the bay of Voïdhokiliá, near Pýlos, sandwiched between sea, rock and lagoon, is one of the most beautiful beaches in Greece. Messinía's notable archeological sites, such as ancient Messene, west of Kalamáta (see page 137) and Nestor's Palace (see page 144) north of Pýlos, rarely see as many visitors as the Argolid sites.



## Brief history

Messinia's history, marked by its cities and battles, showcases the region's enduring importance from ancient to medieval times, reflecting its strategic, military, and cultural significance in Greek history. The region was originally inhabited by Mycenaeans and its strategic location made it a focal point for various powers throughout history.

The Venetians fortified Koróni in the thirteenth century, turning it into a key **maritime and commercial hub**. Its impressive castle, built by the Venetians, still stands as a testament to its historical significance.

Nearby Methóni has a history closely tied to Koróni. Known as Modon in medieval times, it was also fortified by the Venetians and served as an important stop on the maritime route to the Holy Land during the Crusades. Its Castle, one of the largest in the Mediterranean, reflects its historical military significance.

Pýlos on the southwestern coast is famed for the Battle of Navarino in 1827, a pivotal naval battle in the Greek **War of Independence** (see page 741). The town has historical roots stretching back to antiquity, with the nearby Palace of Nestor being a significant Mycenaean site, providing insights into ancient Greek civilization.

**Ancient Messene**, founded in the fourth century BC by the Theban general Epaminondas, was established after the Battle of Leuctra to provide a stronghold for the Messenians against Spartan domination. The city was well-planned and fortified, with impressive structures such as the stadium, theatre, and city walls, many of which are remarkably well-preserved today, offering travellers a glimpse into the region's ancient urban and cultural life.

The region's capital town of **Kalamáta** flourished as a commercial centre during the Turkish period and became one of the first independent Greek towns in 1821; indeed, the first newspaper to be printed on Greek soil was produced here the same year. Throughout the nineteenth and early twentieth centuries, an important port was also established here but as the seat of power subsequently shifted to Athens, the region suffered with emigration and a decline in population. This was further intensified by World War II and then the Civil War. Environmental factors also have played their part on the region's propensity to flourish and in 1986, Kalamáta was near the epicentre of a severe **earthquake** that killed twenty people and left twelve thousand families homeless. But for the fact that the quake struck in the early evening, when many people were outside, the death toll would have been much higher. As it was, large numbers of buildings were levelled throughout the town.

METHÓNI FORT

# Highlights

❶ **Kalamáta Old Town** Wander through the picturesque streets and view the charming historic architecture, vibrant markets, rich cultural heritage and local cuisine of this famous Peloponnese city by the sea. See page 134

❷ **Kalamáta market** Market every Tuesday and Saturday where locals shop for their quality food and the famous black Kalamáta olives. Also has some great street art on display. See page 134

❸ **Church of Agios Apostoloi** Byzantine church in Kalamáta Old Town where Greek revolutionary forces regained control of their city from the Ottomans. See page 135

❹ **Kalamáta Beach** Blue flag awarded beach only a short stroll from the city centre. See page 135

❺ **Ancient Messene** The remains of the former Messinía capital. See page 137

❻ **Koróni citadel** One of the longest held Venetian fortresses in the country with commanding views across the Messenian Gulf. See page 138

❼ **Methóni Fort** Surrounded by the sea on three sides, enter over the stone bridge over its moat and inside you'll find intact the foundations of many houses, a Turkish bath and underground passages. See page 140

HIGHLIGHTS ARE MARKED ON THE MAPS ON PAGES 134 AND 136

# Kalamáta and around

**KALAMÁTA** is by far the largest city in the southern Peloponnese, spreading some 4km back from the sea and into the hills, and it provides quite a metropolitan shock after the small-town life of the rest of the region. As well as the best urban beach this side of Athens, it also boasts plenty of big-town facilities, decent tavernas and a pleasant historic centre. Synonymous for centuries with **olives** (and to a lesser extent figs), Kalamáta today has been boosted by a new international airport and is a resort in itself, as well as being the gateway to the Mani (see page 104) and the southwestern Peloponnese.

## Old town

Kalamata's **old town** is small and attractive especially along its pedestrianized promenades flanked by fin-de-siècle houses. The typical **kástro** (Wed–Mon: winter 8.30am–3.30pm; summer 8am–8pm; Charge; http://odysseus.culture.gr/) makes for a green stroll amid evocative ruins to a small, photogenic chapel. Below the castle, one of the region's most colourful produce **markets** (8am–3pm) takes place

on Wednesdays and Saturdays, across the bridge from the bus station. Come and sample any manner of snacks from the famed Kalamáta black olive to chunks of graviera cheese and local honey for sale, to name but a few produce. There are also some great **street art murals** to be found in the Market, by talented local urban artist Skitsofrenis. His work can also be spotted around the city (http://instagram.com/skitsofrenis/).

The **Archeological Museum of Messinía**, on Benaki & Agiou Ioannou St (Various opening times, check website; Charge; http://archmusmes.culture.gr), has a modest collection with everything informatively labelled and panelled. Meanwhile the sixth century **Metropolitan church of Ypapanti** in Ipapantis Square (Daily; Free) is the city's imposing cathedral with its double domes and bell towers and inside the icon of Panagia Ypapaniti, the patron Saint of Kalamáta and the city's protectress. Annually in early February the icon is paraded through the streets in a celebration.

**Kalamáta** was one of the first Greek towns to gain independence when on 23rd March 1821, Greek revolutionary forces regained control of the town after the Ottomans surrendered. This happened at the **Church of Agios Apostoloi** (daily 7.30am–2pm, 5–8pm; free) in the Old Town – a medieval Byzantine church built in 1317 where after this victory, the local population gathered and held their first mass in over 360 years. The aforementioned street-artist Skitsofrenis has a mural just opposite the church commemorating this victory.

Heading from here straight down towards the port, you'll walk through a pleasant city park, where an **open-air railway museum** (24hr; free) has retired locomotives and train cars lined up to admire.

7

## Beaches

The town boasts some of the most stunning beaches in the Peloponnese. Although the main **Kalamáta Beach** has been awarded Blue Flag status, don't expect white sands as this long stretch along the promenade is a pebbled shoreline with cafés, tavernas and hotels. Nearby, Mikri Mantineia and Almyros offer tranquil spots ideal for swimming and sunbathing. For a more secluded experience, explore the hidden coves of Santova and Archontiko. Each beach promises a perfect blend of relaxation and natural beauty.

### ARRIVAL AND DEPARTURE — KALAMÁTA

**By air** The airport (27210 63805, http://kalamata-airport.airportfield.com), 8km west of Kalamáta on the highway to Messíni and Pýlos, is served by BA and seasonal charter and budget airlines such as Jet2 and easyJet from London and other UK regional airports. Its claim to fame is the fact it featured in the 2013 film *Before Midnight* with facilities including car hire, an ATM and a helpful tourist office, open when flights are due. Buses to the centre leave every thirty minutes (Charge); taxis to the city can be expensive.

**By bus** The bus station (27210 28581; http://ktelmessinias.gr) is at the top of Artemisías, about 1km north of the centre. Destinations Ancient Messini (Hourly; 15min to Messíni then taxi); Athens (10 direct daily; 3hr 15min); Finikoúnda (3 daily; 2hr); Ioánnina (2–4 weekly via Pyrgos or Agrinio; 7hr); Kardhamýli (2 daily; 35min); Kórinthos via Isthmós then taxi (4 daily; 2hr 40min); Koróni (5 daily; 1hr 10min); Messíni (Hourly; 15min); Methóni (3–4 daily; 1hr 40min); Pátra (2 daily; 3hr–3hr 30min); Pýlos (5–6 daily; 1hr 20min); Pýrgos (2 daily; 2hr); Spárti (2 weekly; 1hr 50min); Stoúpa (2 daily to Kardamyli, then taxi; 45min); Thessaloniki (3 weekly direct; 10hr); Trípoli (6–7 daily; 1hr 20min).

**By car** From Athens you'd take the A7 toll road pretty much from Athens Airport all the way through. The journey takes approx. 2hr 40mins–3hrs and driving through Kalamáta is easy, with good sign posting. There are several free parking places or street parking along the promenade and seafront.

### INFORMATION

**Tourist office** The municipal tourist office at Aristomenous 28 (Mon–Fri 8am–9pm; 27213 60754, http://kalamata.gr/en/visitors/tourist-information-office) is helpful and brimming with maps, brochures and books on the area. Trigilidas Travel at Policharous 4 (Mon–Fri 9am–2pm & 6pm–9pm, Sat 9am–2pm; 27210 90900, http://trigilidas.com) is a useful travel agency that can organise tours of the local area including wine harvesting, sea kayaking and arrange transfers.

KALAMÁTA
EATING
Bistroteca 2
Versailles Kitchen Restaurant 3
Vino Banco Tapas 1
ACCOMMODATION
Elektra Hotel & Spa 2
Filoxenia Terma 4
Haïkos 3
Rex 1
Villa Vager Mani 5
HIGHLIGHTS
1 Kalamáta Old Town
2 Kalamáta market
3 Church of Agios Apostoloi
4 Kalamáta Beach
Bus station
Kalamáta Market
OLD TOWN
Metropolitan Church of Ypapanti
Archeological Museum of Messinía
Church of Agios Apostoloi
Explore Messinia
Municipal Railway Park
Open-air Railway Museum
Kalamáta beach
Kalamáta Interntional Airport
N
0 500 metres

### GETTING AROUND

**By bus** There are two bus lines that go around the city, one connecting the city centre with the east beach and the other the city centre with the technical university to the northwest of Kalamáta. Tickets can be bought on board for €1.30.
**By car** There are many car rental places in town, including the reliable Verga Rent A Car, Farón 202 (27210 95190, http://car-rental-kalamata.gr) and Avance Rent A Car, Likourgou 6-8, also at the airport (27210 27211, http://avance.gr). You can rent motorbikes from MotoBastakos at Farón 139 (27210 26638, http://motobastakos.gr).
**By taxi** Radio Taxis on 27210 21112, http://radiotaxi-kalamatas.gr (24hr).

### ACTIVITIES

Explore Messinia, Bouloukou 26 (69718 97640, http://exploremessinia.com) organizes intrepid hikes, kayaking trips and river rafting of the surrounding region and the Máni.

### ACCOMMODATION

SEE MAP PAGE 136

There's an excellent choice of accommodation in Kalamáta, either boutique style hotels tucked in the Old Town or beachside properties. We've listed the best here.

★ **Elektra Hotel & Spa** Psaron 152, at Bouboulinas; http://elektrahotelspa.gr. Convenient for the marina and the ferries, this swish hotel has the largest and most comfortable beds you are likely to sink into in Greece. There's a gym, rooftop pool, sauna and Turkish bath plus a dozen different spa treatments on offer, all adding up to a great stay. Breakfast included. €€

**Filoxenia Terma** Navarínou; http://filoxeniakalamata.com. The best beach resort in Kalamáta, and the only one where you don't have to cross the busy seafront road to get to the beach. A resort style hotel, expect large rooms with balconies, two pools, tennis courts, a sauna, spa and gym plus free parking. Buffet breakfast included; half board extra. €€

**Haïkos** Navarínou 115; http://haikos.gr. A trim, modern hotel with plush rooms by the town beach. All rooms have balconies, a/c and wi-fi, but it's worth paying a little extra to get sea views. Free parking; breakfast included. €€

**Rex** Aristomenous 26; http://rexhotel.gr. Historic old-town hotel built in 1899. Rooms are on the small side, but fresh and well appointed, some with balconies, in a fine Neoclassical building facing the palm-lined promenade. There's also a restaurant and a café. Breakfast included. €€

★ **Villa Vager Mani** Great Mantinia, Mani; http://villavagermani.gr. 15 mins from Kalamáta town and 2 mins from Santova beach lies this luxury, bohemian Historic old neoclassical tower converted into large unique suites, suitable for families and friends. Breakfast included. Apr–Oct. €€€

### EATING AND DRINKING

SEE MAP PAGE 136

The west marina is where you'll find the top restaurants, while the Navarínou waterfront is a good place for popular cafés, bars and ice-cream parlours: the pedestrianized old town is the nightlife hub.

**Bistroteca** Vasileos Georgiou 18; 27210 97431. Café come meal spot for locals and tourists alike. Their burgers are very popular, then come back and hang out in the outside pavement area and sip one of their signature cocktails. €

**Versailles Kitchen Restaurant** Evaggelistrias 46; 27210 81858. Real traditional Greek recipes such as pastitsio, the 'Greek lasagna' served in what looks like a traditional house tucked behind the Marina. Very popular with the locals – only open until 6.30pm so it's great for a spot of lunch. €

★ **Vino Banco Tapas** Diós Ithómata 6; 27210 25160. This tapas wine bar in the old town has taken Kalamáta by storm. They also serve larger dishes such as paella, and pride themselves on being "always open" – we can't guarantee such a claim, but have yet to see it closed. There's a lot going on such as wine tastings and stand-up comedy to while away your time. €€

### DIRECTORY

**Banks** There are banks and ATMs all over the city.
**Post office** The main post office which also operates as a courier is at Filellinon 52 (Mon–Fri 8am–8pm, Sat 8am–2pm).

## Ancient Messene (Ithómi)

Daily: winter 8.30am–3.30pm; summer 8am–8pm • Charge, including museum • 27240 51201, http://ancientmessene.gr • Local bus to Mavromáti from Kalamáta twice daily

Located just 22km northwest of Kalamáta, the substantial remains of **ancient Messene** are spread out just below the village of Mavromáti. This former Messinian capital was founded in 371 BC, following the liberation of the area from Spartan hegemony. The space was originally girded by 9km of Cyclopean **ramparts**, and there are remnants of massive gates. Count on three hours for a complete walkabout. Besides the walls, sights include the agora, a restored theatre, a stadium with its columned entrance, a partial colonnade of the gymnasium, various temple bases and a large Asklepion. There's also a small **museum**, which houses a few very good pieces of statuary found here, including one of **Artemis Orthia**. Apart from some olive groves, most of the area is shadeless, and there are no services, so fill up water bottles at the lovely old **fountain** in the village before setting off.

# Koróni

7

**KORÓNI**, 40km southwest of Kalamáta, occupies one of the more picturesque locations in Greece, stacked against a fortified bluff and commanding grand views across the Messenian gulf. It's a place to relax on the beach, drink wine and amble about a countryside lush with vineyards and olive groves. The town is rustically beautiful with tiled and pastel-washed houses arrayed in a maze of stair-and-ramp streets that have changed little since the medieval **Venetian occupation** (1206–1500). Koróni, along with its sister fortress of **Methóni**, were the Venetians' oldest and longest-held possessions in the Peloponnese.

## The citadel and beaches

Open access • Free

Koróni's **citadel** is one of the least martial-looking in Greece, crowning the town more like a large, pleasantly dilapidated garden. Part of the interior is given over to private houses and garden plots, but the greater part is occupied by the nunnery of **Timíou Prodhrómou**, whose chapels, outbuildings and flower-strewn gardens occupy nearly every bastion. Downhill from the citadel, you reach the rarely crowded **Zánga beach**, which runs into **Mémi beach**, making a 2km stretch of sand with preternaturally clear water.

### ARRIVAL AND INFORMATION — KORÓNI

**By bus** Buses terminate in the main square, one block back from the waterfront where the taxi rank is also located.

**Destinations** Athens (4 daily; 5hr 10min); Kalamáta (5 daily; 1hr 10min).

### ACCOMMODATION — SEE MAP PAGE 138

★ **Camvillia** Vounaria; http://camvillia.com. This luxury hotel is a real treat with its infinity pool, gourmet restaurant,

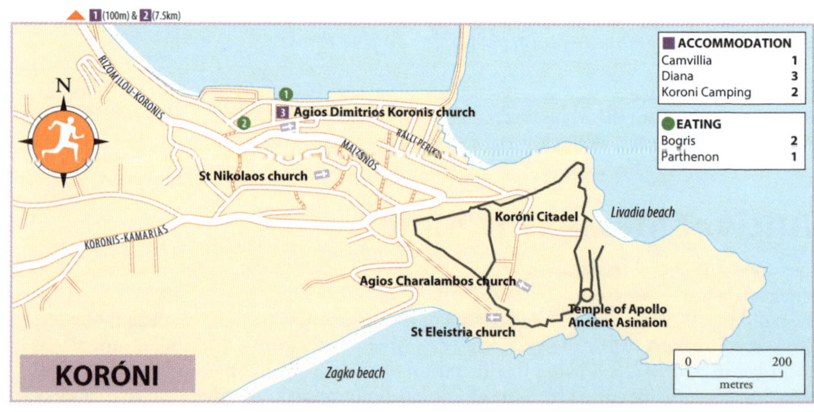

secluded beach access and designer rooms; it also has stunning views over Messinia bay. Breakfast (cooked to order by the chef) included. Mid-May to Sept. €€€

**Diana** Port; http://dianahotel-koroni.gr. Located on a side street as you arrive at the port, this boutique property has modern designer rooms any Koroni hotel would envy. A pull factor is its easy access to the beach. May–Sept. €

**Koroni Camping** 200m north of town; http://koronicamping.com. Just 60m up from a sandy beach, this eucalyptus-shaded campsite offers a pool, bar, an excellent restaurant, minimarket, washing machines and wi-fi. Skygazers can enjoy free use of a telescope. Yoga classes on offer, too. Tents €, caravans €

### EATING AND DRINKING

SEE MAP PAGE 138

**Bogris** Left of the port; 27250 22947. This port-side taverna boasts a romantic garden courtyard. Check the day's offerings on the menu: there are always dozens of grills and a good meze selection. €

**Parthenon** Port; 27250 22146. This restaurant has the best location by the harbour and serves up a classic mix of Greek dishes, notably seafood. Also on offer are good-value 3-course day menus. Also serves breakfast. €

### DIRECTORY

**Banks** Koróni has two banks and ATMs, as well as a post office (Mon–Fri 7.30am–2.30pm).

7

# Finikoúnda

FINIKOÚNDA, 18km west of Koróni, is a small fishing village with seven superb beaches, some of which are in front of the various campsites and the main beach awarded Blue Flag status. It is arguably the best-looking resort between Kalamáta and Yalova, and is popular with British package-holiday companies.

### ARRIVAL AND DEPARTURE

FINIKOÚNDA

**By bus** The bus station is by the village church but in high season buses don't enter the village and stop on the main highway by the entrance roundabout. Finikoúnda is served by the Kalamáta–Pýlos bus (3 daily; 2hr).

### ACCOMMODATION

★ **Estía** 70m from the beach; http://hotelestia.com. Run by a Canadian/Greek couple, this hotel has a roof terrace bar and large Junior suites or Studios with excellent cooking facilities and USB chargers. There's also a gym, plus aromatherapy treatments and yoga classes on offer. May–Oct. €–€€

★ **Finikes Camping** 2km west of the village; http://finikescamping.gr. Set in the middle of nature, this shady campsite is situated along a beautiful beach and has rooms as well. Facilities include a minimarket, bar, restaurant info-kiosk, kitchen and good sanitation services. Camping €, double €

**Fotis Apartments** 150m from the beach; www.finikoundaapartments.gr. This self-catering apartment complex around a central pool is quiet, friendly and owned by a chatty couple who may well share their home-made cakes with you. Every studio has a kitchenette and free wi-fi. May–Sept. €–€€

**Korakakis Beach** Beachfront; http://roomyeti.com/hotel/gr/korakakis-beach.en.html. Medium-sized, quirkily decorated hotel with a bar-restaurant: it also has self-catering bungalows at similar prices, 50m from the beach. Choose top-floor front rooms for maximum views. €–€€

**Loutsa Camping** 1km east of town; http://loutsacamping.gr. This campsite offers ample shade and a garden setting, just steps from a breathtaking, wide sandy beach. There's a minimarket, taverna and free wi-fi, plus washing machines available on-site. Mid-May to mid-Oct. €

### EATING

The eating places tend to all be located along the harbour front. You won't be short of a place to find, but here we've listed some of the better ones.

**Dionysos** Harbourfront; 27230 71229. The best taverna in town after *Elena*, its seafront location is both idyllic and relaxing. Best known for its grills, it also offers excellent lamb dishes such as *kléftiko*. €

★ **Elena** End of the harbour; 27230 71235. This taverna is one of the best in Messinia and counts several VIPs as regulars, including Lord Owen whose holiday home is nearby. They serve vegetables from their own garden and meat from their farm. They also feature live rembétika music three times a week in season. €

**To Karavi** Harbourfront; 27230 71043. Excellent mixture of seafood such as fresh seabass and meat grills, also salads and open all day through from breakfast. €

7

# Methóni

**METHÓNI** is geared more conspicuously to tourism than Koróni and gets very crowded in season, but is still the best value resort along this coastline. The huge Venetian fortress here is as imposing and romantic as they come – massively bastioned, washed on three sides by the sea, and cut off from the land by a great moat. The modern town, which stretches inland for 1km northward, is full of charming back alleys and it meets the sea at a small, pleasant **beach** just on the east side of the citadel.

## Methóni Fortress

Daily (except Tues): winter 8.30am–3.30pm; summer 8am–8pm • Charge

Once used to garrison knights on their way to the Crusades, **Methóni Fortress** is entered across the moat along a stone bridge. Inside are very extensive remains: a Venetian cathedral (the Venetians' Lion of St Mark emblem is ubiquitous), a Turkish bath, the foundations of dozens of houses, a strange pyramid-roofed stone structure, and some awesome, but mostly cordoned-off, underground passages. Walk around the walls, and you'll see a sea gate at the southern end, which leads out across a causeway to the **Boúrtzi**, a small-fortified island that served as a prison and place of execution. The octagonal tower was built by the Turks in the sixteenth century to replace an earlier Venetian fortification.

### ARRIVAL AND INFORMATION METHÓNI

**By bus** KTEL buses stop at the first forked junction in town.

**Destinations** Athens via Kalamáta (every 3 hours to Kalamata; 3hr 15min then 3 daily Kamalanta to Methóni; 1hr 40min); Finikoúnda (3 daily; 20min); Kalamáta (3 daily; 1hr 40min); Pýlos (3–5 daily; 20min).

## ACCOMMODATION

SEE MAP PAGE 140

**Hotel Aris** http://katestravelexperience.eu/aris-methoni-greece. 80m from the castle and 100m from the beach, this simple and clean accommodation in the heart of Methóni offers balconied rooms overlooking the town's square. €€

★ **Niriides Luxury Villas** http://niriidesmessiniahotel.gr. A no-expense-spared housing development 200m up from the end of the beach. It has two pools, landscaped gardens, parking, solar panels, parquet floors, and apartments (sleeping four) with fitted kitchens, American fridges, luxury beds and lots of space. Former guests include the US Ambassador and his entourage, who stayed here in 2016. Apartment €€€, double €€

★ **Ulysses** Kyprou & Bouboulinas; www.ulysseshotel.com. Lovely family hotel with simple, clean rooms, fast wi-fi, TV and fridge with free bottled water: the windows/balconies have mosquito netting. Decoration is by photographer-owner Nikos Markopoulos and the home-made breakfast is served in a large wine-shaded garden, where there are also yoga classes in the summer. Only 100 metres from the beach. March–Oct. €€

## EATING

SEE MAP PAGE 140

The best places to eat are around the castle gate, rather than on the beach square.

**Klimataria** 27230 31544. In a courtyard garden just down from the fortress, this taverna serves fresh, well-prepared dishes (including good, classically Greek veggie options), which you can pick out from the day's offerings. May–Oct. €

**Nikos** http://tavernanikos-methoni.com. Just up from the beach square, this is a high-aspiring taverna with an Athenian chef who will fillet the fish in front of you. Vegetables are grown in the orchard opposite and olive oil comes from their own grove. €

**Sapientza** 27230 31459. 50m from the sea, surrounded by countryside, no menu here – the waiter will invite you to the kitchen to pick that day's offerings. Expect dishes such as *stifado* (beef), chicken, pork and any manner of vegetarian dishes. Popular with the locals. €

## DIRECTORY

**Banks** There are two banks and two ATMs (one on Mézonos and one on Episkópou Grigoríou S).

**Post office** The post office is on Mezonos 40 (Mon–Fri 7.30am–2:30pm).

7

# Pýlos and around

**PÝLOS** is a compact but surprisingly stylish town for rural Messinía; guarded by a pair of medieval castles, it occupies a superb position on one of the finest natural harbours in Greece, the almost landlocked **Navarino Bay**. The main pleasures of Pýlos are exploring the hillside alleys, waterside streets and fortress. Given the town's associations with the **Battle of Navarino**, and, more anciently, with Homer's "sandy Pýlos", the domain of wise **King Nestor** whose alleged palace (see page 144) has been excavated 16km to the north, it makes a good base for exploring this part of the Peloponnese, particularly if you have a car. If you're relying on public transport, you'll find that gaps in services make complex day-trips impractical.

### THE BATTLE OF NAVARINO

In 1827, during the Greek War of Independence, the Great Powers of Britain, France and Russia were attempting to force an armistice on the Turks, having established diplomatic relations with the Greek insurgents. To this end they sent a fleet of 27 warships to **Navarino Bay** below the town of Pýlos, where Ottoman leader Ibrahim Pasha had gathered his forces – 16,000 men in 89 ships. The declared intention was to coerce Ibrahim into leaving Messinía, which he had been raiding ruthlessly.

On the night of October 20, an Egyptian frigate, part of the Turks' supporting force, fired its cannons, and full-scale battle broke out. Without intending to take up arms for the Greeks, the "allies" responded to the attack and, extraordinarily, sank and destroyed 53 of the Turkish fleet without a single loss. There was considerable international embarrassment when news filtered through to the "victors", but the action had nevertheless effectively ended Turkish control of Greek waters and within a year **Greek independence** was secured and recognized.

## Town centre

Shaded by a large plane tree and several of its offspring, **Platía Trión Navárhon** in Pýlos **town centre** is a beautiful public space, encircled by cafés and colonnaded shops. At its head is a **war memorial** commemorating the admirals Codrington, de Rigny and von Heyden, who commanded the British, French and Russian forces in the Battle of Navarino – a decisive naval engagement fought on October 20 1827 during the Greek War of Independence. Allied forces of Britain, France and Russia defeated the Ottoman and Egyptian fleets. This victory was pivotal in securing Greek independence, leading to the establishment of modern Greece.

### Niókastro (Néo Kástro)

Off Methoni Rd • Daily except Tues winter 8.30am–3.30pm; summer 8am–8pm • Charge includes museum

The principal sight in town is the **Niókastro**. The huge "new castle" was built by the Turks in 1572, and you can walk around much of the 1.5km of arcaded battlements. For most of the eighteenth and nineteenth centuries, it served as a prison, and its inner courtyard was divided into a warren of narrow yards separated by high walls. The design was intended to keep Máni clansmen, the bulk of the prison population, from continuing their murderous vendettas inside. Pylos' small but interesting **Archeological museum** is in the Maison building inside the castle and showcases local finds from Neolithic to Roman times. They include the notable Dioscouri twin bronzes plus some exquisitely crafted gold ornaments, precious stone necklaces and delicate glassware.

### René Puaux Museum

Pýlos Port • Daily except Tues winter 8.30am–3.30pm; summer 8am–8pm • Charge

The appealing **René Puaux Museum**, in the former house of a Greek 1912 long jump Olympic champion, houses a surprisingly extensive collection of early nineteenth-century lithographs and cartoons on the Greek War of Independence. They belonged to the French journalist, philhellene and collector René Puaux (1878–1936), who donated them to the Greek state after his death.

## Island of Sfaktiría

(2hr; charge), contact Pylos Cruises at the port (http://pyloscruises.gr) • Boat rental from Pylos Marine by the *Karalis Hotel* (http://pilosmarine.com; 27230 22408)

Memories of the Battle of Navarino can be evoked by a visit to the **island of Sfaktiría. Tours of the bay** land on Sfaktiria to visit various tombs of philhellenes, a chapel and memorials to Russian, British and French sailors. You can also hire a **boat** from the port and snorkel to see the remains of the Turkish fleet lying on the seabed of the island. Sfaktiría was also the site of a battle between a small group of Spartans under siege by the Athenians during the Peloponnesian War – one of the few times that the Spartans surrendered.



## Yiálova

6km north of Pýlos

**Yiálova** has tamarisk trees shading its sandy beach, and makes a delightful base for walkers, beach lovers or bird-watchers drawn by Voïdhokiliá beach and the adjoining nature reserve.

## Paleókastro

At the end of the bay, 5km west of Yiálova

Pýlos's northern castle and ancient acropolis, **Paleókastro** (old castle), stands on a hill ridge almost touching the island of Sfaktiría. It has substantial walls and identifiable courtyards, a mix of Frankish and Venetian designs, set upon ancient foundations. It is currently out of bounds because of subsidence, but you can go up and take in the **view** over Voïdhokiliá, one of the finest beaches in the Peloponnese.

## Voïdhokiliá beach

**Voïdhokiliá beach** is a spectacular crescent of white sand, rolling dunes and turquoise waters 16km north of Pýlos, and it's a highly protected **Natura 2000** area with its unique biodiversity in the Ionian Sea (http://theplanetgreece.com/voidokilia-beach/). Popular with hikers off season, the beach is shaped just like the Omega Greek letter 'O'

### TELEMACHUS TAKES A BATH

King Nestor rates several mentions in Homer's epic, but the scene from *Odyssey* that is set here is the visit of **Telemachus**, son of Odysseus, who had journeyed from Ithaca to seek news of his father from the king. As Telemachus arrives at the beach, accompanied by the disguised goddess Athena, he comes upon **Nestor** with his sons and court sacrificing to Poseidon. The visitors are welcomed and feasted, "sitting on downy fleeces on the sand", and although the king has no news of Odysseus, he promises Telemachus a chariot so he can enquire from Menelaus at Sparta. First, however, the guests are taken back to the palace, where Telemachus is given a bath by Nestor's "youngest grown daughter, beautiful Polycaste", and emerges, anointed with oil, "with the body of an immortal". By some harmonious twist of fate, an actual **bathtub** was unearthed here, rendering the palace ruins as a whole potent ground for Homeric imaginings.

(Ω). The **Gialova lagoon** behind the beach is an important bird conservation area, and vehicles are not allowed on the earth road around its eastern rim. **Turtles** still breed here (and at the beaches of Romanoú and Máti, further north), and there's a tiny population – the only one in mainland Europe – of **chameleons** among the dune shrubs.

## Spílaio toú Néstoros

A path from the southern Voïdhokiliá dunes ascends to the **Spílaio toú Néstoros** (Nestor's Cave), and then to Paleókastro. This impressive bat cave with a hole in the roof is fancifully identified as the grotto in which, according to the *Odyssey*, Nestor and Neleus kept their cows, and in which Hermes hid Apollo's cattle.

## Nestor's Palace

17km from Pýlos • Winter daily 8.30am–3.30pm; summer daily except Tues 8am–8pm • Charge • http://visit-pylos-nestor.gr/castles/

nestors-palace/ • Buses from Pýlos to Hóra stop at the site (4 daily; 20min)

**Nestor's Palace** is the best preserved of all the Mycenaean royal palaces. Flanked by deep, fertile valleys, the palace site looks out towards Navarino Bay – a location that perfectly suits the wise and peaceful king described in Homer's *Odyssey*. The site, which re-opened in 2016 after a three-year restoration, was discovered in 1939 but left virtually undisturbed until after World War II. The site's most important find was a group of 1200 **tablets** inscribed in **Linear B**, which, given their similarity to tablets discovered in Knossós, Crete proved conclusively that there was a link between the Mycenaean and Minoan civilizations. The tablets were baked hard in the fire that destroyed the palace at the time of the Dorian invasion, around 1200 BC, perhaps as little as one generation after the fall of Troy.

### The site

The new 2300-square-metre steel structure that covers the main site and the elevated metal walkway above it were unveiled in late 2016 and work wonders for fully absorbing the scale and structure of Nestor's massive complex. Unlike most Greek sites, it's wheelchair accessible.

The buildings are in three principal groups: the **main palace** in the middle, an earlier and **smaller palace** on the left, and on the right **guardhouses** and an **arsenal**. The basic design will be familiar if you've been to Mycenae or Tiryns: an internal court, guarded by a sentry box, gives access to the main sections of the principal palace that contained some 45 rooms and halls.

On first entering the site, you climb on the walkway in front of the **propylon** in the shape of a letter H. The propylon leads through a double porch to the **megaron** (throne room), with its characteristic open hearth, directly ahead of the entrance. The finest of the frescoes was discovered here, depicting a griffin (perhaps the royal emblem) standing guard over the throne; that work is now in the museum at Hóra. To the right of the megaron lies the famous **bathroom**, with its painted terracotta tub *in situ*, adjoining a smaller complex of rooms, centred on another, smaller, structure, identified as the **queen's megaron**. To the left of the here lie **pantries**, one of which yielded no fewer than 2853 kylikes (drinking vessels), a **canteen** and a **waiting room** for dignitaries with a stone bench still visible. Finally, as you go out behind the car park you can visit a **tholos tomb**, a smaller – but no less impressive – version of the famous ones at Mycenae.

### The Archeological Museum

Housed within Nestor's Palace • Winter 8.30am–3.30pm, summer daily except Tues 8am–8pm • Charge • http://visit-pylos-nestor.gr/castles/nestors-palace/

A browse round the **Archeological Museum** adds significantly to a visit to Nestor's Palace. Pride of place in the display goes to the **palace fresco fragments**, one of which, bearing out Homer's descriptions, shows a warrior in a boar-tusk helmet. You can also see, in a small reproduction, the Nestor Palace's **mosaics** that are not displayed at the site. Lesser finds include much pottery – there are even a few 3300-year-old ceramic baby feeders – some beautiful **gold cups** and other everyday objects, such as loom weights, scales and combs, gathered both from the site and from other Mycenaean tombs in the region.

## ARRIVAL AND DEPARTURE — PÝLOS AND AROUND

**By bus** The bus station is on the main square (27230 22230). The ticket office keeps odd hours, though 8–11am every day is a good bet. Getting your bearings is easy as the town is not large, and the main square facing the port is very much at its heart.

Destinations Athens (4 daily; 5hr); Finikoúnda (5 daily; 40min); Hóra (4 daily; 35min); Kalamáta (every 4 hours; 1hr 20min); Methóni (3 daily; 20min); Yiálova (every 4 hours; 10min).

**By car** Car rental is available through AutoUnion (27230 22393, http://autounion.gr/) on the Kalamáta road.

7

## ACCOMMODATION

### PÝLOS, SEE MAP PAGE 142

**Karalís City** Kalamátas 26; http://hotelkaralis.gr. Located up from the town centre, on the main road to the north, this is an attractive port-view hotel with comfortable modern rooms with balconies, some with jacuzzis. Breakfast included. €

**Karalís Beach** Seafront below the castle; http://karalisbeach.gr. This is the Karalís family's luxury property below the castle, right on the sea, with a comfortable mix of minimalist design and traditional decor. There's no beach though. Buffet breakfast included. April– Oct. €€

**Miramare** Tsamadou 3 Paralia; 27230 22751. This well-located hotel has basic rooms, but all have balconies with views. Models of ancient ships decorate the lobby, there's a well-stocked late bar and a few private parking spaces opposite. Breakfast, a buffet tour de force, is included. April–Oct. €

### YIÁLOVA

**Camping Erodios** 500m west of town; http://erodioss.gr. A modern campsite, with its own sandy beach and a restaurant, bar, minimarket, playground and washing machines. Of particular interest are the self-catering bungalows, as good as any hotel. Mid-April to mid-Oct. Camping €, bungalow €

**Camping Navarino** http://navarino-beach.gr. Large, walled campsite that looks and feels more like a resort. Superb sandy beach, shady palm trees, top-notch facilities, watersports and wi-fi; a good restaurant and supermarket complete the picture. Ten percent discount for stays over six days. April–Oct. €

★ **Zoe Resort** Beach; http://zoeresort.com/en/. An ever-improving luxury eco-resort with spacious, self-catering apartments surrounded by an orchard full of orange, lemon and banana trees, right on the beach. There is also a large pool, a good restaurant (have a dessert, even if it means skipping a starter), a herb and veg garden and several ponds populated with frogs and goldfish. Best buffet breakfast in the area included. April–Oct. €€€

## EATING

### PÝLOS, SEE MAP PAGE 142

**Grigoris** 27230 22621. This warm welcoming, bustling place, at the edge of the port, is renowned for its grilled meats but also offers home-made cooked dishes. €

**Poseidonia** http://pylosposeidonia.gr. Many locals eat here for its inspired Greek cuisine – start with the soup or pie of the day and continue with variations on well-known Greek dishes. To top it all, there's a knockout wine list. €€

### YIÁLOVA

Not many places to choose from in Yiálova, but we've shared the best.

**Spitiko Concept** http://spitikoconcept.gr/. This pleasant and friendly taverna is arguably the best on the Yiálova promenade. It serves up a wide range of dishes, some of them Cypriot, like their owner. For a memorable experience, try the *afélia* – pork in red wine. €–€€

## DIRECTORY

**Banks** There are three banks with ATMs on the central square.

**Post office** The post office is just up from the bus station on Nileos St (Mon–Fri 7.30am–2.30pm).

**Tours** Nikos Lymberópoulos (6974 747 454, nikoslym@otenet.gr) is an English-speaking tour leader for wildlife expeditions and various hikes including Nestor's cave and Paleókastro.

# Olympia and Ilía

SUMMER OLYMPIC GAMES TORCH HANDOVER

# Olympia and Ilía

Dominated by the monumental archeological site of Olympia, gracing the fertile Alfiós valley, the sizeable province of Ilía in the western Peloponnese is, for the most part, flat coastal plains with a series of undistinguished market towns, bordered on the west by long, fine, often underused beaches; the resort to head for here is Arkoúdhi and also the Kyparissia Gulf.

### Brief history

Olympia is one of the most significant archaeological sites in Greece. The site of the ancient Olympic Games, originally part of a religious festival in honor of Zeus, held every four years from 776 BCE to 393 CE, the sanctuary of Olympia included numerous monumental buildings such as the Temple of Zeus housing Zeus' Statue, one of the Seven Wonders of the Ancient World. The games fostered unity among the Greek city-states and were a crucial aspect of Greek culture and identity.

Ilia, the broader region which encompasses Olympia has fertile land and is a strategic location. Ancient Elis, the capital of Ilia, was a powerful city-state that administered the Olympic Games. Ilia's historical significance continued through Roman and Byzantine periods, with its cities serving as important administrative and cultural centres.

8

Over the centuries, Ilia faced invasions and occupations including the Franks, Venetians, and Ottomans, each leaving their mark on the region. Today, Ilia is celebrated for its archaeological treasures and its contribution to the legacy of the Olympic Games, attracting visitors from around the world to explore its historical and cultural heritage.

## Olympia

The historic associations and resonance of **Olympia**, which for over a millennium hosted the most important **Panhellenic Games**, are rivalled only by Delphi or Mycenae. It is one of the largest ancient sites in Greece, spread beside the twin rivers of Alfiós (Alpheus) – the largest in the Peloponnese – and Kládhios, and overlooked by the Hill of Krónos. The site itself is picturesque, but the sheer quantity of ruined structures can give a confusing impression of their ancient grandeur and function. Despite the crowds, tour buses, souvenir shops and other trappings of mass tourism, it deserves a visit with at least an overnight stay at the modern village Arhéa (Ancient) Olymbía.

### The site

Daily Nov–Mar 8.30am–3.30pm; Apr–Oct 8am–8pm • Charge, including the Archeological Museum, the Museum of the History of the Olympic Games in Antiquity and the Museum of the History of Excavations in Olympia • 26240 22517

From its beginnings, the **site** was a sanctuary, with a permanent population limited to the temple priests. At first the games took place within the sacred precinct, the walled, rectangular **Altis**, but as events became more sophisticated a new **stadium** was built adjoining it.

#### Gymnasium and official buildings

The **entrance** to the site, located just 200m from the village, leads along the west side of the Altis wall, past a group of public and official buildings. On the left, beyond some Roman baths, is the **Prytaneion**, the administrators' residence, where athletes stayed and feasted at official expense. On the right are the ruins of a **gymnasium** and a

AERIAL VIEW OF KHLEMOÚTSI

# Highlights

❶ **Ancient Olympia** The site of the original Olympic Games plus the Archaeological Museum. See page 148

❷ **Olympic Torch Lighting Ceremony** If you're lucky enough to be in Olympia the year of any Olympic Games, be sure to try to tie in your visit with the initial Torch Lighting Ceremony. See page 155

❸ **Brintziki Winery** 10-minutes from Ancient Olympia, this family run organic winery is a great place for wine lovers to experience their unique growing methods – zero pesticides. See page 156

❹ **Khlemoútsi Castle** One of the best-preserved Venetian castles in Greece with views across to the Ionian islands. See page 157

HIGHLIGHTS ARE MARKED ON THE MAP ON PAGE 150

**palaestra** (wrestling school), used by the competitors during their obligatory month of pre-games training.

Beyond these stood the Priests' House, the **Theokoleion**, a substantial colonnaded building in whose southeast corner is a structure adapted as a Byzantine church. This was originally the **studio of Fidias**, the fifth-century BC sculptor responsible for the great gold and ivory cult statue in Olympia's Temple of Zeus. It was identified by following a description by Pausanias, and through the discovery of tools, moulds for the statue and a cup engraved with the sculptor's name.

To the south of the studio lie further administrative buildings including the **Leonidaion**, a large and doubtless luxurious hostel endowed for the most important of the festival guests. It was the first building visitors would reach along the original approach road to the site.

## Temple of Zeus

The main focus of the **Altis**, or **sacred precinct**, is provided by the great Doric **Temple of Zeus**. Built between 470 and 456 BC, it was as large as the Parthenon, a fact quietly substantiated by the vast column drums littering the ground. The temple's decoration, too, rivalled the finest in Athens; partially recovered, its sculptures of Pelops in a

chariot race, of Lapiths and Centaurs, and the Labours of Hercules, are now in the museum. In the *cella* was exhibited the (lost) cult statue of Zeus by Fidias, one of the seven wonders of the ancient world. Here, too, the **Olympian flame** was kept alight, from the time of the games until the following spring – a tradition continued at an altar for the modern games.

### Temple of Hera

The smaller **Temple of Hera**, behind the Prytaneion, was the first built in the Altis; prior to its completion in the seventh century BC, the sanctuary had only open-air altars, dedicated to Zeus and a variety of other cult gods. The temple, rebuilt in the Doric style in the sixth century BC, is the most complete building on the site, with some thirty of its columns surviving in part, along with a section of the inner wall. The levels above this wall were composed only of sun-baked brick, and the lightness of this building material must have helped to preserve the sculptures that nineteenth-century excavation uncovered – most notably the *Hermes of Praxiteles*.

### Philippeion

West of the Temple of Hera and bordering the wall of the Altis are remains of the circular **Philippeion**, the first monument in the sanctuary to be built to secular glory. It was begun by Philip II to commemorate his victory at the Battle of Chaeronea, which gave him control over the Greek mainland; the building may have been completed by his son, Alexander the Great.



### Nymphaion (fountain house), treasuries and Metroön

To the east of the Hera temple is a small, second-century AD **Nymphaion**, or **fountain house**, the gift of the ubiquitous Herodes Atticus. Beyond, lining a terrace at the base of the Hill of Krónos, are the state **treasuries**, storage chambers for sacrificial items and sporting equipment used in the games. They are built in the form of temples, as at Delphi; the oldest and grandest, at the east end, belonged to Gela in Sicily. In front of the treasuries are the foundations of the **Metroön**, a fourth-century BC Doric temple dedicated to the mother of the gods.

### Pelopeion

Between the temples of Hera and Zeus is a grove described by Pausanias, and identified as the **Pelopeion**. In addition to a cult altar to the Olympian hero, this enclosed a small mound formed by sacrificial ashes, among which excavations unearthed many of the terracotta finds in the museum. The sanctuary's principal altar, dedicated to Zeus, probably stood just to the east.

### Bouleuterion (council chamber)

The ancient ceremonial entrance to the Altis was on the south side, below a long **stoa** taking up almost the entire east side of the precinct. At the corner was a house built by the Roman emperor Nero for his stay during the games. He also had the entrance remodelled as a triumphal arch, fit for his anticipated victories. Through the arch, just outside the precinct, stood the **Bouleuterion**, or **council chamber**, where before a great statue of Zeus the competitors took their oaths to observe the Olympian rules. These were not to be taken lightly: lining the way were bronze statues paid for with the fines exacted for foul play, bearing the name of the disgraced athlete, his father and city.

### Stadium

The natural focus of the Olympic site is the 200m track of the **stadium** itself, entered by way of a long, arched tunnel. The starting and finishing lines are still there, with the judges' thrones in the middle and seating ridges banked to either side. Originally unstructured, the stadium developed with the games' popularity, forming a model

8

for others throughout the Greek and Roman world. The tiers here eventually accommodated up to twenty thousand spectators, with a smaller number on the southern slope overlooking the **hippodrome** where the chariot races were held. Even so, the seats were reserved for the wealthier strata of society. The ordinary populace – along with slaves and all women spectators – watched the events from the Hill of Krónos to the north, then a natural, treeless grandstand. The stadium was unearthed only in World War II, during a second phase of German excavations between 1941 and 1944, allegedly on the direct orders of Hitler.

## Archeological Museum

200m north of the sanctuary • Charge, including the site, the Museum of the History of the Olympic Games in Antiquity and the Museum of the History of Excavations in Olympia • http://ancientolympiamuseum.com/index

Olympia's site **Archeological Museum** contains some of the finest Classical and Roman sculptures in the country, all superbly displayed. The most famous of the individual sculptures are the **head of Hera** and the **Hermes of Praxiteles**, both dating from the fourth century BC and discovered in the Temple of Hera. The Hermes is one of the best preserved of all Classical sculptures, and remarkable in the easy informality of its pose; it retains traces of its original paint. On a grander scale is the **Nike of Paionios**, which was originally 10m high. Though no longer complete, it hints at how the sanctuary must once have appeared, crowded with statuary.

In the main hall of the museum is the centrepiece of the Olympia finds: statuary and sculpture reassembled from the **Temple of Zeus**. These include a delicately moulded frieze of the **Twelve Labours of Hercules**. Another from the east pediment depicts Zeus presiding over a famous **chariot race** between Pelops and King Oinamaos – the prize the hand of the king's daughter. The king (on the left of the frieze) was eventually defeated by Pelops (on the right), after – depending on the version – assistance from Zeus (depicted at the centre), magic steeds from Poseidon or, most un-Olympian, bribing Oinamaos's charioteer to tamper with the wheels.

The west pediment illustrates the **Battle of the Lapiths and Centaurs** at the wedding of King Peirithous of the Lapiths. This time, Apollo presides over the scene while Theseus helps the Lapiths defeat the drunken centaurs, depicted attacking the women and boy guests. Many of the metope fragments are today in the Louvre in Paris, and some of what you see here are plaster-cast copies.

The last rooms of the museum contain a collection of objects relating to the games – including *halteres* (jumping weights), discuses, weightlifters' stones and other sporting bits

## THE OLYMPIC GAMES

The origins of the games at Olympia are rooted in **legends** – often relating to the mythical hero Pelops, Zeus, or to Hercules. Historically, the contests probably began around the eleventh century BC, growing over the next two centuries from a local festival to the **quadrennial** celebration attended by states from throughout the Greek world. These great gatherings extended the games' importance and purpose well beyond the winning of olive wreaths; assembled under a strict **truce**, nobles and ambassadors negotiated treaties, while merchants did business and sculptors and poets sought commissions.

### EVENTS

From the beginning, the main Olympic **events** were athletic. The earliest was a race over the course of the stadium – roughly 200m. Later came the introduction of two-lap (400m) and 24-lap (5000m) races, along with the most revered of the Olympiad events, the **pentathlon**. This encompassed running, jumping, discus and javelin events, and the competitors were gradually reduced to a final pair for a wrestling-and-boxing combat. It was, like much of these early Olympiads, a fairly brutal contest. One of the most prestigious events was the **pancratium**, where contestants fought each other, naked and unarmed, using any means except biting or gouging. Similarly, the **chariot races** were extreme tests of strength and control; only one team in twenty completed the 7km course.

### RULES AND AWARDS

In the early Olympiads, the **rules** of competition were strict. Only free-born Greek males could take part, and the **rewards** of victory were entirely honorary: a palm, given to the victor immediately after the contest, and an olive branch, presented in a ceremony closing the games. As the games developed, however, the rules were loosened to allow participation by athletes from all parts of the Greek and Roman world. By the fourth century BC, when the games were at their peak, the athletes were virtually all **professionals**, heavily sponsored by their home states and, if they won at Olympia, commanding huge appearance money at games elsewhere. Under the Romans, commercialization accelerated and new events were introduced. Emperor Nero postponed the games by two years to 67 AD just so that he could compete in (and win) special singing and lyre-playing events.

### DECLINE AND FALL

Notwithstanding Roman abuses, the Olympian tradition was popular enough to be maintained for another three centuries, and the games' eventual **closure** happened as a result of religious dogma rather than lack of support. In 393 AD **Emperor Theodosius**, recently converted to **Christianity**, suspended the games as part of a general crackdown on public pagan festivities. This suspension proved final, for Theodosius's successor ordered the destruction of the temples, a process completed by barbarian invasion, earthquakes and, lastly, by the Alfiós River changing its course to cover the sanctuary site. There it remained, covered by 7m of silt and sand, until the first excavation by German archeologists in the 1870s.

and pieces. Also displayed are a number of **funerary inscriptions**, including that of a boxer, Camelos of Alexandria, who died in the stadium after praying to Zeus for victory or death.

### Arhéa Olymbía

**Arhéa Olymbía** is a village that has grown up simply to serve the excavations and tourist trade. It's almost literally a one-horse town – its main street, **Praxitéles Kondhýli**, is lined with shops, and there are just a few short side streets. Nevertheless, it is quite a pleasant place to stay and is preferable by far to Pýrgos, offering the prospect of good countryside walks along the Alfiós River and around the Hill of Krónos.

There are a few somewhat dutiful minor museums, worth a visit if you have time on your hands. The **Museum of the History of the Olympic Games in Antiquity** and the **Museum of the History of Excavations in Olympia** (both daily: 1 Nov–13 Dec 8.00am–5pm; from 14 Dec 8am–3.30pm; Charge, including the site and the Archeological Museum) lie above the coach park at the eastern end of the village, en route to the main site.

#### ARRIVAL AND INFORMATION — ARHÉA OLYMBÍA

**By bus** The bus stop is behind the now unused train station within a block of Arhéa Olymbía village centre.

Destinations from Arhéa Olymbía Athens (Take a taxi to Krestena, then bus 2 daily; 2hr 45min); Pýrgos (7–12 daily; 30min).

**Services** Arhéa Olymbía has three banks on the main avenue and a post office at De Coubertin 2 (Mon–Fri 7.30am–2.30pm).

#### ACCOMMODATION

8

**Europa** Dhroúva 1; www.hoteleuropa.gr. A well-run and comfortable resort hotel situated near the top of the hill to the southwest. There's a large pool, ample parking and a very good restaurant. Excellent choice if you have a car, but if not, note that it's a steep 10min walk from the main street. Breakfast included. €€

**Kronio** Tsoúreka 1; http://hotelsolympia.gr. A comfortable, welcoming hotel with large, basic, airy rooms. As befits the town, the owner was a city marathon runner (and winner). Pick-ups from Pyrgos can be arranged. Breakfast included. €–€€

**Neda** Karamanlí 1; 26240 22563. Nicely furnished and well-managed, this central hotel offers many extras for its price range such as rooms with bathtubs, a decent pool, large private parking area and rooftop restaurant with great views. Breakfast is included. €

★ **Pelops** Varelás 2; http://hotelpelops.gr. Run by a Greek–Australian couple, this pleasant hotel is situated on a square by the church. They offer a popular cooking course (charge for half a day including the resulting meal), as well as courses in painting and creative writing in English. A sumptuous breakfast is available for an extra cost. March–Oct. €

#### EATING

The village is loaded with tavernas and kebab grills, but the best places are off the main drag.

★ **Aegean** Georgiou Douma 4; 26240 22540. This unassuming place serves everything from baked lamb and roast chicken to pizza, but even dedicated carnivores should try the vegetarian stews made with fresh local produce. €

**To Steki tou Vangeli** Stefanopoúlou 13; 26240 22530. Excellent grill house highly recommended by locals and operated by a charming couple. They also supply takeaway dinners to the regional fire service based at Olympia. Try the grilled chicken with lemon & mustard sauce with a litre of house wine. Feb–Nov. €

## Kyparissia

Officially in the Messinia region, it's actually nearer Olymbía at only 33km southwest of it, hence included in this chapter. **Kyparissia** can be found at the westernmost peninsular of the Peloponnese. It's a small town, famous for its beaches and surrounded by high mountains means there's lush vegetation and beautiful scenery. What's left of its Frankish medieval castle, **Kástro** (daily except Tues, 8.30am–3.30pm (http://kastra.eu/castleen.php?kastro=kyparisia; free), stands in the Old Town, guarding over the New Town and surrounding beaches and Ionian Gulf below.

### TORCH LIGHTING CEREMONY

The **Olympic torch lighting ceremony**, held every four years several months before the actual Games in the Olympic Stadium, marks the symbolic start of every Olympic Games. This ancient ritual pays homage to the birthplace of the Olympics and the connection between the ancient and modern games.

The ceremony takes place at the Temple of Hera where a parabolic mirror harnesses the sun's rays to ignite the torch. This method, relying solely on natural sunlight, emphasizes purity and tradition. A high priestess, dressed in traditional Greek attire, uses the mirror to light a flame in a ceremonial cauldron.

Once lit, the flame is passed to the first torchbearer, usually past Olympian winners, thus beginning the Olympic torch relay through the country over eleven days, lit outside the Acropolis then culminating in Athens at the **Panathenaic Stadium.** For the Greeks, the **Olympic Torch Relay** is a highly esteemed symbol of the sacred heritage handed down to them by their ancestors, bearing a message of peace.

This relay then goes on, by plane, to traverse various countries and continents, symbolizing peace, unity and the enduring spirit of the Olympics, before ultimately lighting the cauldron at the host city's Olympic stadium during the opening ceremony.

For the **Paris Olympics 2024** the flame was actually carried by a three-mast schooner, the *Belem*, through the Corinth Canal (see page 49) where it arrived in Marseille on 8th May 2024 and continued its journey on a 69-day relay across France to arrive in Paris for the Opening Ceremony.

8

The most popular beach is the Blue Flag awarded **Ai-Lagoudis**, the nearest to town – about a 5 min walk – with sunbeds, beach volleyball, several species of small plants and where you'll also find tavernas and bars lining its shores.

Just 20km north is the **village of Apollo** by the coast, where **Archelon** (http://archelon.gr/en/volunteer/project-areas/the-peloponnese-kyparissia-bay) has its research field station, working to protect the endangered *Caretta caretta* (sea turtles). Volunteers from around the world and of all ages come to partake in the conservation effort from May to late September and undertake a range of activities such as morning and night beach patrols and nest protection. It's possible to book a 45-minute walk to the **Agiannakis Environmental Station** (see website) and take a Sea Turtle Walk at the nesting beach to learn about these creatures and the NGO's work with an ARCHELON volunteer.

## ARRIVAL AND DEPARTURE — KYPARISSIA

**By bus** The bus station is about a 4 minute walk from Ai-Lagoudis beach in town at Nosokomiou 6 (27610 022260, http://ktelmessinias.gr/).

Destinations Athens (4 daily; 4hr); Kalamáta (every 3 hours; 1hr); Kyllíni (via Pýrgos; 1 daily then 3 daily; 2hr 5min); Olympia (via Pýrgos; 1 daily then every 1hr; 40min); Pátra (1 daily; 2hr 35min); Pýrgos (1–2 daily; 1hr 20min).

## ACCOMMODATION

**Apollo Art Resort Hotel** Farmaka; http://apollo-hotel.gr/. 1.5km away from the city centre, this resort style hotel with large pool and nearest beach 200m away offers a choice of single, double, twin and triple rooms as well as a range of activities from olive oil tastings to cookery classes. Full buffet breakfast (included) with all the Greek favourites. €€

**Apollo Village Camping** Zacharo; http://apollovillagecamping.gr/. Space for your own tent/caravan with excellent facilities such as water and power supply. Possible to book one of their own little cottages onsite with either a private or shared bathroom. The best location for the Archelon NGO Research Station. Open May–Sep. €

**Kyparissia Beach Hotel** Port Kyparissia; http://kyparissiabeachhotel.gr/. Great location by the Port with marina views from most of its 28 simple yet pleasantly decorated rooms. Visitors can enjoy their large pool, as well as the bar and café. The hotel can also arrange agrotourism tours, to taste olive oil on an organic farm, for example. Breakfast included. €€

### ORGANIC WINERY

**Brintziki Organic Winery**, just a 10-minute drive from the ancient site near the village of Lantzoi, is a family run winery renowned for its dedication to producing high-quality organic wines. It specialises in crafting red, white, and rosé wines from indigenous Greek grape varieties such as Agiorgitiko and Assyrtiko, alongside international varieties like Merlot and Cabernet Sauvignon.

What makes it particularly special is its commitment to sustainability and environmental stewardship. Organic farming practices are used, avoiding the use of synthetic pesticides and fertilizers in order to preserve the natural ecosystem. Additionally, it is the first winery in Greece to utilize geothermal energy, reducing its carbon footprint significantly.

Fires in the region in 2017 destroyed much of their crops, yet once the fires stopped raging, what was left was harvested to make a distinctive vintage called the **Diapyros**. Only 2,400 bottles were made and no two labels on the bottles are the same, except for the fact they're handmade using real gold depicting a phoenix – a symbol of a bird that never dies and always rises.

Brintziki's wines are celebrated for their unique expression of the local soil, combining traditional methods with modern techniques to produce elegant and flavourful wines. The combination of organic principles and innovative energy solutions underscores Brintziki's position as a leader in sustainable viticulture.

8

### EATING

**Kyparissia Arkadia Gefsipoleio** Eleni Chameri 9, Old Town; 27610 24522. Expect traditional Greek fair in this old style taverna. Have a strong stomach for dishes such as kokoretsi – lamb or goat intestines wrapped around seasonal offal, or a more gentle meat dish of kontosouvli (chunks of pork marinaded then skeward with peppers). €

**Palia Agora** Eleni Chameri 3, Old Town; http://palia-agora.com.gr/. Meaning 'Old Market' and located at the highest point in the Old Town, a 3-minute walk from the Castle, this is more of a restaurant than a taverna, open from lunch and for dinner. Serving fish delights such as shrimp saganaki, the ubiquitous meatballs and homemade fries and vegetarians will love their fried courgettes with yogurt sauce. €€

# Pýrgos

**Pýrgos** is a large, modern business town and the capital of Ilía province. A public transport hub, it's pleasant enough in parts, though with little appeal for tourists. The town has a grim history. When the Germans withdrew at the end of World War II, it remained under the control of Greek Nazi collaborators. They negotiated a surrender with the Greek Resistance, who were met by gunfire as they entered the town. Full-scale battle erupted and for five days the town burned.

### ARRIVAL AND DEPARTURE — PÝRGOS

**By bus** The bus station is to the west of town (26210 20600, http://ktelileias.gr).

**Destinations** Athens (Taxi to Tholó then bus; 2 daily;2hr 40min); Kalamáta (1 daily; 2hr 5min); Kyllíni (2–3 daily; 1hr); Olympia (7–12 daily; 30min), Pátra (7–9 daily; 1hr 30min).

### ACCOMMODATION & EATING

**Boutique Hotel Anagennisis** Patroklou 12; http://hotelanagennisis.gr/index.php/en/. Situated in a neoclassical mansion house, this ornate boutique hotel in the centre of the town has double rooms through to Junior Suites and Triples (good for families). Breakfast included, some dishes may be extra and there's a restaurant onsite too. €€

**Olympos** Karkavitsa 2, at Patron; http://hotelolympos.gr. This modern high-rise hotel has handsome rooms and is located right in the city centre, not far from parks and shopping. Facilities include satellite TV, car rental and private parking. Bathrooms are small, but some have hot tubs. Breakfast included. €

# Cape Tripití and around

About 25km to the north of Pýrgos, near the point where this most westerly coast of the Peloponnese forms **Cape Tripití**, is **Arkoúdhi**, a compact village resort that has something of an island feel to it, and a fine sandy bay enclosed by a rocky promontory. Using Arkoúdhi as a base, it's worth taking time to drive or climb to the village of **Kástro**, at the centre of the cape.

## Khlemoútsi Castle

Kástro • Daily 8.30am–3.30pm • Charge • http://visitkastro.com/chlemoutsi

Looming above Kástro village and visible from many kilometres around is the Frankish **Khlemoútsi Castle**, one of the best-preserved Venetian castles in Greece, with a vast hexagonal structure built (1220–23) by Geoffrey de Villehardouin. Its function was principally to control the province of Ahaïa, though it also served as a strategic fortress on the Adriatic. Haze permitting, there are sweeping views across the straits to Zákynthos, and even to Kefaloniá and Itháki, from the well-preserved and restored ramparts.

## Kyllíni

Heading north from Kástro, you'll pass a rather clinical spa resort, **Loutra Kyllínis**, on the way to the northern tip of the cape. Here, the cheerless little port of **Kyllíni** has little more to offer than its **ferry connections** to Zákynthos and Kefaloniá.

8

### ARRIVAL AND DEPARTURE — KYLLÍNI

**By bus** KTEL buses from Athens and Pátra to Kyllíni continue on the ferry to Zákynthos (http://ktel-zakynthos.gr).

Destinations Athens (via Pyrgos 3 daily; 1hr, Pyrgos to Athens 5 daily; 2 hr 40 min); Pátra (5 daily; 1hr 30min).

**By ferry** Ferries from Kyllíni are run by the Ionian Group (http://ioniangroup.com) and Kefalonian Lines (http://kefalonianlines.com).

Destinations Póros, Kefaloniá (10 daily; 1hr 30min); Zákynthos (10–12 daily; 1hr 15min). These are summer frequencies; a heavily reduced service operates year-round.

### ACCOMMODATION AND EATING

**Almira** Arkoúdhi; http://almira-hotel.gr. Luxury hotel and spa right on the sandy beach, this is a three-star with higher aspirations: there's a sauna, gym, pool and a lively beach bar-restaurant. Rooms with sea views are only slightly more expensive than those without. Parking and breakfast included. €€

**Grecotel LUXME Olympia Oasis & Aqua Park** Loutrá Killinis; http://rivieraolympia.com/olympiaoasis. Luxury resort hotel popular with package tourism, but great if you want to base yourself right on the beach and usually requires a week's stay or more. Selection of rooms with garden or sea views and family style accommodation, some with private pools and a large outdoor pool for all, its beachside location means you probably won't need it. Facilities include spa and kids club. Buffet breakfast included. €€€

**Ionion Beach Camping** near Glyfa, Elis; https://www.ionion-camping.gr/. Super campsite with a beautiful beachfront location with pitches for tents, caravans and modern bungalows and apartments to rent. Pool, pool bar, restaurant serving traditional Greek food and supermarket on site as well as showers and wood-fired barbecues and children's play area. €

**R.Q.D. Paradise Bar** Arkoúdhi; 26230 96167. Located right down on the beach, this is more of a bar than restaurant, though the food is gourmet and pricey, especially their burgers. You're paying for the location really, which can't be faulted as the atmosphere crackles with summer energy. June–Sept. €€€

# Pátra and Ahaïa (the north coast)

TRAIN RIDE THROUGH THE VOURAÏKÓS GORGE

9

# Pátra and Ahaïa (the north coast)

The capital of the large northern province of Ahaïa, Pátra is the largest city in the Peloponnese and third most populous in Greece. At first glance it offers little to visitors, however there are a few decent beaches including a sensational one at Kalogriá, and from the small town of Dhiakoftó you can opt for a trip on a picturesque rack-and-pinion railway which follows the dramatic Vouraïkós Gorge up to Kalávryta, a ski centre, one of few that exist in Greece.

### Brief history

Pátra and the **Ahaïa region's** history spans several millennia, starting from the Mycenaean period. In antiquity, Pátra was an important trade centre due to its strategic coastal location. It flourished during the Roman period, becoming a key economic and cultural hub of the region. It's thought The Apostle Andrew was martyred in Pátra with the city is home to the impressive St Andrew's Cathedral, one of the largest in the Balkans.

In ancient times, **Ahaïa** was part of the Achaean League, a confederation of Greek city-states that played a significant role in resisting Macedonian, and later Roman, domination. The region prospered during the Roman and Byzantine periods, with its cities becoming centres of commerce and culture.

During the Middle Ages **Ahaïa** came under Frankish, Venetian, and Ottoman control, each period leaving distinct cultural and architectural influences. Patra played a crucial role in the Greek War of Independence in the nineteenth century, being one of the first cities, along with Kalamáta, to revolt against Ottoman rule.

Today, Pátra is a vibrant city known for its port, which connects Greece with Italy and the rest of Europe, as well as its annual Carnival, one of the largest in Greece, reflecting its enduring cultural vibrancy.

## Pátra

**PÁTRA** (Patras) is a major Greek port, from where you can catch ferries to Italy and Corfu. The pedestrianization of its centre has added much character to the town, and there are now several new chic restaurants and cafés to while away your time until late in the evening or until your ferry. The relative lack of tourists and the presence of its large **university** makes Pátra a good place to meet Greeks outside a touristy environment. It's also home to Greece's largest and best-known **carnival** (http://carnivalpatras.gr/en/), which starts on St Anthony's Day (Jan 18) and ends on the Sun before Clean Monday (Katharí Dheftéra) with a thirty thousand-strong grand parade through the city centre attended by half a million people, making it one of the biggest in Europe. The city is also the gateway to **Kalogriá** (see page 166), with its dunes and stunning beach.

### Kástro

Frouriou 56 • Summer daily except Tues 8.30am–4pm; Winter daily except Tues 8.30am–3.30pm • Free

The **Kástro**, a mainly Frankish–Byzantine and partly restored citadel, is built around the sixth century AD, a fifteen minutes' walk uphill from the water at the highest point of the town making it up and away from the city bustle. It makes for a nice respite from the city as a small park surrounds it, with woodland extending beyond.

MÉGA SPILÉOU MONASTERY

# Highlights

❶ **Turkish Hammam** Take a steam and treatment in Europe's oldest operational hammam, located in Pátra. See page 162

❷ **Kalogriá** Best beach near Patra, 7km long and part of the 22-square-kilometre Strofyliá Forest-Kotýkhi Wetland National Park. See page 166

❸ **Museum of the Sacrifice of the People** A sobering museum in the old Primary Town just outside of Kalávryta Town where many young men where shot during the German occupation of the town in WWII. See page 168

❹ **Odontotós** Rack-and-pinion railway that goes from the coastal town of Dhiakoptó cutting through the Vouraïkós Gorge up to Kalávryta. See page 167

❺ **Vouraïkós Gorge** Dark, narrow gorge carved out of rock where the Odontotós Rack-and-pinion railway cuts through. See page 167

❻ **Méga Spiléou Monastery** Known as the 'Great Cave', on the Odontotós route is the oldest monastery in Greece, nestled into a 120m cliff. See page 167

HIGHLIGHTS ARE MARKED ON THE MAP ON PAGE 162

## Turkish hammam

Boukaoúri 29 • Charge • http://xamampatron.gr/el/ • 2610 274 267

Just beneath the Kástro is Europe's oldest, still-functioning **Turkish hammam**, built in 1400. The benefits of hammams' are well known, from treating salts in the body, arthritis, rheumatism and toxin elimination and after six hundred and twenty years, this one is still good for a steam, renovated and upgraded over time.

## Archeological Museum

Pátras–Athens National Rd 38–40 • Daily • Charge • http://ampatron.gr

Located about 3km from the centre, at the north end of the city, the crisply contemporary **Archeological Museum** is second only in size to Athens' Acropolis Museum. Themed exhibits include a vast quantity of everyday objects from Ahaïa dating from the Mycenaean to the Roman eras, most of which have been in storage for the past thirty years. Though it houses one of Greece's biggest Roman mosaic collections, there's no single item of great importance and its approach in general is a little too didactic for most.

## New and old churches of Áyios Andhréas

Daily: new 7am–8pm, old 8am–1am • Free

The **new and old churches of Áyios Andhréas** (St Andrew–the Patron Saint of the city) stand next to each other at the southwest end of the waterfront. The old basilica, restored in 1835, lies on the spot where St Andrew is said to have been martyred in 69 AD, and

where an ancient temple to Demeter once stood. The saint's tomb is housed within, but the relics (returned by the Vatican in 1964, after the crusaders plundered it in 1204) are housed in the grand eclectic-style church built in 1903 with elements of Art Nouveau.

## Roman Odeon

Platiá Áyios Yeóryios • Temporarily closed for upgrades

The impressive **Roman Odeon**, dating from the first century AD and restored in 1956, lies in the north end of the square of Áyios Yeóryios (25 March). It was once the centre of ancient Pátra; ruins of the Roman stadium can also be seen on the south side of the square. The Odeon is still used occasionally for music performances during the summer.

## Church of Pandokrátor

Pandokrátoros • Sun Mass only • Free

Further up from the Odeon, the **Church of Pandokrátor** is one of the most striking Greek Orthodox basilicas in the city. Dating from 900 AD, its current multi-dome shape belies the fact that it was converted into the city mosque during the Ottoman era.

### ARRIVAL AND DEPARTURE — PÁTRA

**By bus** The main bus station (2610 623 886/8, http://ktelachaias.gr) is next to the InfoCenter Patras at Agora Argýri. Buses for Mesolóngi and Náfpaktos leave from the old Deck 5 at Iröon Polytechníou 42 (2610 421 205), about 15min walk north.

**Destinations** Athens (2 hourly, 2hr 30min–3hr); Náfplio

via Isthmos (1 hourly for Isthmos, every 2 hours Isthmos–Náfplio; 4hr); Igoumenítsa via Agrinio and Árta (Every 4 hours to Agrinio, 1 daily to Árta then twice daily to Igoumenítsa; 6hr 20min); Itéa, for Delphi (1 daily; 2hr); Ioánnina (2 daily; 5hr 30min); Kalamáta (2 daily; 3hr); Kalávryta (1 daily; 2hr); Kalogriá (5–6 daily in season; 1hr 15min); Kyllíni (every 4 hours daily to Pýrgos, then 3 daily; 2hr 30min); Mesolóngi (every 4 hours daily; 45mins); Náfpaktos (5 daily; 30min); Pýrgos (4–5 daily; 1hr 30min); Thessaloníki (2 daily; 6hr); Vólos (2 weekly; 4hr).

**By train** The train station, on Óthonos & Amalías, serves only the commuter line Pátra–Rio. The Proestiakós rail line to Athens is currently under construction: in the meantime, there are replacement buses to Kiáto, where you can pick up the Athens suburban train.

**By ferry** All ferries leave from Néo Limáni (New Port) at the south of the city. Pátra is the gateway to the Ionian islands of Kefalonia, Corfu and Ithaca and also Italian destinations. You can take a taxi to the centre and bus #18 will also take you through the centre to the KTEL station (hourly 10.30am–5.30pm; charge). Italy-bound ferries (see page 22) leave from early afternoon to late evening. You must check in at the agent's embarkation booth at least 2hr before departure (http://patrasport.gr).

Destinations Ancona (3–4 weekly; 24–25hr); Bari (5 weekly; 16hr 30min–17hr); Brindisi (1 weekly; 6hr 30min); Corfu (1-2 weekly; 6hr 30min); Ithaca (1 daily; 4hr 10min); Kefalonia (1 daily; 3hr 30min); Venice (2 weekly; 34hr 30min).

**By car** Pátra is linked to the mainland by the suspension bridge across the gulf from Río to Andírio (5min; charge, car toll). If you're going beyond Pátra, you can take a fast bypass to the east. From Pátra you can reach Kórinthos in 1hr 25min along the national highway; the onward journey to Athens takes another 45min.

## INFORMATION

**Tourist office** The Office of Tourism in Patras at Othonos Amalias 6 (Daily 8am–10pm; 2610 461 740; http://patrasinfo.com) offers maps & info.

**Bike Rental** Voukelatos Bros at Panepistimiou 242 (Sat, Mon & Wed 9am–3pm, Tue, Thurs & Fri 9am–2.30pm & 5.30pm–9pm; https://voukelatos-bikes.com/) rent bicycles.

## GETTING AROUND

**By bus** Local buses go from Óthonos & Amalías north of the main bus station; tickets are also available from kiosks. Check https://astikopatras.gr/ for the local timetable.

**By car** The traffic and one-way system in Pátra is no less frustrating for drivers than in Athens. Car rental is available from: Lalas (Ayíou Andhréou 1; 2610 273 667); Dirent A Car (Athinon 16; http://direntacar.gr); Avis (Óthonos Amalías 33; 2610 275 547; http://avis.gr); Hertz (Aktí Dhymaíon 40; 2610 220 990; http://hertz.gr); Patras Car Rental (28 October 16; 2617 742 113; http://patrasrentacar.gr); Enterprise (Ag. Dionisiou 2; 2610 625 659; http://enterprise.gr).

## ACCOMMODATION

SEE MAP PAGE 164

**Adonis** Kapsáli 9, at Zaïmi; http://adoniscityhotel.gr. This large high-rise hotel is well maintained, though showing its age, and rooms and bathrooms are small. It feels like a cheap overall option, but is conveniently located by the bus station. Breakfast included. €

★ **Astir** Ayíou Andhréou 16; 2610 277 502. Pleasantly modernist styling within Pátra's public spaces, spacious rooms, great harbour views plus a rooftop terrace restaurant with a pool (summer only) and sauna make this the best choice in the centre of town. Breakfast and secure parking included. €€

**Atlanta** Zaïmi 10; http://hotelatlanta.gr/. Plain but central hotel, just across from the bus station, with small rooms. Breakfast included. €

★ **Galaxy City Center** Ayíou Nikoláou 9; http://galaxyhotel.com.gr. Well-placed for the nightlife, this hotel is clean and old-fashioned, with a sleek modern lobby and more than decent rooms with balconies and flat-screen TVs. The rooms not facing the street are quieter. Breakfast costs extra. €

**Olympic Star** Ayíou Nikoláou 46; 2610 224 103. Stylish hotel with large rooms, each with its own balcony, LCD TV, and bathroom with a classy jet shower. If you can afford it, ask for the suite – it's almost an apartment. Breakfast included. €€

## EATING

SEE MAP PAGE 164

Stroll and choose among shoulder-to-shoulder bars and restaurants in the pedestrianized section along Ríga Feréou and along the seafront, plus the Old Town.

**Argo** Iroon Politechniou 78; http://argopatras.gr/. Great place along the waterfront, opposite the DEI electricity building. It has a selection of dishes ranging from typical meze such as zucchini balls and gruyere with chili sauce to seafood dishes such as grilled farmed bream. €-€€

**Asteria** Mentoros 1 & Leukipphs; http://asteria.com.gr/en. Popular fish taverna with indoor and outsoor seating overlooking the Gulf of Patras. Expect fresh and frozen dishes such as fried and grilled calamari, shrimp saganaki or octopus in vinegar. €-€€

**Terra Bistro** Kanari kai Ríga Feraíou; 2610 313 000. Cosy restaurant in the Old Town serving up a whole range of dishes from Angus steaks, pasta dishes and Greek salads. Great for lunch and dinner. €

**Troufa** Patreos 83; 2610 623 717. Another Old Town favourite with outdoor and indoor seating, Greek dishes changing daily and on display at the kitchen counter for you to choose from. It's a cooperative kitchen meaning all people who work there are involved in the planning and preparation of dishes. Great value. Try their home-made burgers and fries. €

## DRINKING

SEE MAP PAGE 164

**Beer Bar Q** Riga Feraiou 182; 2610 346 097. Serves a range of 60+ labels of bottled beers plus 17 different draft beers in an outdoor seating environment along the Old Town's main drag for nightlife. Some cocktails and occasional live music nights – Greek music and bands.

**Bodegas** Riga Feraiou 147; 2610 221 113. Pricey-but-

9

worth-it wine bar with food, situated on the main nightlife drag in the Old Town, serving a wide selection from local vineyards. Try the veal burger with three-pepper sauce. €

**Mare Mare** Platia Terpsithéas; 2610 428 851. Set up on the seafront in the summer offering the best sunset views in the city from their bar-restaurant. Great cocktails with a view and try their beefsteak or seafood risotto. Book in advance if you're coming for the sunset and note that the service gets easily overwhelmed. €€

### DIRECTORY

**Banks and exchange** There are plenty of banks and ATMs in Pátra.

**Consulate** Britain, Vótsi 2; 2610 277 329, https://british-consulate.net/uk/United-Kingdom-Consular-Assistance-Patras.

**Post office** Mézonos & Záïmi 23; 2610 620 594 (Mon–Fri 7.30am–8.30pm).

**Tourist police** Goúnari 52; 2610 695 073 (daily 7am–11pm).

# The north coast

The resorts and villages lining the **north coast** are modest, but at least not overdeveloped. Generally you'll find little more than a narrow strip of beach, a campsite, a few rooms for rent and a couple of seasonal tavernas. About 35km west of Pátra is **Kalogriá**, the best beach in the area. To the east is **Dhiakoftó**, from where you can stop for the old **Kalávryta railway** ride up into the picturesque **Vouraïkós Gorge** via quaint **Zakhloroú**. After Dhiakoftó, if you're unhurried, it's worth taking the old **coast road** along the Gulf of Kórinthos; this runs below the national highway, often right by the sea.

## Kalogriá

**KALOGRIÁ** (locally Kalógria) is the best **beach** near Pátra: a 7km strand, partly naturist, bordered by a swathe of umbrella pine forests. A fair proportion of Pátra, including the gay community, descends here at the weekend. The whole area is protected as part of the 22-square-kilometre **Strofyliá Forest-Kotýkhi Wetland National Park**, which covers beach dunes, a pine, cedar and myrtle forest, as well as lagoons with their rare birdlife. Blissfully any permanent development remains low-key. Kalogriá is not actually a village – the nearest bona fide town is Metóhi – but rather a small cluster of hotels and stores. Behind what hotels there are, the 200m outcrop Mávra Vouná has a number of hiking routes.

### ARRIVAL AND DEPARTURE — KALOGRIÁ

**By bus** Hourly buses run from Pátra to Káto Achaía, then taxi; 45min.

### ACCOMMODATION

**Kalogria Beach** http://kalogriahotel.gr. Extensive but dated, this family resort on a stunning stretch of the beach has every sort of facility you could wish for: restaurant, beach sunbeds with umbrellas and three large pools. Wi-fi is patchy. Rate includes three meals a day. June–Sept. €€

★**Verde Al Mare** 350m from the beach; http://verdealmare.gr. This is a great-looking boutique hotel-cum-resort with two good pools and an even better upmarket restaurant. They rent mountain bikes and offer bird-watching activities and guided tours of the national park. Breakfast included. €€

## Río

Local bus #6 from Pátra (every 30min; 30min)

**RÍO** signals the beginning of swimmable water east of Pátra, though most travellers pass through for the **suspension bridge** across the gulf to Andírio (5min; charge if going by car).

## THE KALÁVRYTA EXPRESS (ODONTOTÓS)

The 22km **rack-and-pinion railway** from **Dhiakoftó** to **Kalávryta** (26910 43206, http://odontotos.com) is a crazy feat of Italian engineering, rising at gradients of up to one in seven as it cuts inland through the Vouraïkós Gorge. The journey can be hot, crowded and uncomfortable, but the route is a toy-train fantasy of tunnels, bridges and precipitous overhangs, and well worth experiencing.

The railway was built between 1889 and 1896 to bring minerals from the mountains to the sea. Its 1896 steam locomotives were replaced some years ago – one (O Moutzouris) remains by the line at Dhiakoftó station with other relics, and another at Kalávryta – but the track itself retains all the charm of its period. The tunnels, for example, have delicately carved window openings, and the narrow bridges zigzagging across the Vouraïkós seem engineered for sheer virtuosity.

It takes around 45 minutes to get from Dhiakoftó to **Zakhloroú** (listed on timetables as **Méga Spíleo)** and about another 20 minutes from there to Kalávryta. In peak season the ride is very popular, so plan to buy tickets in advance of your preferred departure (Mon–Fri 3 daily, Sat & Sun 5 daily).

# Dhiakoftó

From **DHIAKOFTÓ** (officially Dhiakoptó) an old **rack-and-pinion railway**, the **Kalávryta express** (see box, page 167) heads south up into the **Vouraïkós gorge** and terminates at **Kalávryta**. Dhiakoftó itself is somewhat drab, but there's a narrow pebble beach along the eastern side.

### ARRIVAL AND DEPARTURE — DHIAKOFTÓ

**By bus** Athens–Pátra buses stop at Éyio about 10km west, then the local buses connect to Dhiakoftó (2 daily; 20min). You can then take a taxi. Or travel from Athens via Corinth (every hour; 1hr 50min) then to Éyio (2 daily; 20 mins) then as above.

### ACCOMMODATION AND EATING

**Chris Paul** http://chrispaul-hotel.gr. Friendly and well-located hotel situated by the entrance of the rack-and-pinion railway, whose highlight is a pool among a gorgeous lemon and orange grove. It's convenient too; there's private parking, a café, and a/c, though it may be for heating rather than cooling. Breakfast included. €

**Koursaros** Dhiakoftó Achaias; 698 810 2102. Beachside club serving basic food such as club sandwiches. Good for a snack and a place to base yourself on their sun loungers and while away the day. €

**Lemonies** Filipopoulou 323; 2691 041 229. Friendly, family run hotel by Dhiakoftó beach with somewhat simple yet clean and comfortable rooms. Free parking onsite. Breakfast included. €

**Taverna Kosta** Main Road; 697 595 1711. Very popular taverna a short walk from the railway serving good Greek fare. Owner (Kosta) will invite you to the display to pick your dish – very popular with vegetarians. Try their *imam* (grilled aubergines with vegetables) or *gemista* (stuffed tomato or peppers with rice). €

**Theasi Hotel** Trapeza Achaias http://theasi.gr/en/. 8 spacious double or family units in the village of Trapeza, about an 8 min drive from Dhiakoftó nestled up a small hill slope overlooking the bay. Some units have a fireplace. Breakfast included. €

# Zakhloroú

**Zakhloroú** is as perfect a train stop as could be imagined: a tiny hamlet echoing with the sound of the **Vouraïkós River,** which splits it into two neighbourhoods. It's a lovely, peaceful place with an old hotel (see page 168).

## Méga Spiléou Monastery

Daily • **Museum** Charge • 45min walk from Zakhloroú village, up a rough donkey track along the hillside • Usual monastery dress code applies i.e. cover legs and shoulders

The eight-storey **Méga Spiléou Monastery** ("Great Cave") near Zakhloroú is the oldest monastery in Greece and spectacularly sited under a 120m cliff. The view of the gorge valley from the monastery is for many the principal attraction – sadly the monastery itself has been burned and rebuilt so many times that it now resembles nothing so much as a 1970s hotel – however, its treasury, arranged as a small **museum**, is outstanding. In the main **church**, among its icons is a charred black wax and mastic image of the Virgin, one of three in Greece said to be by the hand of St Luke (but probably from the tenth century); a smaller chapel houses a remarkable collection of body parts from various saints, all encased in precious materials. The monastery was founded by Saints Theodhoros and Simeon, after a vision by the shepherdess Euphrosyne in 362 AD led to the discovery of the icon in the cave (Ayíazma) behind the site of the later church.

**ACCOMMODATION AND EATING** **ZAKHLOROÚ**

Only one place to stay and eat in this tiny hamlet. It's the perfect get away from it all.

**Olympios Zeus** http://olympioszeus.gr. Built with traditional stone and wood, this luxury hotel caters for winter clients at the Helmós ski resort, so winter prices are higher. Worth staying overnight if you are going to Kalávryta for the grand views of Mt Helmós. Breakfast included. €€

# Kalávryta

Despite its beautiful position amid gorgeous greenery at the end of the little train line, with Mount Helmós as a backdrop, **KALÁVRYTA** retains an air of both melancholy and poignancy due to its tragic history during **World War II**. On December 13, 1943, the town's German occupiers shot the entire male population over the age of twelve and set fire to the town, killing around seven hundred in reprisal for partisan activity. By the end of the war, the local death toll had risen to around twelve hundred.

Greeks come here out of a sense of **patriotic pilgrimage** – it's crowded with school parties during the week and with families at weekends – and the attitude to foreigners is business-like rather than overtly friendly. It is worth remembering and respecting their history in order to understand this. Still, the town tries hard to generate a resort feel; everything's well turned out, with lots of souvenir shops and cafés and restaurants, and from here there's a winding scenic road of 10km north to Méga Spiléou and on to the coast, as well as a road deep into Arcadia in the other direction.

## Remembrance sights and shrines

The first and last sight you're likely to encounter is a mural, opposite the train station, that reads: "Kalávryta, founding member of the Union of Martyred Towns, appeals to all to fight for world peace." The left clocktower on the central church stands fixed at 2.34pm – the hour of the massacre. In the old primary school is the somber **Museum of the Sacrifice of the People of Kalávryta** (closed Mon; http://www.dmko.gr/; Free), while outside of town is a shrine to those massacred, with the single word "Peace" (*Iríni*), as well as the historically significant **Ayías Lávras Monastery**.

### Ayías Lávras Monastery

6km southwest of Kalávryta • Daily • http://agialavra.gr • Free

The tenth-century **monastery of Ayías Lávras,** and the last stop on the Odontotós train, was the site where Yermanos, Archbishop of Pátra, raised the flag to signal the **War of Independence**. Destroyed in World War II, it has since been rebuilt into an impressive monastery and features a small historical **museum**.

**ARRIVAL AND DEPARTURE** **KALÁVRYTA**

**By bus** The new bus station is 1km outside of town, on the road to Pounda; it's more convenient to get on and off

the bus at the stop by the train station. For information & timetables call 26920 22224.

Destinations Athens direct (3 weekly; 3hr) (via Isthmos 1 daily then hourly; 2hr 55min); Éyio (1–2 daily; 55min).

**By train** The train station is at Andréa Lóndou street, by Platía Fotéla in the centre of town.

Destinations Dhiakoftó (3–5 daily; 1hr).

## ACCOMMODATION AND EATING

SEE MAP PAGE 169

If you miss the last train out, you can stay at several hotels here, open all year since the town is a ski resort in winter. There are several adequate restaurants around the square as well as on the main pedestrian drag.

**Filoxenia** Ethnikís Andístasis 10; http://hotelfiloxenia.gr. This is a chalet-like hotel which verges on being luxurious, with good amenities, including wi-fi, and winter pluses such as a hammam, sauna and Jacuzzi. Add forty percent to prices in winter. Breakfast included. €

**Revi Mountain Resort** Chondrogianneon; http://revimountainresort.gr/. Luxurious resort with heated outdoor pool, rooms and suites all have mountain views. There's also onsite gym. A great treat if you choose to stay in the town, especially during ski season. Breakfast included. €€

**Spitiko** Paleon Patron Germanou 7; 2692 024 260. Meaning 'home', Spitiko lives up to its name with home cooked, prepared on the spot dishes such as lamb, pork and cannelloni just like you'd get at home. Their spicy feta spread is popular. €

**Stani** 25th March 3; http://kalavrita-stani.gr. Located off the main square, this taverna attracts more tourists than most, for good reason. Its menu consists of grilled and baked farm-to-table pork, lamb and goat dishes. €

STATUES FROM THE TEMPLE OF ZEUS

# Contexts

# History

The Peloponnese was home to some of the most powerful rulers in ancient Greece. During the Mycenaean period (around 2000–1100 BC), the peninsula hosted the legendary kingdoms of Agamemnon at Mycenae, Nestor at Pýlos and Menelaus at Sparta. In the Dorian and Classical eras, the region's principal city-state was Sparta, which, with its allies, brought down Athens in the ruinous Peloponnesian War. Under Roman rule, Corinth was the capital of the southern Greek province.

## Prehistoric Greece: to 2100 BC

Evidence of human habitation in Greece goes back half a million years, as demonstrated by the skeleton of a **Neanderthal** youth in the **Petralóna Cave**, 50km east of the northern city of Thessaloníki, along with the earliest known site of a man-made fire in Europe.

Only very much later, about **40,000 years ago**, did **Homo sapiens** make their first appearance in Greece after migrating out of Africa. At several sites in **Epirus** in northwest Greece, Homo sapiens used tools and weapons of bone, wood and stone to gather wild plants and hunt. Even between **20,000 and 16,000 years ago**, when the Ice Age was at its peak, **Stone Age man** continued to make a home in Greece, though only when the glaciers finally receded about **10,000 BC** did a considerably warmer climate set in, which altered the Greek environment to something more like that of present times.

### The Neolithic period

**Agricultural communities** first appeared in northern Greece around **6500 BC**. Whether agriculture developed indigenously or was introduced by migrants from Asia Minor is much debated: what is certain, however, is its revolutionary effect.

An assured supply of food enabled the Stone Age inhabitants of Greece to settle in fixed spots, and they built mud-brick houses on stone foundations. Though still reliant on stone implements, this new farming culture marked a significant break with the past, so a "new stone age" or **Neolithic period** is said to have begun. As the flint needed for weapons and tools was rare in Greece, mainlanders imported obsidian from the island of **Melos** (Mílos) in the southern Cyclades. The earliest **seaborne trade** known anywhere in the world, this clearly involved a mastery of building and handling boats.

### Cycladic culture and the beginnings of the Greek Bronze Age

Around **3000 BC** a new people settled in the **Cyclades**, probably from Asia Minor, bringing with them the latest metallurgical techniques. While continuing the old trade in obsidian, they also developed a **trade in tin** and were making prodigious voyages westwards as far as Spain by 2500 BC. The mining of **gold and silver** in the Cyclades may have dated from this period, too. Long before Crete or the Greek mainland, these new islanders became specialists in **jewellery-making**, **metalwork** and **stone-cutting**.

| c. 6000 BC | c. 2100 BC | c. 1600 BC | c. 1200 BC |
|---|---|---|---|
| Earliest human settlements in the Peloponnese | The Greek language is heard in Greece for the first time | Rise of the Mycenaean civilization in Mycenae and other sites in the Peloponnese | The Trojan War: connections to Mycenae and sites |

From the abundant marble of the Cyclades, they sculpted statuettes, mostly of female figures. Slender, spare and geometric, these **Cycladic sculptures** are startlingly modern in appearance, and were exported widely, to Crete and mainland Greece, along with other ritual objects.

In about 3000 BC, the introduction of bronze technology to the mainland, also from the Cyclades, marked the start of the **Bronze Age** in Greece. By **2500 BC** the widespread use of bronze had transformed farming and fighting throughout the Eastern Mediterranean and the Middle East. Because tin (which when alloyed with copper creates bronze) came from so far afield – in the east from the Caucasus, Persia and Afghanistan, in the west from Cornwall, Brittany, northwest Spain and northern Italy – the Aegean became an important trade route. This resulted in a burst of development along the eastern coast of **central Greece** and the **Peloponnese**, and on the **Aegean islands** which linked the Greek mainland to Asia Minor and the Middle East.

It is uncertain what **language** was spoken at this time, but one thing is clear: it was not yet Greek. Indeed, when **Greek-speaking people** did arrive on the mainland in about 2100 BC, their destructive impact paralysed its development for five hundred years.

### The coming of the Greeks

The destruction of numerous mainland sites in about **2100 BC**, followed by the appearance of a new style of pottery, has suggested to archeologists the violent arrival of a **new people**. They domesticated the horse, introduced the potter's wheel and possessed considerable metallurgical skills. These newcomers replaced the old religion centred on female fertility figures with **hilltop shrines**, thought to have been dedicated to the worship of male sky gods like Zeus. And with them came a new language, an early form of **Greek**, though they were obliged to adopt existing native words for such things as olives, figs, vines, wheat and the sea, suggesting that these new migrants or invaders may have come from distant inland steppes where they had been pastoral highlanders, not farmers, fishermen or sailors.

## Minoan and Mycenaean civilizations: 2100–1100 BC

The history of the Aegean during the second millennium BC can be seen as a struggle between the **Mycenaean culture** of the Greek mainland and the **Minoan culture** of Crete. Situated halfway between mainland Greece and Egypt, Crete exploited the Bronze Age boom in trade to become the dominant power in the Aegean by the start of the second millennium BC. Its influence was felt throughout the islands and also on the mainland, where the Greek-speaking invaders were "Minoanized", gradually developing a culture known as Mycenaean (after Mycenae, a principal mainland Bronze Age site) that owed a lot to Crete.

### Mycenaean dominance

However, around **1500 BC**, the Mycenaeans gained control of the palace of Knossós and were soon in full possession of Crete. How this happened is unknown, but it probably marked the culmination of a growing rivalry between the Mycenaeans and the Minoans for control of the Aegean trade.

| **c. 1100 BC** | **776 BC** | **498 BC** | **479 BC** |
|---|---|---|---|
| Collapse of Mycenaean civilization, ushering in a Dark Age | First Olympic Games held in Olympia | Rebellious Ionian Greeks burn the city of Sardis, provoking a Persian invasion of Greece | Persians are defeated at the Battle of Plataea and forced out of Greece |

### THE TROJAN WAR

For the Greeks, the story of the **Trojan War** was the central event in their early history, and in their minds Homer's **Iliad** was not just a poem of heroic deeds sung at noble courts, but the epic of their first great national adventure.

Excavations in the late nineteenth century by Heinrich Schliemann uncovered many Troys of several periods, but the layer known as **Troy VIIa** clearly suffered violent destruction in about 1220 BC. The Mycenaeans are the likeliest perpetrators, though the abduction of a Greek beauty called **Helen** would not have been the only reason they launched a thousand ships against the Trojans. Mycenaean prosperity greatly depended on trade with the Eastern Mediterranean, where increasingly unsettled conditions made it imperative that they secure their lines of **trade and supply**. Troy commanded a strategic position overlooking the Hellespont, the narrow waterway (today called the Dardanelles) dividing Europe and Asia and linking the Aegean to the Black Sea, where it controlled important trade routes.

The capture of Troy was the last great success of the Mycenaeans, and perhaps for that reason it was long remembered in poetry and song. It inspired later generations of Greeks to dream of overseas expansion, culminating in the fourth century BC when Alexander the Great carried a copy of the *Iliad* as he marched across Asia, founding Greek cities as he went, and stood with his army on the banks of the Indus River.

**Greek** now became the language of administration at Knossós and the other former Minoan palaces, as well as on the mainland – indeed, this is the earliest moment that Greek language can definitely be identified, as the palace records on Crete are from now on written in a script known as **Linear B**, which, when deciphered in 1953, was shown to be a form of Greek. Having wrested control of the Aegean trade from the Minoans, the **Mycenaeans** were dominant for another three hundred years. At the end of that period, in about 1220 BC, they famously laid siege to, and destroyed, yet another rival, the city of **Troy**.

Yet within a generation, the Mycenaean world was overwhelmed by a vast **migration** of northerners from somewhere beyond the Black Sea. Probably victims of a catastrophic change in climate that brought drought and famine to their homelands, these **Sea Peoples**, as the ancients called them, swept down through Asia Minor and the Middle East and also crossed the Mediterranean to Libya and Egypt, disrupting trade routes and destroying empires as they went. With the palace-based Bronze Age economies destroyed, the humbler **village-based economies** that replaced them lacked the wealth and the technological means to make a mark in the world. Greece was plunged into a Dark Age, and knowledge of the Minoan and Mycenaean civilizations slipped into dim memory.

## The Dark Age and the rise of the city-state: 1150–491 BC

The poverty and isolation that characterized Greece for the next five hundred years did have one lasting effect: **emigration**. Greeks spread to the Dodecanese islands, to Cilicia along the south coast of **Asia Minor**, and to **Cyprus**. Later, around 1000 BC, they also settled in large numbers along the western coast of Asia Minor. Even in the Dark Age

| 447–438 BC | 431–404 BC | 399 BC | 395 AD |
|---|---|---|---|
| Parthenon, the symbol of Athens' Golden Age, is constructed | Peloponnesian War between Athens and Sparta, with Sparta winning | Socrates condemned to death for corrupting the minds of the youth of Athens | The Roman Empire splits; Greece becomes part of the Byzantine Empire |

### THE ILIAD AND THE ODYSSEY

The **Iliad** and the **Odyssey**, the oldest and greatest works in Greek literature, were the brilliant summation of five centuries of poetic tradition, first developed by nameless bards whose recitations were accompanied by music. Completed by 725 BC, they are far older than the *Pentateuch*, the first five books of the Old Testament, which achieved their finished form only around 400 BC. The whole Greek world knew the **Homeric epics**, and their influence upon the subsequent development of Greek literature, art and culture in general cannot be overstated. Few works, and probably none not used in worship, have had such a hold on a nation for so long.

The *Iliad* is the story of a few days' action in the tenth and final year of the **Trojan War**, which in its tales of heroic exploits recalls the golden age of the Mycenaeans. The *Odyssey* begins after the war and follows the adventures of **Odysseus**, who takes ten years to return to his island home of Ithaca on the western side of Greece. The story of his voyages demonstrates the new Greek interest in the area around the Black Sea and in Italy and Sicily to the west. They are also a celebration of an emerging **Hellenic identity**, of a national adventure encompassing both shores of the Aegean and beyond.

there were a few glimmers of light: **Athens**, for example, escaped the destruction that accompanied the fall of Mycenaean civilization, and maintained trading links abroad. It became the route through which the **Iron Age** was introduced to mainland Greece with the importation of iron weapons, implements and technological know-how around 1100 BC. A new cultural beginning was also made in the form of pottery painted in the **Geometric style**, a highly intricate and controlled design that would lie at the heart of later Greek architecture, sculpture and painting. But it was the **Phoenicians**, sailing from Sidon and Tyre in present-day Lebanon, who really re-established trading links between the Middle East and the Aegean world in the eighth century BC, and Greeks followed swiftly in their wake.

With wealth flowing in again, Greek civilization developed with remarkable rapidity; no other people achieved so much over the next few centuries. The institution most responsible for this extraordinary achievement, the **city-state** or **polis**, came into being at a time of rapidly growing populations, greater competition for land and resources, increasing productivity and wealth, expanding trade and more complex relationships with neighbouring states. The birthplace of **democracy** and of equality before the law, the city-state became the Greek ideal, and by the early seventh century BC it had spread throughout Greece and wherever Greeks established colonies overseas.

Trade also acted as a cultural stimulus; contact with other peoples made the Greeks aware of what they shared among themselves, and led to the development of a **national sentiment**, notably expressed and fostered by the **panhellenic sanctuaries** that arose during the eighth century BC, of Hera and Zeus at **Olympia** and of Apollo and Artemis at **Delos**, as well as the **oracles** of Zeus at **Dodona** and of Apollo at **Delphi**.

## Expansion and colonization

Around 750 BC, Greeks began to found **colonies** in the Western Mediterranean – in **Sicily** and **southern Italy** especially – while a century later, around 650 BC, further

| 362 BC | 359 BC | 215–213 BC | 200–197 BC |
|---|---|---|---|
| Battle of Mantinea in the Peloponnese, signaling the decline of Theban power | Philip II becomes king of Macedonia | First Macedonian War extends Roman influence | Second Macedonian War, culminating in the Roman victory at Cynoscephalae |

colonies were established round the shores of the **Black Sea**. By the fifth century BC, Greeks seemed to sit upon the shores of the entire world, in Plato's words like "frogs around a pond".

One impetus for expansion was competition between the Greeks and the Phoenicians over trade routes; but there was also rivalry among the Greek city-states themselves. **Chalkis**, **Eretria** and **Corinth** were the major colonizers in the west, while the **Ionian Greeks** were the chief colonizers around the Black Sea. When the Spartans needed more land, they conquered neighbouring Messenia in 710 BC, but generally land shortage drove Greeks overseas.

### Democracy, tyranny and slavery

In the city-states, political tensions were building between the **aristocratic rulers** and the **people**. A large class of farmers, merchants and the like was excluded from political life but forced to pay heavy taxes. The pressure led to numerous reforms and a gradual move towards **democracy**. Ironically, the transition was often hastened by **tyrants**. Despite the name – which simply means they seized power by force – many tyrants were in fact champions of the people, creating work, redistributing wealth and patronizing the arts. **Peisistratos,** tyrant of Athens during the sixth century BC, is perhaps the archetype. Successful and well-liked by his people, his populist rule ensured Athenian prosperity by gaining control of the route into the Black Sea. He also ordered that Homer's works be set down in their definitive form and performed regularly, and encouraged the theatrical festivals where Greek drama was born.

## Athens and the Golden Age: 490–431 BC

**Democracy** was a very long way from universal. The population of **Athens** and surrounding Attica amounted to some 400,000 people, of whom about 80,000 were slaves, 160,000 foreigners, and another 160,000 free-born Athenians. Out of this last category came the **citizens**, those who could vote and be elected to office, and their number amounted to no more than 45,000 adult men.

Yet if the powers of democracy were in the hands of the few, the energy, boldness and creative spirit that it released raised Athens to greatness. Throughout the **fifth century BC** the political, intellectual and artistic activity of the Greek world was centred on the city. In particular, Athens was the patron of **drama**, both tragedy and comedy. Athenian tragedy always addressed the great issues of life and death and the relationship of man to the gods. And the Athenians themselves seemed to be conscious of living out a high drama as they fought battles, argued policy, raised temples and wrote plays that have decided the course and sensibility of Western civilization.

### The Persian Wars

The wars between Greece and Persia began with a revolt by Ionian Greeks in Asia Minor. Athens and Eretria gave them support, burning the city of Sardis in 498 BC. Provoked by their insolence, **Darius**, the Persian king, launched a punitive expedition. The **Persians'** unexpected repulse at **Marathon** in 490 BC persuaded Darius to hurl his full military might against Greece, to ensure its subjection once and for all to the Persian Empire.

| **146 BC** | **49–52 AD** | **117–138** | **395** |
|---|---|---|---|
| Roman conquest of Greece; Corinth is destroyed by Rome | St Paul lives and preaches in Corinth and Athens; he introduces Greece to Christianity | The reign of Emperor Hadrian, a Hellenophile who left many monuments, above | Roman Empire splits; Greece becomes part of the eastern, or Byzantine, Empire; Olympic Games suppressed |

## BIG IDEAS: SOCRATES, PLATO AND ARISTOTLE

The Golden Age of Athens under Pericles, and the city-state rivalry after the Peloponnesian War, saw the **birth of Western philosophy** under the towering figures of Socrates, Plato and Aristotle.

### SOCRATES (C.470–399 BC)

The son of an Athenian sculptor, **Socrates** was for a time a sculptor himself, and fought bravely for Athens as a hoplite in the Peloponnesian War. In his twenties, he turned to philosophy, which he practised in his own peculiar style, asserting ceaselessly, the supremacy of reason. Often, in the streets of Athens, he would ask some self-regarding Athenian of the older generation questions, then pick his answers to pieces, until he came up with a definition that held water or, more likely, the victim confessed his own **ignorance** before crowds of Socrates' mirthful young supporters.

By this "Socratic method" he asked for definitions of familiar concepts such as piety and justice; his technique was to expose the ignorance that hid behind people's use of such terms, while acknowledging his own similar ignorance. Indeed, when the Delphic oracle proclaimed that no man was wiser than Socrates, he explained this by saying wisdom lies in knowing how little one really knows. Because he valued this question-and-answer process over settling on fixed conclusions, Socrates never wrote anything down. Yet his influence was pivotal; before his time, philosophical enquiry concerned itself with speculations on how the natural world was formed and how it operates; afterwards, it looked to **ethics** and the **analysis of concepts**.

Socrates' method could be irritating, especially when he questioned conventional morality, and this, coupled with powerful friendships with unpopular oligarchs, led to a backlash. Having tried him for impiety and corrupting the young, and sentenced him to death, the city gave him the option of naming another penalty, probably expecting him to choose exile. Instead, Socrates answered that if he was to get what he deserved, he should be maintained for life at public expense. At this the death penalty was confirmed, but even then it was not to be imposed for two months, with the tacit understanding that Socrates would escape. Instead Socrates argued that it was wrong for a citizen to disobey even an unjust law, and in the company of his friends he drank the cup of hemlock. "Such was the end," wrote Plato, "of our friend; of all the men of his time whom I have known, he was the wisest and justest and best."

### PLATO (C.427–C.347 BC)

As a young man, **Plato** painted, composed music and wrote a tragedy, as well as being a student of Socrates. He intended a career in politics, where his connections would have ensured success, but Socrates' death made Plato decide that he could not serve a government that had committed such a crime, and his mission became to exalt the memory of his teacher. In Plato's writings, many of them **dialogues**, Socrates is frequently the leading participant,

After Darius died in 486 BC, his son **Xerxes** took over. In 483 BC, he began preparations that lasted two years and were on a fabulous scale. Bridges of boats were built across the Hellespont for Persia's vast imperial army to parade into Europe, and a canal was cut for the fleet through the Athos peninsula. Though the Greek historian

| 600–700 | 730 | 1071 | 1095 |
|---|---|---|---|
| the Christianization of Greece marks the end of the Ancient Greek era | Icons and other images banned in the Orthodox Church for being idolatrous; the height of the iconoclastic controversy | Byzantine army defeated by the Turks | First Crusade drives back the Turks |

while at the **Academy** in Athens, which Plato founded, the Socratic question-and-answer method was the means of instruction.

Plato's philosophy is elusive, though certain themes recur. He believed that men possess **immortal souls** separate from their mortal bodies. **Knowledge**, he believed, was the recollection of what our souls already know; we do not gain knowledge from experience, rather by using our reasoning capacity to draw more closely to the realm of our souls. The true objects of knowledge are not the transient, material things of this world, which are only reflections of a higher essence that Plato called **Forms** or **Ideas**. Forms are objects of pure thinking, cut off from our experience; but Forms also motivate us to grasp them, so that the reasoning part of us is drawn to Forms as a kind of mystic communion.

Plato's notion of a mystic union with a higher essence would play an important role in later religious thought. But, more immediately, his teachings at the Academy concerned themselves with logic, mathematics, astronomy and above all **political science**, for its purpose was to train a new ruling class. Prominent families sent him their sons to learn the arts of government. Plato taught that the best form of government was a constitutional monarchy, at its head a wise and just philosopher-king. Though it was a utopian vision, Plato's political philosophy helped prepare the intellectual ground for the acceptance of an absolutist solution to the increasing uncertainties of fourth-century BC Greece.

### ARISTOTLE (384–322 BC)

**Aristotle** grew up in Pella, the capital of an increasingly powerful Macedonia, where his father was doctor to King Amyntas II; it is therefore not unlikely that Amyntas' son, the future Philip II, and Aristotle were boyhood friends. Aged seventeen, Aristotle was sent to Plato's Academy in Athens, and he remained there, first as a student, then as a teacher, a faithful follower of Plato's ideas. His independent philosophy matured later, during the years he spent at Pella, as tutor to Alexander the Great, and later still, after 335 BC, when he founded his own school, the **Lyceum**, in Athens.

Aristotle came to reject Plato's dualism. He did not believe that the soul was of a substance separate from the body, rather that it was an aspect of the body. Instead of Plato's inward-looking view, Aristotle sought to explain the physical world and human society from the viewpoint of an outside observer. Essentially a **scientist and realist**, he was bent on discovering the true rather than establishing the good, and he believed sense perception was the only means of human knowledge. His vast output covered many fields of knowledge – logic, metaphysics, ethics, politics, rhetoric, art, poetry, physiology, anatomy, biology, zoology, physics, astronomy and psychology. Everything could be measured, analysed and described, and he was the first to classify organisms into **genera and species**.

The exactitude of Aristotle's writings does not make them easy reading, and Plato has always enjoyed a wider appeal owing to his literary skill. All the same, Aristotle's influence on Western intellectual and scientific tradition has been enormous.

**Herodotus** claimed that Xerxes' army held one million eight hundred thousand soldiers, his figure is probably a tenfold exaggeration. Even so, it was a massive force, an army of 46 nations, combined with a fleet of eight hundred triremes carrying almost as many sailors as there were soldiers in the army.

| **1204** | **1261** | **1453** | **1571** |
|---|---|---|---|
| Fourth Crusade; the Peloponnese is taken over by Frankish Crusaders | Byzantine forces reclaim parts of the Peloponnese from Latin occupiers | Constantinople falls to the Ottoman Turks, the Peloponnese gradually falls under Ottoman rule | Battle of Lepanto – the first significant military defeat for the Ottoman Empire |

Despite their numerical superiority, the might of Asia was routed both at sea off **Salamis** in 480 BC and on land at **Plataea** the following year. Within a few days of that second battle came another naval victory at **Mycale**, off Sámos, when Xerxes' subject Ionians defected to join their fellow Hellenes. Xerxes could do no more than return to Susa, his capital deep in Persia, leaving the entire Aegean free.

This sudden shift in the balance of power between East and West, notwithstanding occasional reversals, endured for the next 1500 years. Within 150 years, **Alexander the Great** achieved in Asia what Xerxes had failed to achieve in Europe, and the Persian Empire succumbed to a Greek conqueror.

### Themistocles and the rise of sea power

The greatest Athenian statesman, and architect of the victory over Persia, was **Themistocles**. Following the Ionian revolt, he understood that a clash between Persia and Greece was inevitable, and he had the genius to recognize that Athens' security and potential lay in its command of the sea. Thus he began in 493–492 BC to develop **Piraeus** (Pireás) as the harbour of Athens. Though his initial pretext was the hostility of the island of Aegina (Égina), his eyes were always on the more distant but far greater Persian danger.

When the Persians marched into Attica in the late summer of 480 BC, the oracle at Delphi told the Athenians to trust in their wooden wall. Many took that to mean the wooden wall around the citadel of the Athenian Acropolis, but Themistocles argued that it referred to the Athenian fleet. Determined to fight at sea, Themistocles warned his Peloponnesian allies against retreating to the Isthmus, where they too had built a wall, threatening that if they did, the entire citizenry of Athens would sail to new homes in southern Italy, leaving the rest of Greece to its fate. On the eve of the **Battle of Salamis**, as the Persians stormed the Acropolis, slaughtering its defenders and burning down its temples, the taunt came back from the Peloponnesians that Athens had no city anyway. Themistocles replied that so long as the Athenians had two hundred ships, they had a city and a country.

The naval victory at Salamis that he masterminded cut the Persians' maritime lines of supply and contributed to their defeat at Plataea the following year. It gave Athens and its allies command of the sea, ensuring their eventual victory throughout the Aegean. For his pains the Athenians later drove Themistocles into exile.

## Decline of the city-state: 431–338 BC

The **Peloponnesian War** that began in **431 BC** was really a continuation of earlier conflicts between Athens and its principal commercial rivals, Corinth and Aegina and their various allies in the Peloponnese. Sparta had earlier stood aside, but by 432 BC, when Corinth again agitated for war, the **Spartans** had become fearful of growing Athenian power.

## City-state rivalries

The Peloponnesian War left **Sparta** the supreme power in Greece, but those whom the Spartans had "liberated" swiftly realized that they had simply acquired a new and

| **1821** | **1827** | **1832** |
|---|---|---|
| Greek War of Independence begins in the Peloponnese, with significant battles at Tripoli, Kalamata, and Navarino | Battle of Navarino; a decisive naval battle in the Peloponnese that leads to Greece gaining independence | Independent Greek state established, with its capital in Náfplio |

### THUCYDIDES: THE FIRST MODERN HISTORIAN

The writing of history began among the Greeks, first with **Herodotus**, then with Thucydides. Whereas Herodotus gives the impression that he prefers telling a good story, and that he still inhabits Homer's world of epic poetry, for **Thucydides** the paramount concern is to analyse events. In that sense Thucydides is the first modern historian; wherever possible he seeks out primary sources, and his concern is always with objectivity, detail and chronology. Not that there is anything dry about his writing; its vividness and insight make reading him as powerful an experience as watching a Greek drama.

Thucydides began writing his history at the outset of the **Peloponnesian War**. He intended to give an account of its whole duration, but for reasons unknown, he abruptly stopped writing in the twentieth year, though he is thought to have survived the war by a few years, living until about 400 BC. Born into a wealthy, conservative Athenian family in around 455 BC, he was a democrat and an admirer of Pericles; his reconstruction of Pericles' speeches presents the most eloquent expression of the Athenian cause. But when Thucydides was **exiled** from his city seven years into the war, it was the making of him as a historian. As he put it, "Associating with both sides, with the Peloponnesians quite as much as with the Athenians, because of my exile, I was thus enabled to watch quietly the course of events".

Thucydides was himself a **military man**, who understood war at first hand. Hence his concern for method in his research and analysis in his writing, for he intended his book to be useful to future generals and statesmen. For these reasons, we have a better understanding of the Peloponnesian War than of any ancient conflict until Julius Caesar wrote his own first-hand accounts of his campaigns. And for these reasons too, Thucydides' history stands on a par with the greatest literature of ancient Greece.

inferior master, one that entirely lacked the style, ability and intelligence of Athens. Meanwhile, Athens had lost its empire but not its trade, and as it rapidly rebuilt its navy, its mercantile rivals faced no less competition than before.

## Rise of the Athenian Empire: 478–431 BC & its relevance to the Peloponnese

The first consequence of the Greek victory against the Persians was not, as might have been expected, the rise of **Sparta**, the pre-eminent Greek military power, whose soldiers had obediently sacrificed themselves at Thermopylae and won the final mainland battle at Plataea. Instead, many Greek city-states voluntarily placed themselves under the leadership of Athens.

This Aegean confederation was named the **Delian League**, after the island of Delos where the allies kept their treasury. Its first task was to protect the Greeks of Asia Minor against a vengeful Xerxes. This was the opposite of the policy proposed by Sparta and its Peloponnesian allies, which called for the abandonment of Greek homes across the Aegean and the resettlement of Asian Greeks in northern Greece.

That typified the Spartan attitude throughout the Persian crisis, in which Sparta had shown no initiative and acted only at the last minute. Its policy was provincial, protecting its position in the Peloponnese rather than pursuing the wider interests of

| 1881 | 1896 | 1924 | 1935 |
|---|---|---|---|
| Following military action and treaties, much of northern Greece added to the new nation | Modern Olympic Games are revived, inspired by the ancient games in Olympia | Plebiscite abolishes the monarchy and establishes a republic | Monarchy restored under George II |

Greece. Sparta persistently lacked vision, adventure and experience of the sea, believing that what could not be achieved by land was impossible. Thus, over the coming decades Sparta lost prestige to Athens, which Themistocles had established as a maritime power and whose imperial potential was realized under Pericles.

This was the **Athenian Golden Age**, and indeed a golden age for all Greece. The fifty years following Salamis and Plataea witnessed an extraordinary flowering in architecture, sculpture, literature and philosophy, whose influence is felt to this day. Greeks of the time recognized the historical importance of their experience and gave it realization through the creative impulse. Just as **Herodotus**, the "father of history", made the contest between Europe and Asia the theme of his great work, so **Aeschylus**, who fought at Marathon, made Xerxes the tragic subject of *The Persians* and thereby brought the art of drama to life. Indeed, in the intoxicating Athenian atmosphere, the warriors who turned back the Persian tide seemed to have fought in the same cause as Homer's heroes at Troy. In thanksgiving and celebration, the temples upon the Acropolis that the Persians had destroyed were rebuilt – most notably with the building of the **Parthenon**.

Yet Athens was still just one among numerous city-states, each ready to come together during a common danger but reasserting its sovereignty as the foreign threat receded. This was illustrated by the ten-year struggle from 461 BC onwards between Athens and various **Peloponnesian states**, itself a warning of a yet greater war to come between Athens and Sparta.

## Ottomans, Middle Ages & Byzantines

From the decline of the Roman Empire to the Ottoman conquest, the Peloponnese pursued a more complex, individual course from the rest of Greece. A succession of **occupations and conquests**, with attendant outposts and **castles**, left an extraordinary legacy of medieval remains. It retained a nominally Roman civilization well after colonial rule had dissipated, with Corinth at the fore until two major earthquakes destroyed it in the fourth and sixth centuries.

In the Middle Ages, the region was known as the **Moreas**, due to the resemblance of its outline to the leaf of a mulberry tree (*mouriá*). The **Byzantines** established their courts, castles and towns from the ninth century onward; their control, however, was only partial. The **Venetians** dominated the coast, and founded trading ports at Monemvasiá, Pýlos and Koróni which endured, for the most part, into the fifteenth century. The **Franks**, fresh from the sacking of Constantinople in the Fourth Crusade, arrived in 1204 and swiftly conquered large tracts of the peninsula, dividing it into feudal baronies under a prince of the Moreas.

## The rise of Islam and the Crusades

Towards the mid-thirteenth century, there was a remarkable **Byzantine renaissance**, which spread from the court at Mystra to reassert control over the peninsula. Yet the worst fears of the Byzantines were borne out in 1204 when the **Fourth Crusade** attacked and sacked **Constantinople** itself. Greece as a country was shared out between Franks, Venetians and many others in a bewildering patchwork of feudal holdings. Amid

| 1941–1944 | 1944–49 | 1952 | 1952 |
|---|---|---|---|
| German occupation of Greece, with resistance movements in the Peloponnese | German withdrawal is followed by the outbreak of bitter civil war | Greece joins NATO | New constitution establishes a parliamentary democracy, with king as Head of State |

### GREEK TRAGEDY

**Greek tragedy** has its roots in a fertility ritual celebrating the life and death of Dionysus, the god of the vine. Because goats were sacrificed in his honour, this ritual, in which a chorus danced and sang, was called *trag-odia*, a goat-song. Around 520 BC, an actor was introduced who came and went, changing costumes and playing different roles in successive episodes.

**Aeschylus** transformed matters by introducing a second actor and increasing the amount of dialogue, while reducing the size and role of the chorus. Thus tragedy became drama, driven by exchanges of words and actions. That Aeschylus had fought at Marathon and, probably, Salamis, may explain the urgency of his play, *The Persians*, the oldest surviving Greek tragedy. Although a religious man who believed in the overwhelming power of the gods, Aeschylus makes clear that it is man himself, through the free choices he makes, who steps into the appalling conflicts of the tragic situation. His later work, the *Oresteia*, a great drama of revenge, focused on Agamemnon's return home from the Trojan War and his murder. By now, Aeschylus was using a third actor and painted scenery, ideas taken from **Sophocles**, his younger rival.

Sophocles' innovation made it possible to present plots of considerable complexity. His was a world of inescapable consequences – in *Oedipus Rex*, for example, to be unseeing is not enough, while *Antigone* presents the ultimate tragic conflict, between right and right.

The effect of the tragedies of Aeschylus and Sophocles was to leave their audiences with an enhanced sense of pity or of terror. The unspoken moral was "You are in this too", the cathartic experience leaving everyone stronger – as though Athens, democratic, confident and imperial, was preparing itself to meet the blows of destiny.

endless infighting in the West a new Turkish dynasty, the **Ottomans**, emerged in the late thirteenth century.

By 1400, they had conquered all of Byzantine Greece except Thessaloníki and the Peloponnese. In 1452, they invaded the Peloponnese as a diversion to the main attack on **Constantinople**, which fell on May 29, 1453 and in 1460 the **Peloponnese** was captured. A last flicker of "Greek" rule, it was eventually extinguished by the **Turkish conquest** between 1458 and 1460, and was to lie dormant, save for sporadic rebellions in the perennially intransigent Máni, until the nineteenth-century **Greek War of Independence**.

## War of Independence: 1821–32

The **ideology** behind the **War of Independence** came from the Greeks of the diaspora, particularly those merchant colonies in France, Italy, Austria and Russia who had absorbed new European ideas of nationalism and revolution. Around 1814, assorted such Greeks formed a secret society, the **Filikí Etería** (Friendly Society). Their sophisticated political concepts went uncomprehended by the peasantry, who assumed the point of an uprising was to exterminate their religious adversaries. And so when war finally broke out in **spring 1821**, almost the entire settled **Muslim population of Greece** – farmers, merchants and officials – was **slaughtered** within weeks by roaming bands of Greek peasants armed with swords, guns, scythes and clubs. They were often

| **1964** | **1974** | **1981** | **2002** |
|---|---|---|---|
| The film of *Zorba the Greek* released, its soundtrack going on to grace (or blight) every Greek restaurant ever since | Greece transitions to a republic; Peloponnesian towns celebrate the return to democracy | Greece joins the EU | Greece adopts the euro, consigning Europe's oldest currency, the drachma, to history after some 3000 years |

## THE ORIGINS OF THE ORTHODOX CHURCH

The split between the Orthodox and Catholic Churches is traditionally dated to the "**Great Schism**" of 1054. But in practice the Churches had been diverging for centuries, and arguably the final break came much later. The causes of the split were as much linguistic – following the division of the Roman Empire, the language of the Church in Rome was Latin, while in the East it was Greek – and political as they were doctrinal, though there were certainly significant theological differences. Chief among these were the **iconoclastic controversy** – over the use of images in worship – the use of leavened (in the East) or unleavened bread (in the West) in the liturgy, and the Roman adjustment of the Creed, in 1014, to include the word "filioque" (and the Son).

The final schism was precipitated by the pope's claim to **supremacy over the Church**. While the patriarch in Constantinople and other Orthodox leaders accepted the bishop of Rome as "first among equals", they were not prepared to accept his ultimate authority over all the Church – or his subsequent claims to infallibility. In 1054, papal legates went to Constantinople to press the patriarch, Michael Celaurius, to accept Rome's claims. When he refused, Cardinal Humbert, leader of the Latin contingent, excommunicated Celaurius, who responded by in turn excommunicating Humbert and his colleagues.

Any hope of reconciliation disappeared with the sacking of Constantinople during the Fourth Crusade, when Orthodox churches were looted by Catholic crusaders and forcibly converted to Catholic worship, and by the centuries of separation which followed the fall of Constantinople, when much of the Orthodox East came under Ottoman rule.

led by Orthodox priests, and some of the earliest Greek revolutionary flags portrayed a cross over a severed Turkish head.

While the Greeks fought to rid themselves of the Ottomans, their further aims differed widely. Landowners sought to reinforce their traditional privileges; the peasantry saw the struggle as a means towards land redistribution; and westernized Greeks were fighting for a modern nation-state. Remarkably, by the end of **1823**, the Greeks appeared to have won their independence. Twice the sultan had sent armies into Greece; twice they had met with defeat. Greek guerrilla leaders, above all **Theodhoros Kolokotrónis** from the Peloponnese, had gained significant military victories early in the rebellion, which was joined by a thousand or so **European Philhellenes**, almost half of them German, though the most important was the English poet, **Lord Byron.**

But the situation was reversed in 1825, when formidable Egyptian forces loyal to the sultan invaded the **Peloponnese**. Thus far, aid for the Greek struggle had come neither from Orthodox Russia, nor from the Western powers of France and Britain, both wearied by the Napoleonic Wars and suspicious of a potentially anarchic new state. But the death of Lord Byron from a fever while training Greek forces at **Mesolóngi** on the west coast of the Greek mainland in 1824 galvanized European public opinion. When Mesolóngi fell to the Ottomans in 1826, Britain, France and Russia finally agreed to seek autonomy for certain parts of Greece, and sent a combined fleet to put pressure on the sultan's army in the **Peloponnese** and the Turkish-Egyptian fleet harboured in Navarino Bay. Events took over, and an accidental naval battle at **Navaríno** in October 1827 resulted in the destruction of almost the entire Ottoman fleet. The following

**2004**

Triumphant Athens Olympics and Greece wins the Euro football tournament

**2008**

Rioting in Athens brings Greek economic crisis to world attention

**2012**

Uneasy New Democracy-led coalition agrees to bailout with imposed austerity measures spring, Russia itself declared war on the Ottomans, and Sultan Mahmud II was forced to accept the existence of an autonomous Greece.

At a series of conferences from 1830 to 1832, **Greek independence** was confirmed by the Western powers, and borders were drawn in 1832. These included just eight hundred thousand of the six million Greeks living within the Ottoman Empire, and territories that were largely the poorest of the classical and Byzantine lands: **Attica**, the **Peloponnese** and the islands of the **Argo-Saronic**, the **Sporades** and the **Cyclades**. The rich agricultural belt of **Thessaly, Epirus** in the west and **Macedonia** in the north remained in Ottoman hands, as did the Dodecanese and Crete.

## The nineteenth and twentieth centuries

The Peloponnese played a major part in the revolt against the Turks, with local heroes **Theodhoros Kolokotrónis** and **Petros Mavromihális** becoming important military

### IMMIGRATION AND THE REFUGEE CRISIS

Since 1990, well over a million **immigrants** have arrived in Greece, a huge burden for a country of just over ten million citizens, creating a permanent economic underclass. The three largest groups are Albanians, Bulgarians and Romanians, followed by Poles, Pakistanis, Bangladeshis, Syrians, Filipinos, Ukrainians, Russians, Equatorial Africans, Kurds and Georgians.

Since the summer of 2015, numbers have increased exponentially with the flood of **refugees** escaping the war in Syria and other turmoil in the Middle East. These desperate people risked life and limb to make the crossing in flimsy boats from the Turkish coast to the closest Greek islands, with Lésvos, Híos and Kos bearing the brunt of the arrivals. Many did not survive the journey, such as the toddler Alan Kurdi, the image of whose drowned body provoked an international outcry. Those who did were initially put up in makeshift camps on the islands, with many then moved to larger but poorly equipped camps outside Athens, Thessaloníki or near the Macedonian border.

At first, the majority of the refugees stayed in Greece only temporarily before heading, often on foot, towards northern Europe. When this "**Balkan corridor**" was closed in March 2016, however, around 60,000 people were effectively trapped in squalid conditions, putting further strain on Greece's ailing economy. Although Greece was granted more than €400 million in aid to deal with the **refugee crisis**, the situation remained critical for several years after its peak. Indeed, its after effects still linger and the country's longstanding homogeneity is definitely in the past.

The Greek response has been decidedly mixed, with some openly welcoming and helping the refugees, and others protesting against programmes to integrate their children into the national education system. Overall, the Albanians and other eastern Europeans have become largely established in Greece and are not as reviled as they were originally, yet immigrants are still blamed for all manner of social ills. For the first time, **crime** – especially burglary and mugging – is a major issue. Equally worryingly, the understandable concerns of ordinary Greeks have been accompanied by a significant rise in support for the utterly repugnant **fascist party** Golden Dawn, now criminalised, and latterly the Spartiates (Spartans), who constantly seek to stoke fears and create divisions.

**2015**

A coalition led by radical leftwing SYRIZA wins two elections but is forced to continue many austerity measures

**2019**

New Democracy return to power amidst continuing austerity

leaders. At Pýlos, the international, but accidental, naval battle at **Navarino Bay** in 1827 decided the war, and the **first Greek parliament** was convened at Náfplio. After independence, however, power swiftly drained away from the Peloponnese to Athens, where it wzas to stay. The Maniots in Náfplio disaffected the peninsula, highlighted by the assassination of Kapodhístrias, the first Greek president.

Throughout the **nineteenth** and **early twentieth centuries**, the region developed important ports at Pátra, Kórinthos and Kalamáta, but its interior reverted to backwater status, which started a population decline that has continued up to the present. It was little disturbed until **World War II**, during which the area saw some of the worst German atrocities; there was much brave resistance in the mountains, but also some of the most shameful collaboration. The subsequent **civil war** left many of the towns polarized and physically in ruins; in its wake there was substantial **emigration** from both towns and countryside, to North America and Australia in particular. **Earthquakes** still cause considerable disruption, as at Kórinthos in 1981, Kalamáta in 1986, and Éyio in 1995.

Today, the Peloponnese is a captivating blend of the ancient and contemporary. Visitors can walk through the majestic ruins of ancient cities such as **Sparta** and **Corinth**, explore the grandeur of **Epidaurus' theatre**, and marvel at the fortifications of medieval cities such as **Mystras.** The region's natural beauty is equally compelling, with rugged mountains, olive groves, and pristine coastlines that invite adventure and relaxation.

**2020**

Covid-19 sweeps the world causing widespread lockdowns and closures; Greece's government is praised for imposing tough restrictions early, keeping case and death numbers relatively low

**2024**

The Olympic torch is lit at Olympia for the Paris games. Wolves are discovered in the Peloponnese for the first time in a century.

# Archeology

Until the second half of the nineteenth century, archeology was a very hit-and-miss, treasure-hunting affair. The early students of antiquity went to Greece to draw and make plaster casts of the great masterpieces of Classical sculpture. Unfortunately, a number soon found it more convenient or more profitable to remove objects wholesale and might be better described as looters than scholars or archeologists.

## Early excavations

The **British Society of Dilettanti** was one of the earliest promoters of Greek culture, financing expeditions to draw and publish antiquities. Founded in the 1730s as a reputedly drunken club for young aristocrats who had completed the Grand Tour (among them Sir Francis Dashwood, founder of the Hellfire Club), the society was the first body organized to sponsor systematic research into Greek antiquities, though it was initially most interested in Italy, as Greece was then still a backwater of the Ottoman Empire.

## The new nation

The Greek War of Independence (1821–32) and the establishment of a modern Greek nation changed all this. As a result of the selection of Prince Otto of Bavaria as the first king of modern Greece in 1832, the **Germans**, whose education system stressed classical learning, were at the forefront of archeological activity.

The Greeks themselves had begun to focus on their ancient past when the first stirrings of the independence movement were felt. In 1813, the **Philomuse Society** was formed, aiming to uncover and collect antiquities, publish books and assist students and foreign philhellenes. In 1829, an orphanage on the island of Égina became the first **Greek archeological museum.**

In 1837, the **Greek Archeological Society** was founded by **Kyriakos Pittakis.**

## The great Germans

Although King Otto was deposed in 1862 in favour of a Danish prince, Germans remained leaders of Greek archeology in the 1870s. Two men dominated the scene: Ernst Curtius and Heinrich Schliemann.

**Ernst Curtius** was a traditional classical scholar. He had come to Athens originally as tutor to King Otto's family and in 1874 returned to Greece to secure permission to conduct excavations at **Olympia.** He set up a **German Archeological Institute** in Athens and negotiated the **Olympia Convention**, under the terms of which the Germans were to pay for and have total control of the dig; all finds were to remain in Greece, though the excavators could make copies and casts; and all finds were to be published simultaneously in Greek and German.

This was an enormously important agreement, which almost certainly prevented the treasures of Olympia and Mycenae going to a German museum.

At **Olympia**, digging began in 1875 on a site buried beneath river mud, silt and sand. Only one corner of the **Temple of Zeus** was initially visible, but within months the excavators had turned up statues from the east pediment. Over forty magnificent sculptures, as well as terracottas, statue bases and a rich collection of bronzes, were uncovered, together with more than four hundred inscriptions. The laying bare of this huge complex was a triumph for official German archeology.

## TOP ARCHEOLOGICAL SITES IN THE PELOPONNESE

Greece as a country has such a wealth of ancient remains, the Peloponnese being no exception. Here are some of the most famous and unmissable sites of the region.

**Mycenae** The citadel of King Agamemnon and cavernous tholos tombs never fail to impress. See page 58

**Olympia** The birthplace of the Olympic Games is a vast and impressive site, centred around the ancient stadium. See page 148

**Epidaurus** An ancient theatre with incredible acoustics, where performances of Classical drama are a highlight of the annual Athens and Epidaurus Festival. See page 70

**Bassae** This superbly well-preserved temple is enhanced by its stunning location in the Arcadian mountains. See page 127

Three years later, Schliemann turned his attentions to **Mycenae**, again inspired by Homer, and once more following a hunch. Alone among contemporary scholars, he sought and found the legendary graves of Mycenaean kings inside the existing Cyclopean wall of the citadel rather than outside it, in the process unearthing the magnificent treasures now displayed in the Mycenaean Halls of the National Archeological Museum in Athens.

Almost single-handedly, and in the face of continuing academic obstruction, Schliemann had revolutionized archeology and the study of Greek history and civilization. Although some of his results have been shown to have been deliberately falsified in the sacrifice of truth to beauty, his achievements remains enormous.

The last two decades of the nineteenth century saw the discovery of other important Classical sites, including the beginning of excavations at **Epidaurus** in 1881 under the Greek archeologist **Panayiotis Kavvadias**, who made it his life's work.

# Wildlife

For anyone who has seen Greece as a country, including the Peloponnese, only at the height of summer will have experienced its brown parched hillsides and desert-like ambience. Yet the richness of the wildlife – in particular the flora – may come as a surprise to the regional visitor. As winter warms into spring, the countryside transforms into a mosaic of coloured flowers attracting a plethora of insect life followed by birds. Isolated coastal and mountainous areas such as the mountains of Arcadia have had many thousands of years to develop species. The total flora of the Peloponnese, including Kithira, is estimated as roughly 2630 species, most of them endemic to the Taigetos and Parnon mountain ranges in the south and on Chelmos in the north.

## Plants

Greece as a country has a rich biodiversity, with the Peloponnese holding a particular variety of flora that's adapted to its rugged mountains and sometimes harsh environment, Mediterranean climate, and coastal plains, with many species found to be endemic to the region meaning the Peloponnese celebrates a unique ecological heritage.

### The Maliachoria Tulip (Tulipa goulimyi)

One of the Peloponnese's most distinctive endemic species is the **Maliachoria tulip** (*Tulipa goulimyi*), found primarily in the Máni Peninsula (see page 104). It's distinguished by its vibrant red or pink petals and compact size, making it an eye-catching addition to the rocky terrain. Blooming in early spring, it paints the landscape with splashes of colour against a backdrop of olive groves and limestone crags. Botanists consider it one of the most unique tulips globally due to its limited range and resilient nature meaning it has survived in challenging soil and climatic conditions.

### The Arcadian Bellflower (Campanula andrewsii)

The **Arcadian bellflower** (*Campanula andrewsii*) in the heart of the Peninsular is a delicate yet resilient species that thrives on the rocky slopes of the Arcadian mountains (see page 124). Known for its bell-shaped flowers in colours of purple and blue that bloom each spring, it clings to crevices in limestone cliffs, making it a true survivor in a rugged landscape. Its stems and petals give it an ethereal appearance, especially when backlit by sunlight.

### The Argolic Iris (Iris attica)

Named after the ancient city of Argos, the **Argolic iris** (*Iris attica*) symbolises both the natural and historical allure of the Peloponnese. It can be found near Mycenae (see page 58), an area rich in archaeological history. Its blue and white petals add a touch of colour to this ancient landscape, where legends and natural beauty come together. The plant's specific habitat requirements make it sensitive to environmental changes, underscoring the importance of conservation efforts in preserving Greece's native flora.

### The Messenian Peony (Paeonia clusii subsp. russoi)

The **Messenian peony** (*Paeonia clusii subsp. russoi*), endemic to the Messenia region in southwestern Peloponnese (see page 132), is known for its large, fragrant pink flowers and blooms in late spring, thriving in cool, shaded valleys and forests where it's protected under oak and pine trees. Ancient Greek texts often reference it as a symbol of beauty and healing, yet it's vulnerable to extinction, making it a priority for conservationists.

### The Taygetus Mouse-ear Hawkweed (Hieracium taygeticum)

Growing in the high altitudes of the **Taïyetos mountain range** (see page 113), and especially seen in the Vyros Gorge region of the Mani Peninsula (see page 114), the **Taïyetos mouse-ear hawkweed** (*Hieracium taygeticum*) is a tiny yellow-flowering plant that blooms at elevations over 1,500 metres where it endures harsh winds, intense sunlight, and poor soil conditions. Named due to its tiny, mouse-ear-shaped leaves, this hawkweed is adapted to survive in rocky alpine zones, often found nestled among larger rocks that provide shelter from the elements. Its bright yellow flowers bloom in summer, offering a splash of colour in an otherwise stark landscape.

### The Aroanian Parnassia (Parnassia parnassifolia)

Around the mountains of Aroania in the Northern Peloponnese, grows the **Aroanian parnassia** (*Parnassia parnassifolia*). This alpine plant is known for its distinctive white flowers; five delicate petals and a central ring of yellow-tipped stamens. Unlike most of the endemic species of the region that thrive in rocky areas, this flower prefers damp, marshy ground near streams, making it a rare sight in the typically dry Mediterranean landscape, blossoming in the late summer.

### Peloponnesian Wild Olive (Olea europaea var. sylvestris)

The **Peloponnesian wild olive** (*Olea europaea var. sylvestris*) is a direct ancestor of the cultivated olive tree with immense cultural and economic significance in Greece. The hardy, twisted trees grow throughout the region and produces small, bitter olives that are not typically harvested for consumption. However, the wild olive plays a critical ecological role by providing food and shelter for native wildlife. Its roots stabilise soil, reduce erosion, and as a resilient species it's capable of withstanding extreme drought. This remarkable ancient tree is a reminder of the peninsula's long-standing relationship with olive cultivation and the resilience of native species.

## Animals

The region's rugged mountains, dense forests and extensive coastline provides habitats for numerous species. Among the mammals, the **Peloponnesian wild goat** (Capra aegagrus cretica) and the **European hare** are notable. It is also home to the elusive **Eurasian otter** and the **golden jackal. Birdlife** is abundant with raptors such as the golden eagle and the **Bonelli's eagle**. Wetlands and coastal areas attract the **Dalmatian pelican**, and **herons** can be found in the marshes of Greece's only fjord, **Gerakas**, 30 minutes from Monemvasiá. **Reptiles** thrive in the Mediterranean climate, and include the Greek tortoise, the Peloponnesian wall lizard and the Balkan green lizard.

**Marine life** along the coast is equally impressive. **Loggerhead sea turtles** nest on beaches such as the Bay of Kyparissia on the Peloponnese's west coast, only 90km south east of the island of Zakynthos which is also home to a large population of the animal.

**NOTABLE PLANT SPECIES ENDEMIC TO THE PELOPONNESE**

**Campanula andrewsii subsp. Hirsutula** A type of bellflower.
**Aubrieta gracilis** A delicate flowering plant often found on rocky cliffs.
**Cephalaria ambrosioides** A herbaceous perennial.
**Centaurea athoa** A species of knapweed.
**Erysimum olympicum** A wallflower native to high altitudes.
**Lomelosia hymettia** A member of the honeysuckle family.

# Music

Music is ubiquitous in the whole of modern Greek culture; even the most indifferent visitor can't fail to notice it in tavernas and other public spaces across the country, let alone the Peloponnese. Like so many aspects of the country, it amalgamates "native" and eastern styles, with occasional contributions from points west, and flourishes alongside and often in preference to Western pop. Many traditional songs can trace their roots back to Byzantine religious chants or to the popular music of the Ottoman Empire, though more nationalist-minded musicologists claim their original descent from the now-lost melodies of ancient Greece.

In the **Peloponnese**, many folk songs – known as **paliá dhimotiká** – hark back to the Ottoman occupation and the War of Independence; others, in a lighter tone, refer to aspects of pastoral life. Instruments such as the bouzouki, lyra, and **klaríno** (clarinet) play central roles in creating its distinctive sound which reached Greece during the 1830s, introduced either by Gypsies or King Otto's Bavarian entourage. Backing was traditionally provided by a *koumpanía* consisting of *kythára* (guitar), *laoúto*, *laoutokythára* (a hybrid instrument) and *violí*, with *toumberléki* (lap drum) or *défi* (tambourine) for rhythm. These folk songs and dances are often characterized by vibrant rhythms and poignant melodies. The region's musical heritage includes "Klephtic" songs, which narrate tales of the Greek War of Independence and celebrate the bravery of the klephts–Greek guerrilla fighters.

Many mainland melodies are **dances**, divided by rhythm into such categories as *kalamatianó* (a line dance), *tsámiko*, *hasaposérviko* or *syrtó*, the quintessential circle dance of Greece. Those that aren't danceable include the slow, stately *kléftiko*, which relate, baldly or in metaphor, incidents or attitudes from the Ottoman era and the fight for freedom.

Peloponnesian festivals and celebrations frequently feature live music, preserving and passing down these traditional tunes through generations, ensuring that the region's musical legacy remains vibrant and influential.

# Books

## TRAVEL/IMPRESSIONS

**Patrick Leigh Fermor** *Roumeli: Travels in Northern Greece and Mani: Travels in the Southern Peloponnese.* Sir Patrick – knighted in 2004 for his writing and contribution to British-Greek relations – is an aficionado of rural Greece's vanishing minorities and customs. These two volumes, written in the late 1950s and early 1960s respectively, are scholarly travelogues interspersed with strange yarns. Despite self-indulgent passages, they remain among the best books on modern Greece. *A Time of Gifts* and *Between the Woods and the Water* are two other earlier (1933/34) noteworthy books, the first two in this series transcribing his travels across Europe to Greece on foot.

**John Humphrys and Christopher Humphrys** *Blue Skies and Black Olives: A Survivor's Tale of Housebuilding and Peacock Chasing in Greece*. The irascible BBC presenter and his son, a cellist with a Greek orchestra, give their contrasting versions of the frustrations involved in building a holiday home in the Peloponnese. Enjoyable, if a bit familiar.

## GREEK FICTION

**Panos Karnezis** Karnezis has become the most accessible, and feted, Greek writer since the millennium. He grew up in Greece but now lives in London and writes in English; however, his concerns remain utterly Greek. *Little Infamies* is a collection of short stories set in his native Peloponnese during the late 1950s and early 1960s; *The Maze* is a darker-shaded, more successful novel concerning the Asia Minor Catastrophe. More recent works include *The Birthday Party*, based on events in the life of Aristotle Onassis and daughter Christina, and *The Convent*, a gentle whodunnit with nuns.

## PHRASEBOOKS AND DICTIONARIES

**Collins Pocket Greek Dictionary** *Harry T. Hionides*. Very nearly as complete as the *Pocket Oxford* and probably better value for money. The inexpensive *Collins Gem Greek Dictionary* (UK only) is palm-sized but identical in contents – the best day-pack choice.

**The Pocket Oxford Greek Dictionary** *J. T. Pring*. A bit bulky for travel, but generally considered the best Greek–English, English–Greek paperback dictionary.

**Rough Guide Phrasebook: Greek** Current, accurate and pocket-sized, with phrases that you'll actually need. The English–Greek section is transliterated, though the Greek–English part requires mastery of the Greek alphabet.

# Greek

So many Greeks have lived or worked abroad that you will find English-speakers in much of the Peloponnese region, especially among the younger generation where English is a second language and a necessity for the tourism industry, although venture into the mountains where only elderly locals reside and you might find this a challenge. Add the thousands attending language schools or working in the tourist industry – English is the lingua franca of most resorts – and it's easy to see how so many visitors return home having learned only minimal restaurant vocabulary. You can certainly get by this way, but it isn't very satisfying, and the willingness and ability to say even a few words will transform your status from that of dumb "tourístas" to the more honourable one of "xénos/xéni", which can mean foreigner, traveller and guest all combined.

## Learning basic Greek

**Greek** is not an easy language for English-speakers but it is a very beautiful one, and even a brief acquaintance will give you an idea of the debt owed to it by Western European languages. Greek **grammar** is predictably complicated; **nouns** are divided into three genders, all with different case endings in the singular and in the plural, and all adjectives and articles have to agree with these in gender, number and case. To simplify things, all adjectives are cited in the neuter form in the lists on the following pages. **Verbs** are even more complex; they're in two conjugations, in both active and passive voices, with passively constructed verbs often having transitive sense. As a novice, it's best to simply say what you want the way you know it, and dispense with the niceties.

### TEACH-YOURSELF GREEK COURSES

**Anne Farmakides** *A Manual of Modern Greek, 1, for University Students*. If you have the discipline and motivation, this is among the best for learning proper, grammatical Greek.

**Hara Garoufalia et al** *Read & Speak Greek for Beginners* (book & CD). Unlike many quickie courses, this provides a good grammatical foundation.

**David Holton et al** *Greek: A Comprehensive Grammar of the Modern Language*. A bit technical, so not for rank beginners, but it covers almost every conceivable construction.

**Alison Kakoura and Karen Rich** *Talk Greek* (book and 2 CDs). Probably the best in-print product for beginners' essentials, and for developing the confidence to try them.

**Aristarhos Matsukas** *Complete Greek: Teach Yourself* (book and optional cassettes or CDs). Another complete course; touches on idiomatic expressions as well.

## The Greek alphabet: transliteration and accents

Besides the usual difficulties of learning a new language, Greek has an entirely separate **alphabet**. Despite initial appearances, this is in practice fairly easily mastered – a skill that will help enormously in getting around independently. In addition, certain combinations of letters have unexpected results. This book's **transliteration system** (see below) should help you make intelligible noises, but remember that the correct **stress** (marked throughout the book on any words of more than one syllable with an acute accent or sometimes dieresis) is crucial. With the right sounds but the wrong stress people will either fail to understand you, or else understand something quite different.

The **dieresis** (¨) is used in Greek over the second of two adjacent vowels to change the pronunciation; often in this book it can function as the primary stress. In the word *kaïki* (caique), the use of a dieresis changes the pronunciation from "keh-key" to "ka-ee-key". In the word *païdhákia* (lamb chops), the dieresis changes the sound of the first syllable from "peh" to "pah-ee", but in this case the primary stress is on the third syllable. It is also, uniquely among Greek accents, used on capital letters in signs and personal-name spellings in Greece, and we have followed this practice on our maps.

### GREEK TRANSLITERATION PRONOUNCED

**Α, α** a *a* as in cat
**Β, β** v *v* as in vet
**Γ, γ** y/g *y* as in yes except before consonants or a, o or ou when it's a breathy *g*, approximately as in gap
**Δ, δ** dh *th* as in then
**Ε, ε** e *e* as in get
**Ζ, ζ** z *z* sound
**Η, η** I *i* as in ski
**Θ, θ** th *th* as in theme
**Ι, ι** I *i* as in ski
**Κ, κ** k *k* sound
**Λ, λ** l *l* sound
**Μ, μ** m *m* sound
**Ν, ν** n *n* sound
**Ξ, ξ** x *ks* sound, never *z*
**Ο, ο** o *o* as in box
**Π, π** p *p* sound
**Ρ, ρ** r *r* sound, lightly rolled as in Scottish
**Σ, σ, ς** s *ss* sound, except *z* before m or g
**Τ, τ** t *t* sound
**Υ, υ** y *i* as in ski
**Φ, φ** f *f* sound
**Χ, χ** h before vowels, denoted harsh *h* sound like *ch* in loch kh before consonants but pronounced the same
**Ψ, ψ** ps *ps* as in lips
**Ω, ω** o *o* as in box, indistinguishable from *o*

#### COMBINATIONS AND DIPHTHONGS

**ΑΙ, αι** e *e* as in get
**ΑΥ, αυ** av/af *av* before voiced consonants and vowels *af* before voiceless consonents
**ΕΙ, ει** I *i* as in ski
**ΕΥ, ευ** ev/ef *ev* before voiced consonants and vowels *ef* before voiceless consonents
**ΟΙ, οι** I *i* as in ski
**ΟΥ, ου** ou *ou* as in tourist
**ΓΓ, γγ** ng *ng* as in angle; always medial
**ΜΠ, μπ** b/mb *b* at start of a word, *mb* if medial
**ΝΤ, ντ** d/nd *d* at start of a word, *nd* if medial

## Polite forms and questions

Greek makes the distinction between the **informal** (*esý*) and **formal** (*esís*) second person, like the French "tu" and "vous". Young people and country people often use *esý* even with total strangers, though it's best to address everyone formally until/unless they start using the familiar with you, to avoid offence. By far the most common greeting, on meeting and parting, is *yiásou/yiásas* (literally "health to you").

To ask a **question**, it's simplest, though hardly elegant, to start with *parakaló* (please), then name the thing you want in an interrogative tone.

### GREEK WORDS AND PHRASES

#### ESSENTIALS

**Hérete/Yiásas** Hello
**Kaliméra** Good morning
**Kalispéra** Good evening
**Kaliníkhta** Goodnight
**Adío** Goodbye
**Tí kánis/Tí kánete?** How are you?
**Kalá íme** I'm fine
**Ke esís?** And you?
**Ne** Yes
**Óhi** No
**Parakaló** Please
**Efharistó (polý)** Thank you (very much)
**Sygnómi** Sorry/excuse me
**Miláte angliká?** Do you speak English?
**(Dhén) Katalavéno** I (don't) understand
**Parakaló, na milísate pió sigá** Speak slower, please
**Pos léyete aftó sta Elliniká?** How do you say it in Greek?
**Pos se léne?** What's your name?
**Me léne ...** My name is ...
**Kýrios/Kyría** Mr/Mrs
**Dhespinís** Miss
**Parakaló, o ...?** Where is the ...?

## THE QUEST FOR "PURE" GREEK

When Greece achieved independence in 1832, its people were mostly illiterate, and the spoken language – **dhimotikí**, "demotic" or "popular" Greek – had undergone enormous change since the Byzantine and Classical eras. The vocabulary had numerous loan words from the languages of the various invaders and conquerors – especially Turks, Venetians and Slavs – and the grammar had been considerably streamlined since ancient times.

The leaders of the new Greek state, filled with romantic notions of Greece's past glories, set about purging the language of foreign words and reviving its Classical purity. Accordingly, they created what was in effect an artificial language, **katharévoussa** (literally "cleansed" Greek). Long-forgotten words and phrases were reintroduced and complex Classical grammar reinstated. *Katharévoussa* became the language of the schools, government, business, the law, newspapers and academia. Everyone aspiring to membership in the elite strove to master it.

The split between *katharévoussa* and *dhimotikí* quickly took on a **political** dimension, with intellectuals and left-wing politicians championing the demotic form, while the right, notably the colonel's junta of 1967–74, insisted on the "purer" *katharévoussa. Dhimotikí* returned permanently after the fall of the colonels, though the Church and the legal profession still persist with *katharévoussa.*

All this has reduced, but not eliminated, confusion. The Metaxás dictatorship of the 1930s changed scores of village names from Slavic, Turkish or Albanian words to Greek ones – often reviving the name of the nearest ancient site. These official **place names** still hold sway on most road signs and maps – even though the local people may use the *dhimotikí* or non-Greek form. Thus for example you will see "Plomárion" or "Ypsoúnda" written, though everyone actually says "Plomári" or "Stemnítsa" respectively.

**Dhen xéro** I don't know
**Tha se dho ávrio** See you tomorrow
**Kalí andhámosi** See you again
**Páme** Let's go
**Parakaló, na me voithíste** Please help me
**(Dhen) Trógo/píno** I (don't) eat/drink
**(Dhen) Mou arési** I (don't) like
**Stinyásas!** Cheers!
**Málista** Certainly
**Endáxi** OK, agreed
**Anikhtó** Open
**Klistó** Closed
**Méra** Day
**Níkhta** Night
**Edhó** Here
**Ekí** There
**Grígora** Quickly
**Sigá** Slowly
**Pou?** Where?
**Pos?** How?
**Póte?** When?
**Yiatí?** Why?
**Ti óra ... ?** At what time ... ?
**Ti íne/Pió íne ... ?** What is/Which is ... ?

### ACCOMMODATION

**Parakaló, éna dhomátio** A room, please
**yiá éna/dhýo/tría átoma** for one/two/three people
**yiá mía/dhýo/tris vradhiés** for one/two/three nights
**me dhipló kreváti** with a double bed
**me dous** with a shower
**Xenodhohío** Hotel
**Xenónas** Guesthouse
**Xenónas neótitas** Youth hostel
**Zestó neró** Hot water
**Krýo neró** Cold water
**Klimatismós** Air conditioning
**Anemistíras** Fan
**Boró na to dho?** Can I see it?
**Boroúme na váloume ti skiní edhó?** Can we camp here?
**Kámping/Kataskínosi** Campsite

### SHOPPING AND SERVICES

**Póso (káni)?** How much (does it cost)?
**Tí óra aníyi/ klíni?** What time does it open/close?
**Parakaló, éna kilo portokália?** May I have a kilo of oranges?
**Pósi, póses or pósa?** How many?
**Aftó** This one
**Ekíno** That one
**Kaló** Good
**Kakó** Bad
**Megálo** Big
**Mikró** Small
**Perisótero** More

**Ligótero** Less
**Lígo** A little
**Polý** A lot
**Ftinó** Cheap
**Akrivó** Expensive
**Mazí (me)** With (together)
**Horís** Without
**Magazí** Shop
**Farmakío** Pharmacy
**Tahydhromío** Post office
**Gramatósima** Stamps
**Venzinádhiko** Petrol station
**Trápeza** Bank
**Leftá/Khrímata** Money
**Toualéta** Toilet
**Astynomía** Police
**Yiatrós** Doctor
**Nosokomío** Hospital

## ON THE MOVE

**Parakaló, o dhrómos yiá … ?** Can you show me the road to … ?
**Aeropláno** Aeroplane
**Leoforío, poúlman** Bus, coach
**Aftokínito, amáxi** Car
**Mihanáki, papáki** Motorbike, scooter
**Taxí** Taxi
**Plío/vapóri/karávi** Ship, ferry
**Tahyplóö, katamarán** High-speed boat, catamaran
**Dhelfíni** Hydrofoil
**Tréno** Train
**Sidhirodhromikós stathmós** Train station
**Podhílato** Bicycle
**Otostóp** Hitching
**Mé ta pódhia** On foot
**Monopáti** Trail, path
**Praktorío leoforíon KTEL** Bus station
**Stási** Bus stop
**Limáni** Harbour
**Ti óra févyi?** What time does it leave?
**Ti óra ftáni?** What time does it arrive?
**Pósa hiliómetra?** How many kilometres?
**Póses óres?** How many hours?
**Pou páte/pas?** Where are you going?
**Páo sto …** I'm going to …
**Thélo na katévo sto …** I want to get off at …
**O dhrómos yiá …** The road to …
**Kondá** Near
**Makriá** Far
**Aristerá** Left
**Dhexiá** Right
**Katefthía/ísia** Straight ahead
**Éna isitírio yiá …** A ticket to …
**Éna isitírio apló/mé epistrofí** A ticket one-way/return
**Paralía** Beach
**Spiliá** Cave
**Kéndro** Centre (of town)
**Eklissía** Church
**Thálassa** Sea
**Horió** Village

## NUMBERS

**énas/mía/éna** 1
**dhýo** 2
**tris/tría** 3
**tésseri/tésseres/téssera** 4
**pénde** 5
**éxi** 6
**eftá** 7
**okhtó** 8

## GREEK'S GREEK

There are numerous words and phrases that you will hear constantly, even if you don't have the chance to use them. These are a few of the most common.
**Éla!** Come (literally) but also Speak to me! You don't say! etc.
**Oríste!** Literally, Define!; in effect, What can I do for you? Say that again, when used interrogatively. Also used as phone response.
**Embrós!/Léyete!** More phone responses
**Tí néa?** What's new?
**Tí yínete?** What's going on?
**Étsi k'étsi** So-so
**Ópa!** Whoops! Watch it!
**Po-po-po!** Expression of dismay or concern, like French "O là là!"
**Pedhí moú** My boy/girl, sonny, friend, etc.
**Maláka(s)** Literally "wanker", but often used (don't try it!) as an informal term of address
**Sigá sigá** Take your time, slow down
**Kaló taxídhi** Bon voyage

**ennéa (or, in slang, enyiá)** 9
**dhéka** 10
**éndheka** 11
**dhódheka** 12
**dhekatrís/ía** 13
**dhekatésseri/es/a** 14
**dhekapénde** 15
**íkossi** 20
**íkossi éna** 21
**triánda** 30
**saránda** 40
**penínda** 50
**exínda** 60
**evdhomínda** 70
**ogdhónda** 80
**enenínda** 90
**ekató** 100
**ekatón penínda** 150
**dhiakósies/ia** 200
**pendakósies/ia** 500
**hílies/hília** 1000
**dhýo hiliádhes** 2000
**prótos/próti/próto** first
**dhéfteros/i/o** second
**trítos/i/o** third

### TIME AND DAYS OF THE WEEK

**Tóra** Now
**Argótera** Later
**Símera** Today
**Ávrio** Tomorrow
**Khthés** Yesterday
**Tó proï** In the morning
**Tó apóyevma** In the afternoon
**Tó vrádhi** In the evening
**Kyriakí** Sunday
**Dheftéra** Monday
**Tríti** Tuesday
**Tetárti** Wednesday
**Pémpti** Thursday
**Paraskeví** Friday
**Sávato** Saturday
**Tí óra íne?** What time is it?
**Mía iy óra/dhýo iy óraa/trís iy ór** One/two/three o'clock
**Tésseres pará íkosi** Twenty minutes to four
**Eftá ke pénde** Five minutes past seven
**Éndheka ke misí** Half past eleven
**Se misí óra** In half an hour
**S'éna tétarto** In a quarter-hour
**Se dhýo óres** In two hours

### MONTHS AND SEASONS

**Yennáris/Ianouários** January
**Fleváris/Fevouários** February
**Mártis/Mártios** March
**Aprílis** April
**Maïos** May
**Ioúnios** June
**Ioúlios** July
**Ávgoustos** August
**Septémvris/ios** September
**Októvris/ios** October
**Noémvris/ios** November
**Dhekémvris/ios** December
**Therinó dhromolóyio** Summer schedule
**Himerinó dhromolóyio** Winter schedule

## A FOOD AND DRINK GLOSSARY

### BASICS

**Katálogos** Menu
**O logariasmós** The bill
**Merídha** Portion
**Zestó** Hot
**Krýo** Cold
**(Horís) ládhi** (Without) oil
**Hýma** Bulk (wine, olives etc)
**Varelísio/a** Barrelled wine/beer
**Hortofágos** Vegetarian
**Kréas** Meat
**Lahaniká** Vegetables
**Neró** Water
**Psári(a)** Fish
**Thalassiná** Seafood
**Mezédhes** Small plates of various food, dips etc
**Orektiká** Starters
**Pikilía** Mixed selection on plate
**Aláti** Salt
**Pipéri** Pepper (condiment)
**Avgá** Eggs
**Méli** Honey
**Psomí ...** Bread
**Olikís** Wholemeal
**Sikalísio** Rye
**Kalambokísio** Corn
**Tyrí** Cheese
**Yiaoúrti** Yoghurt
**Záhari** Sugar
**Zaharíni** Sweetener

### FOOD SHOPS, RESTAURANTS AND BARS

**Baráki** Bar
**Estiatório/Inomayirío** Old-style restaurant mainly featuring baked dishes
**Exohikó kéndro** Out-of-town restaurant

**Foúrnos** Bakery
**Galaktopolío** Café specializing in dairy products
**Mezedhopolío** Restaurant specializing in *mezédhes*
**Ouzerí** Restaurant specializing in ouzo and *mezédhes*
**Patsatzídhiko** Restaurant specializing in tripe soup
**Psarotavérna** Specialist fish taverna
**Psistariá** Grill house
**Souvlatzídhiko** *Souvláki* shop
**Tsipourádhiko** Restaurant specializing in *tsípouro* and *mezédhes*
**Zaharoplastío** Patisserie, confectionary shop

## COOKING TERMS

**Akhnistó** Steamed
**Frikasé** Stew, either lamb, goat or pork, with celery
**Iliókafto** Sun-dried
**Kokkinistó** Cooked in tomato sauce
**Kourkoúti** Egg-and-flour batter
**Krasáto** Cooked in wine sauce
**Ladherá** Vegetables cooked in an oily sauce
**Ladholémono** Oil and lemon sauce
**Makaronádha** Any spaghetti/pasta-based dish
**Mayireftá** Traditional oven-baked dish
**Pastó** Fish marinated in salt
**Petáli** Butterflied fish, eel, shrimp
**Psitó** Roasted
**Saganáki** Cheese-based red sauce; also fried cheese
**(Tis) Skáras** Grilled
**Sti soúvla** Spit-roasted
**Sto foúrno** Baked
**Tiganitó** Pan-fried
**Tís óras** Grilled/fried to order
**Yakhní** Stewed in oil and tomato sauce
**Yemistá** Stuffed (squid, vegetables, etc)

## SOUPS, STARTERS AND SNACKS

**Avgolémono** Egg and lemon soup
**Bouréki, bourekákia** Courgette/zucchini, potato and cheese pie
**Dolmádhes, yaprákia; yalantzí** Vine leaves stuffed with rice and mince; with vegetables
**Fasoládha** Bean soup
**Fáva** Purée of yellow peas
**Féta psití** Baked feta cheese slabs with chilli
**Galotýri** Curdled creamy dip
**Hortópita** Pastry stuffed with greens
**Kápari** Pickled caper leaves
**Kopanistí, khtypití** Pungent, fermented cheese purée
**Kreatópita** Meat pie, usually with mince
**Lahanodolmádhes** Stuffed cabbage leaves
**Loukanoukópita** Sausage roll
**Mavromátika** Black-eyed peas
**Melitzanosaláta** Aubergine/eggplant dip
**Piperiés florínes** Marinated sweet peppers
**Rengosaláta** Herring salad
**Revythokeftédhes** Chickpea/garbanzo patties
**Skordhaliá** Garlic dip
**Soúpa** Soup
**Spanakópita** Spinach pie, usually with cheese
**Strapatsádha** Eggs scrambled with tomato and onions
**Taramosaláta** Cod roe pâté
**Tiganópsomo** Toasted oiled bread
**Trahanádhes** Crushed wheat and milk soup, sweet or savoury
**Tyrokafterí** Cheese dip with chilli
**Tyrópita** Cheese pie
**Tyropitákia** Small fried cheese pies
**Tzatzíki** Yoghurt and cucumber dip
**Tzirosaláta** Cured mackerel dip

## VEGETABLES

**Ambelofásola** Runner beans
**Angináres** Artichokes
**Angoúri** Cucumber
**Ánitho** Dill
**Bámies** Okra/ladies' fingers
**Briám, tourloú** Ratatouille
**Domátes** Tomatoes
**Fakés** Lentils
**Fasolákia** French (green) beans
**Fasóles** Small white beans
**Horiátiki (saláta)** Greek salad (with olives, feta etc)
**Hórta** Steamed greens
**Kolokythákia** Courgette/zucchini
**Koukiá** Broad fava beans
**Láhano** Cabbage
**Maroúli** Lettuce
**Melitzánes imám/Imám baïldí** Aubergine/eggplant slices baked with onion, garlic and copious olive oil
**Patátes** Potatoes
**Patzária** Beetroot
**Piperiés** Peppers
**Pligoúri, pinigoúri** Bulgur wheat
**Radhíkia** Wild chicory
**Róka** Rocket, arugula
**Rýzi/Piláfi sáltsa** Rice (usually with sauce)
**Saláta** Salad
**Spanáki** Spinach
**Yígandes** White haricot beans

## FISH AND SEAFOOD

**Ahini, foúskes** Sea urchins
**Astakós** Lobster
**Atherína** Sand smelt
**Bakaliáros** Cod or hake, usually the latter
**Barbóuni** Red mullet
**Fangrí** Common bream

**Galéos** Dogfish
**Garídhes** Shrimp, prawns
**Gávros** Mild anchovy
**Glóssa** Sole
**Gónos, gonákia** Any hatchling fish
**Gópa** Bogue
**Hokhlí** Sea snails
**Kakaviá** Bouillabaisse
**Kalamarákia** Baby squid
**Kalamária** Squid
**Karavídhes** Crayfish
**Koliós** Chub mackerel
**Koutsomoúra** Goatfish (small red mullet)
**Lakérdha** Light-fleshed bonito, marinated
**Lithríni** Red bream, pandora
**Melanoúri** Saddled bream
**Ménoula** Sprat
**Mýdhia** Mussels
**Okhtapódhi** Octopus
**Petalídhes** Limpets
**Platý** Skate, ray
**Psarósoupa** Fish soup
**Sardhélles** Sardines
**Sargós** White bream
**Seláhi** Skate, ray
**Sfyrídha** White grouper
**Skáros** Parrotfish
**Skathári** Black bream
**Skoumbrí** Atlantic mackerel
**Soupiá** Cuttlefish
**Strídhia** Oysters
**Thrápsalo** Large, deep-water squid
**Tónos** Tuna
**Tsipoúra** Gilt-head bream
**Xifías** Swordfish
**Yermanós** Leatherback
**Yialisterés** Smooth Venus shellfish

### MEAT AND POULTRY

**Arní/arnáki** Lamb
**Bekrí mezé** Pork chunks in spicy pepper sauce
**Biftéki** Hamburger
**Brizóla hiriní** Pork chop
**Brizóla moskharísia** Beef chop
**Exohikó/Kléftiko** Lamb baked in tin foil or in pastry
**Frigadhéli** Minced meat dumplings
**Gourounópoulo** Suckling pig roast on a spit
**Hirinó** Pork
**Kalamáki** Small kebab on a wooden skewer
**Katsíki/Yídha** Goat
**Keftédhes** Meatballs
**Kókoras krasáto** Coq au vin
**Kokorétsi** Liver/offal roulade, spit-roasted
**Kondosoúvli** Spit-roasted pork
**Kopsídha** (Lamb) shoulder chops
**Kotópoulo** Chicken
**Kounéli** Rabbit
**Loukánika** Spicy course-ground sausages
**Moskhári** Veal
**Moussakás** Aubergine/eggplant, potato and lamb-mince casserole with béchamel topping
**Païdhákia** Rib chops, lamb or goat
**Pantséta** Pork belly
**Papoutsákia** Stuffed aubergine/eggplant "shoes"
**Pastítsio** Macaroni "pie" baked with minced meat
**Pastourmás** Cured, highly spiced beef
**Patsás** Tripe soup
**Patsitsádha** beef with pasta in wine sauce
**Provatína** Female mutton
**Psaronéfri** Pork tenderloin medallions
**Salingária** Garden snails
**Sofríto** beef fried in garlic sauce
**Soutzoukákia** Minced meat rissoles/beef patties
**Souvláki** Any type of kebab
**Spetzofáï** Sausage and pepper stew
**Stifádho** Meat stew with tomato and boiling onions
**Sykóti** Liver
**Tiganiá** Pork chunks fried with onions
**Yiouvétsi** Baked clay casserole of meat and pasta
**Yíros** Rotisserie meat, usually pork

### SWEETS AND DESSERT

**Baklavás** Honey and nut pastry
**Bergamóndo** Bergamot
**Bougátsa** Sweet cream pie served warm with sugar and cinnamon
**Galaktoboúreko** Custard pie
**Glyká koutalioú** Spoon sweet (syrupy fruit preserve)
**Halvás** Semolina- or sesame-based sweet
**Kataïfi** Honey-soaked "shredded wheat"
**Karydhópita** Walnut cake
**Kréma** Custard
**Loukoumádhes** Dough fritters in honey syrup and sesame seeds
**Pagotó** Ice cream
**Pastélli** Sesame and honey bar
**Ravaní** Sponge cake, lightly syruped
**Rizógalo** Rice pudding
**Sandiyí** Whipped cream

### FRUITS

**Akhládhi** Big pear
**Aktinídhi** Kiwi fruit
**Fystíkia** Pistachio nuts
**Fráoules** Strawberries
**Karpoúzi** Watermelon
**Kerásia** Cherries
**Krystália** Miniature pears

**Kydhóni** Quince
**Lemóni** Lemon
**Mílo** Apple
**Pepóni** Melon
**Portokáli** Orange
**Rodhákino** Peach
**Sýka** Figs
**Stafýlia** Grapes

## CHEESE

**Ayeladhinó** Cow's-milk cheese
**Féta** Salty, creamy white cheese
**(Kefalo) graviéra** (Extra-hard) *Gruyère*-type cheese
**Katsikísio** Goat cheese
**Kasséri** Medium-sharp cheese
**Myzíthra** Sweet cream cheese
**Próvio** Sheep cheese

## DRINKS

**Boukáli** Bottle
**Býra** Beer
**Gála** Milk
**Galakakáo** Chocolate milk
**Kafés** Coffee
**Krasí** Wine
**...áspro/lefkó** ...white
**...kokkinélli/rozé** ...rosé
**...kókkino** ...red
**Limonádha** Lemonade
**Metalikó neró** Mineral water
**Portokaládha** Orangeade
**Potíri** Glass
**Rakí/Tsikoudhiá** Clear Cretan spirit
**Retsína** Wine made with added pine resin
**Tsáï** Tea
**Tsáï vounoú** "Mountain" (mainland sage) tea
**Tsípouro** Clear strong spirit

# Glossary

**Acropolis** Ancient, fortified hilltop.

**Agora** Market and meeting place of an ancient Greek city; also the "high street" of a modern village (**agorá** in modern Greek).

**Amphora** Tall, narrow-necked jar for oil or wine.

**Áno** Upper; common prefix of village names.

**Apse** Curved recess at the east end of a church nave.

**Archaic period** Late Iron Age period, from around 750 BC to the start of the Classical period in the fifth century BC.

**Arhondikó** A lordly stone mansion, often restored as boutique accommodation.

**Astikó** (Intra) city, municipal, local; adjective applied to phone calls and bus services.

**Ayíasma** A sacred spring, usually flowing out of church foundations.

**Áyios/Ayía/Áyii** (m/f/plural). Saint or holy. Common place-name prefix (abbreviated Ag or Ay), often spelled **Agios** or **Aghios**.

**Bema** Rostrum for a church oratory.

**Bouleuterion** Auditorium for meetings of an ancient town's deliberative council.

**Bouzoúki** Most common Greek stringed musical instrument.

**Capital** The flared top, often ornamented, of a column.

**Cavea** Seating curve of an ancient theatre.

**Cella** Sacred room of a temple, housing the cult image.

**Classical period** From the end of the Persian Wars in 480 BC until the unification of Greece under Philip II of Macedon (338 BC).

**Conch** Concave semi-dome surmounting a church apse, often frescoed.

**Corinthian** Decorative columns, festooned with acanthus florettes; any temple built in this order.

**Dhimarhío** Town hall.

**Dhomátia** Rooms for rent in purpose-built block, without staffed reception.

**Dorian** Northern civilization that displaced and succeeded the Mycenaeans and Minoans through most of Greece around 1100 BC.

**Doric** Minimalist, unadorned columns, dating from the Dorian period; any temple built in this order.

**Drum** Cylindrical or faceted vertical section, usually pierced by an even number of narrow windows, upholding a church cupola.

**Entablature** The horizontal linking structure atop the columns of an ancient temple; same as **architrave**.

**Eparhía** Subdivision of a modern province, analogous to a county.

**Exedra** Display niche for statuary.

**Exonarthex** The outer vestibule or entrance hall of a church, when a true **narthex** is present.

**Forum** Market and meeting place of a Roman-era city.

**Frieze** Band of sculptures around a temple. Doric friezes consist of various tableaux of figures (**metopes**) interspersed with grooved panels (**triglyphs**); Ionic ones have continuous bands of figures.

**Froúrio** Medieval citadel; nowadays, can mean a modern military headquarters.

**Garsoniéra/es** Studio villa/s, self-catering apartment/s.

**Geometric period** Post-Mycenaean Iron Age era named for its pottery style; starts in the early eleventh century BC with the arrival of Dorian peoples. By the eighth century BC, with development of representational styles, the **Archaic period** begins.

**Hellenistic period** The last and most unified "Greek empire", created in the wake of Alexander the Great's Macedonian empire and finally collapsing with the fall of Corinth to the Romans in 146 BC.

**Heroön** Shrine or sanctuary-tomb, usually of a demigod or mortal; war memorials in modern Greece.

**Hóra** Main town of an island or region; literally it means "the place".

**Ierón** The sanctuary between the altar screen and the apse of a church, reserved for priestly activities.

**Ikonostási** Wood or masonry screen between the nave of a church and the altar, supporting at least three icons.

**Ionic** Elaborate, decorative development of the older **Doric** order; Ionic temple columns are slimmer, with deeper "fluted" edges, spiral-shaped capitals and ornamental bases.

**Kafenío** Coffee house or café.

**Kaïki** (plural **kaïkia**) Caique, or medium-sized boat, traditionally wooden and used for transporting cargo and passengers; now refers mainly to island excursion boats.

**Kalderími** A cobbled mule-track or footpath.

**Kámbos** Fertile agricultural plain, usually near a river mouth.

**Kantína** Shack, caravan or even a disused bus on the beach, serving drinks and perhaps sandwiches or quick snacks.

**Kástro** Any fortified hill, but most often the oldest, highest, walled-in part of an island hóra, intended to protect civilians.

**Katholikón** Central church of a monastery.

**Káto** Lower; common prefix of village names.

**Kendrikí platía** Central square.

**Kouros** Nude Archaic statue of an idealized young man, usually portrayed with one foot slightly in front of the other.

**Megaron** Principal hall or throne room of a Mycenaean palace.

**Meltémi** North wind that blows across the Aegean in summer, starting softly from near the mainland and hitting the Cyclades, the Dodecanese and Crete full on.

**Metope** see **Frieze**.

**Minoan** Crete's great Bronze Age civilization which dominated the Aegean from about 2500 to 1400 BC.

**Moní** Formal term for a monastery or convent.

**Moreas** Medieval term for the Peloponnese; the peninsula's outline was likened to the leaf of a mulberry tree, *mouriá* in Greek.

**Mycenaean** Mainland civilization centred on Mycenae and the Argolid from about 1700 to 1100 BC.

**Naos** The inner sanctum of an ancient temple; also, the central area of an Orthodox Christian church.

**Narthex** Western vestibule of a church, reserved for catechumens and the unbaptized; typically frescoed with scenes of the Last Judgement.

**Neolithic** Earliest era of settlement in Greece; characterized by use of stone tools and weapons together with basic agriculture. Divided arbitrarily into Early (c.6000 BC), Middle (c.5000 BC) and Late (c.3000 BC).

**Néos, Néa, Néo** "New" – a common prefix to a town or village name.

**Nomós** Modern Greek province – there are more than fifty of them. Village bus services are organized according to their borders.

**Odeion** Small theatre, used for musical performances, minor dramatic productions or councils.

**Orchestra** Circular area in a theatre where the chorus would sing and dance.

**Palaestra** Gymnasium for athletics and wrestling practice.

**Paleós, Paleá, Paleó** "Old" – again a common prefix in town and village names.

**Panayía** Virgin Mary.

**Pandokrátor** Literally "The Almighty"; generally refers to the stern portrayal of Christ in Majesty frescoed or in mosaic in the dome of many Byzantine churches.

**Paniyíri** Festival or feast – the local celebration of a holy day.

**Paralía** Beach, or seafront promenade.

**Pediment** Triangular, sculpted gable below the roof of a temple.

**Pendentive** Triangular sections of vaulting with concave sides, positioned at a corner of a rectangular space to support a circular or polygonal dome; in churches, often adorned with frescoes of the four Evangelists.

**Períptero** Street kiosk.

**Peristereónes** Pigeon towers, in the Cyclades.

**Peristyle** Gallery of columns around a temple or other building.

**Pinakothíki** Picture gallery, ancient or modern.

**Pithos** (plural **pithoi**) Large ceramic jar for storing oil, grain, etc. Very common in Minoan palaces and used in almost identical form in modern Greek homes.

**Platía** Square, plaza.

**Polygonal masonry** Wall-building technique of Classical and Hellenistic periods, using unmortared, closely joined stones; often called "Lesvian polygonal" after the island where the method supposedly originated. The much-(ab)used term **Cyclopean** refers only to Bronze Age mainland sites such as Tiryns and Mycenae.

**Propylaion** Monumental columned gateway of an ancient building; often used in the plural, **propylaia**.

**Pýrgos** Tower or bastion; also tower-mansions found in the Máni.

**Skála** The port of an inland island settlement, nowadays often larger and more important than its namesake, but always younger since built after the disappearance of piracy.

**Skyládhiko** Rough-and-ready live bouzouki club.

**Squinch** Small concavity across a corner of a columnless interior space, which supports a superstructure such as a dome.

**Stele** Upright stone slab or column, usually inscribed with an edict; also an ancient tombstone, with a relief scene.

**Stoa** Colonnaded walkway in Classical-to-Roman-era marketplaces.

**Távli** Backgammon; a favourite café pastime, especially among the young. There are two more difficult local variations (*févga* and *plakotó*) in addition to the standard international game (*pórtes*).

**Telestirion** Shrine associated with ancient mystery rituals.

**Témblon** Wooden altar screen of an Orthodox church, usually ornately carved and painted and studded with icons; more or less interchangeable with **ikonostási**.

**Temenos** Sacred precinct of ancient temple, often used to refer to the sanctuary itself.

**Theatral area** Open area found in most of the Minoan palaces with seat-like steps around. Probably a type of theatre or ritual area.

**Tholos** Conical or beehive-shaped building, eg a Mycenaean tomb.

**Triglyph** see **Frieze**.

**Tympanum** The recessed space, flat or carved in relief, inside a pediment.

**Yperastikó** Long-distance – as in bus services.

# Small print and index



## ABOUT THE AUTHOR

**Rebecca Hall** is a travel writer, author and freelance journalist known for her extensive work on travel-related topics, particularly focusing on Greece. She has lived and worked in Greece for many years, making her an expert on the country's culture, history, and everyday life. As well as a being a proud contributor to the Rough Guide series, her debut novel *Girl Gone Greek* can be found on Amazon and you can follow her adventures at www.lifebeyondbordersblog.com with its rich focus on sharing immersive experiences and detailed guides. Her deep connection with Greece has made her a respected authority on travel within the country. Her writing style is often praised for its vivid descriptions and the ability to transport readers vicariously to the places she writes about.

## A ROUGH GUIDE TO ROUGH GUIDES

Published in 1982, the first Rough Guide – to Greece – was a student scheme that became a publishing phenomenon. Mark Ellingham, a recent graduate in English from Bristol University, had been travelling in Greece the previous summer and couldn't find the right guidebook. With a small group of friends he wrote his own guide, combining a contemporary, journalistic style with a thoroughly practical approach to travellers' needs.

The immediate success of the book spawned a series that rapidly covered dozens of destinations. And, in addition to impecunious backpackers, Rough Guides soon acquired a much broader readership that relished the guides' wit and inquisitiveness as much as their enthusiastic, critical approach and value-for-money ethos. These days, Rough Guides include recommendations from budget to luxury and cover more than 120 destinations around the globe, from Amsterdam to Zanzibar, all regularly updated by our team of roaming writers.

Browse all our latest guides, read inspirational features and book your trip at **roughguides.com**.

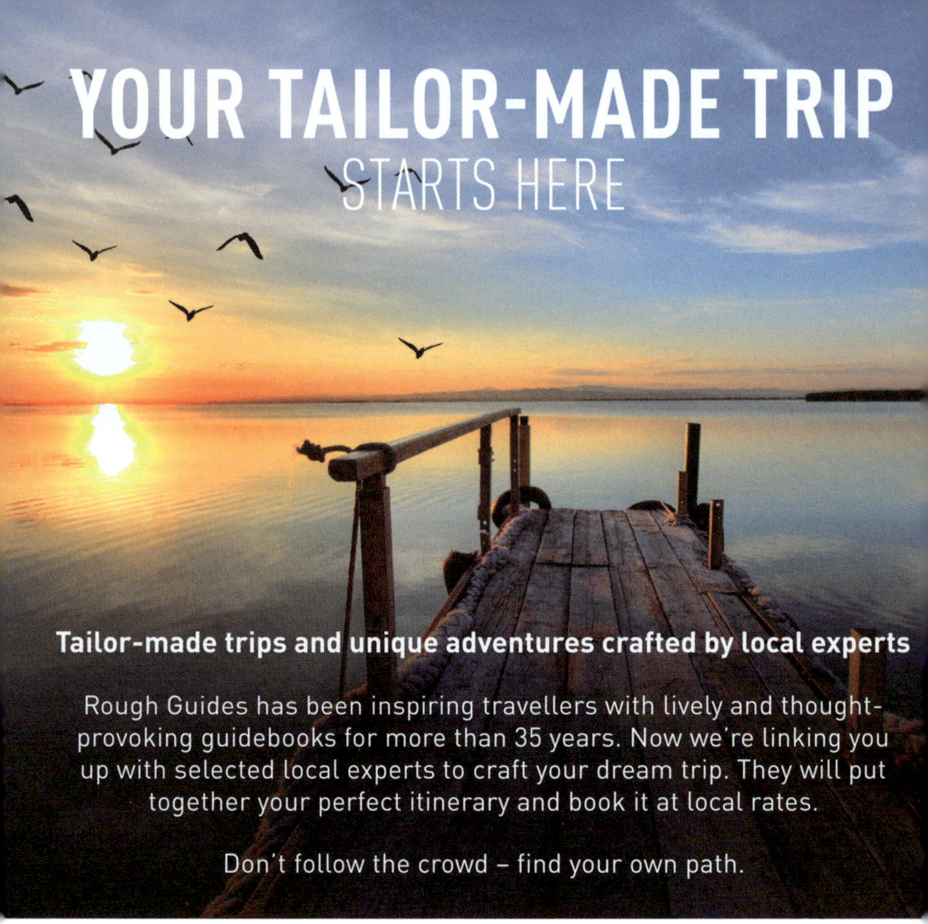


## HOW ROUGHGUIDES.COM/TRIPS WORKS

**STEP 1**

Pick your dream destination, tell us what you want and submit an enquiry.

**STEP 2**

Fill in a short form to tell your local expert about your dream trip and preferences.

**STEP 3**

Our local expert will craft your tailor-made itinerary. You'll be able to tweak and refine it until you're completely satisfied.

**STEP 4**

Book online with ease, pack your bags and enjoy the trip! Our local expert will be on hand 24/7 while you're on the road.

## Rough Guide credits

**Editor:** Kate Drynan
**Cartography:** Katie Bennett
**Picture editor:** Piotr Kala
**Picture Manager:** Tom Smyth
**Layout:** Ankur Guha
**Publishing technology manager:** Rebeka Davies
**Production operations manager:** Katie Bennett
**Head of Publishing:** Sarah Clark

## Publishing information

First edition 2025

**Distribution**
*UK, Ireland and Europe*
Apa Publications (UK) Ltd; sales@roughguides.com
*United States and Canada*
Ingram Publisher Services; ips@ingramcontent.com
*Australia and New Zealand*
Booktopia; retailer@booktopia.com.au
*Worldwide*
Apa Publications (UK) Ltd; sales@roughguides.com

**Special Sales, Content Licensing and CoPublishing**
Rough Guides can be purchased in bulk quantities at discounted prices. We can create special editions, personalised jackets and corporate imprints tailored to your needs. sales@roughguides.com.
roughguides.com

Printed in Czech Republic

This book was produced using **Typefi** automated publishing software.



A catalogue record for this book is available from the British Library



## Help us update

We've gone to a lot of effort to ensure that this edition of **The Rough Guide to The Peloponnese** is accurate and up-to-date. However, things change – places get "discovered", transport routes are altered, restaurants and hotels raise prices or lower standards, and businesses cease trading. If you feel we've got it wrong or left something out, we'd like to know, and if you can direct us to the web address, so much the better.

Please send your comments with the subject line "**Rough Guide The Peloponnese Update**" to mail@uk.roughguides.com. We'll acknowledge all contributions and send a copy of the next edition (or any other Rough Guide if you prefer) for the very best emails.

## Acknowledgements

There are many people that help pull a book together of this magnitude, especially a first edition. I'd like to thank the people of the Peloponnese whom I met through my travels, and how they shared their stories, opened their homes and ensured I was well-fed. Kate Drynan, my editor, has been an invaluable source of support, as has Head of Publishing, Sarah Clark, who knew I was the right fit for the job. And all those behind the scenes at Rough Guides who make sure a guide collates to the final product. It's what you see here and looks great. Thank you for making my wish of being a sole author of a guidebook come true.

## Photo credits

(Key: T-top; C-centre; B-bottom; L-left; R-right)

All images **Shutterstock**

**Cover:** Gerolimenas village, Mani region, Lakonia **iStock**

# Index

# L



# M



# N

# P



# R



# S

# Map symbols

The symbols below are used on maps throughout the book

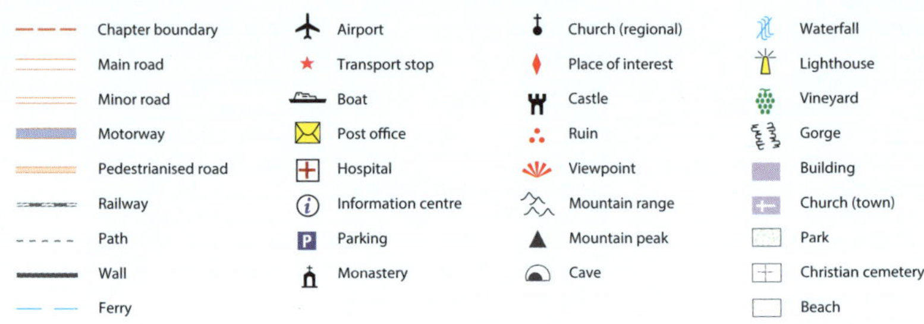


## Listings key

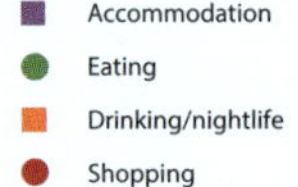


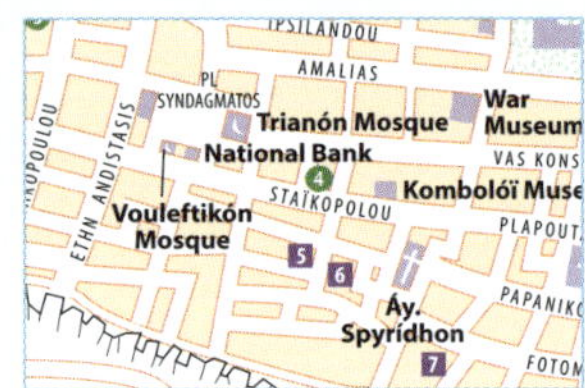